Soci   ..ural
Intelligence

Sociocultural Intelligence

A New Discipline in Intelligence Studies

Kerry Patton

continuum

The Continuum International Publishing Group
The Tower Building   80 Maiden Lane
11 York Road   Suite 704
London SE1 7NX   New York, NY 10038

www.continuumbooks.com

ISBN: 978-1-4411-2848-5 (HB)
      978-1-4411-5531-3 (PB)

Library of Congress Cataloging-in-Publication Data
Patton, Kerry.
   Sociocultural intelligence : a new discipline in intelligence studies / by Kerry
Patton.
       p. cm.—(Continuum intelligence studies series)
   Includes bibliographical references and index.
   ISBN-13: 978-1-4411-2848-5 (hardcover : alk. paper)
   ISBN-10: 1-4411-2848-4 (hardcover : alk. paper)
   ISBN-13: 978-1-4411-5531-3 (pbk. : alk. paper)
   ISBN-10: 1-4411-5531-7 (pbk. : alk. paper) 1. Intelligence service. 2. War
and society. 3. Guerrilla warfare—Social aspects. 4. Counterinsurgency—Social
aspects. I. Title. II. Series.
   JF1525.I6P395 2010
   327.12—dc22   2010000335

Typeset by Newgen Imaging Systems Pvt Ltd, Chennai, India
Printed and bound in the United State of America by Sheridan Books, Inc

This book is dedicated to all those brave men and women along with their families who have sacrificed everything for this great nation. May God continuously embrace you and look over you.

Contents

Acknowledgements

The following individuals must be recognized for their efforts and assistance with the production and insights needed for this book. Dr. Michael Corcoran (Henley Putnam University) and Dr. Brian Carso (Misericordia University) have been nothing but stellar in their feedback and insights for the peer review requirements along with all other bits of information provided in making this a successful journey. Dr. Katherine Shelfer and her entire team at Saint Johns University for all their hard work ensuring every piece of this puzzle was put together properly. Librarians are wonderful tools! Dr. Janice Laurence (Temple University) and Dr. Montgomery McFate for having faith in me to fulfill the demanding requirements while working a very unique assignment in Afghanistan; without such an assignment the majority of this writing would never have occurred. Dr. Drew Bowman, you are a true friend, teacher, mentor, and leader. We started as simple co-workers, transitioned that relationship into an incredible friendship, and today, I take honor in calling you one of my brothers. Major General Gregory Schumacher has provided invaluable mentorship and sincere interest about this specific topic, which will hopefully assist in socially conditioning the Intelligence Community in an attempt to promote this philosophy. Mr. Wayne Simmons as he is truly a "super patriot." He is a man I wish every American would strive to be pertaining to his love of country, willingness of sacrifice, and understandings of National Security needs and demands. To my wife, you truly are my soul mate. Throughout our relationship, I have witnessed you transition into a warrior within by understanding my desires to continue with my passion of fulfilling any role deemed appropriate to assist National Security demands. Because my family has grown so large over the years, I will not go about thanking them all individually; instead I thank each and every one of you for understanding and putting up with me and all my adventures through life. And lastly, I must thank God for looking over me and all my teammates.

Foreword

After serving almost three decades with the Central Intelligence Agency in some of the most unique and dangerous capacities of Clandestine and Covert Operations my life often depended upon the knowledge and implementation of what the author of this book describes as Sociocultural Intelligence. The fundamental concepts and understanding of how societal systems and networks operate around the world have proven key in the preservation and maintenance of the freedoms of the United States and the western world. Virtually all of my years of academic training were spent attempting to understand human behavior and every facet of human reaction to other humans, known in the intelligence world as the Human Intelligence discipline or Humint. I have discovered through personal experiences and by witnessing asymmetric terrorist threats worldwide that social and cultural understanding is crucial to the success of military and civilian intelligence agencies in the Global War on Terror.

Patton outlines numerous historical implementations of what he refers to as Sociocultural Intelligence further proving that this innovative concept is being utilized by intelligence organizations throughout the world. Relying solely on technical intelligence disciplines such as Electronic Intelligence (Elint), Image Intelligence (Imint), and Signal Intelligence (Sigint) has crippled operational successes in our National Defense capabilities. As Patton deftly notes, human interaction is imperative for sound intelligence collection. The discipline of Human Intelligence, Humint, is not for the cerebrally weak or those with a flawed character. It is a special individual who can perform such tasks; one who is physically and mentally disciplined, ethical, adaptive, flexible, and willing to take risks. The character strengths of those working in the realms of Human Intelligence should be the blueprint for the Sociocultural operative.

No country is capable of competing with the United States in our commitment to National Security. This does not mean that we have reached perfection. We strive every day to achieve it but are still far from it. The dynamic and forward-thinking ideas and suggestions made by Patton to create a formalized, stand alone, Sociocultural Intelligence discipline comes at a time in world history when intelligence agencies are screaming out for new and innovative tools to help understand and defeat the asymmetric and unconventional terrorist threats that we face today. The implementation of Patton's directives will clearly help drive America in its quest to achieve this goal.

Wayne Simmons
CIA (Ret.)
Fox News Terrorism and Intelligence Analyst
November, 2009

Preface

Intelligence is a discipline that is crucially needed and depended upon for insights on threats to National Security. Today, the United States benefits from superior technological advancements to improve intelligence collection and analysis requirements. We can track conventional movements across the globe with ease. Intercepting communications among our adversaries has never been so simple. Our abilities to formulate decisions based on such advancements have become second nature. With such advanced systems, an individual with interest must wonder why then the war in Afghanistan continues. Some would claim that the United States has and will continue to fail in its attempts to defeat unconventional and asymmetric threats, not just in Afghanistan but globally due to technological dependency.

Our failures exist due to many reasons, and reliance on technological advancements of intelligence related instruments is one of them. Many would say that we have not failed at all, but with a war going on for over eight years in Afghanistan, arguments can be made otherwise. Eight years into such a war with no sign of victory in the future and the expenditures of billions of dollars along with the continued loss of American and coalition lives—this war should have been over long ago. Mistakes have been made and will continue to be made. These mistakes will impair our successes. They can be prevented, partially, though through the incorporation of a very old yet unofficial tool. That tool is called Sociocultural Intelligence (SOCINT).

Currently, this intelligence discipline does not officially exist because those in leadership positions fail to respect and value the components, fundamentals, and results that can exist through the incorporation of such an intelligence discipline. Maybe they do understand the need and importance, but maybe they have just become so overwhelmed by the unnecessary demands of numbers showing how many High Valued Targets (HVT's) have been killed or captured. Either way, a new intelligence discipline that focuses on social and cultural principles throughout areas of concern is needed.

This book aims to give the reader an opportunity to understand the historical situations where the discipline of SOCINT has been unofficially utilized. Historically, a lot can be learned when attempting to implement new ideas. Through the historical lessons learned, advancements in the approach of implementation, training, and needs have also been addressed. For the most part, all sections have been created with a breadth of knowledge to provide a very broad-based understanding of the subject. Following virtually every breadth of knowledge, a depth of research and writings has been added to provide the reader with greater insight to the topics discussed in the subsections. The first section of this book includes a unique case study about a very strong and encouraging individual with whom I had the chance of interacting while in Afghanistan. This case study was designed to hone the mental demands of the reader in understanding how this proposed new discipline could be implemented internationally. The conclusion adds insight about our domestic issues which will assist in understanding how SOCINT can be used both internationally and domestically.

To help understand the key points, numerous examples are offered throughout, most of which relate to Afghanistan. Our politicians and media alike have provided great misconceptions about Afghanistan. The Afghan people as a whole are peaceful, respectable, and worthy of seeing their country become an internationally successful nation. It has been torn apart by historical episodes of war, and its people have paid the ultimate price. If SOCINT were ever officially formalized into one of the several intelligence disciplines, we as a nation would better understand the truths about those places of concern, domestically and internationally, like the Islamic Republic of Afghanistan.

List of Acronyms

AAF	Anti Afghan Forces
AC	Area of Concern
AO	Area of Operation
CARVER	Criticality, Accessibility, Recuperability (which is argued by many to truly mean Recoverability), Vulnerability, Effects on Population, and Recognizability
CCIR	Commanders Cultural Intelligence Requirements
CCTV	Close Circuit Television
CF	Coalition Forces
CI	Counter Intelligence
CIA	Central Intelligence Agency
CIPB	Cultural Intelligence of the Battlefield
COIN	Counterinsurgency or Counterinsurgency Operations
DA	Direct Action
DHS	Department of Homeland Security
DIA	Defense Intelligence Agency
DOD	Department of Defense
DOS	Department of State
DROC	Democratic Republic of Congo
EBO	Effects Based Operations
FAO	Foreign Area Officer
G2	General Staff Office for Military Intelligence
GIRoA	Government of the Islamic Republic of Afghanistan
GPS	Global Positioning System
HIG	Hezb Islami Gullbidine

HIQ	Hezb Islami Haqqani or simply the Haqqani Network
HSCB	Human, Social, Cultural, Behavioral Modeling Program
HTS	Human Terrain System
HUMINT	Human Intelligence
HVI's	High Valued Individuals
HVT's	High Valued Targets
IC	Intelligence Community
IDP	Internationally Displaced Person
IED	Improvised Explosive Device
IMINT	Imagery Intelligence
IO	Information Operations
IPB	Intelligence Preparation of the Battlefield or Battle-space
IT	Information Technology
JSOU	Joint Special Operation University
LeT	Lashkar e Toiba or can also be spelt as Lashkar e Teiba
MAAG	Military Assistance Advisory Group
MACV-SOG	Military Advisor Corp Vietnam Studies and Observation Group
MASINT	Measures and Signatures Intelligence
MRE's	Meals Ready to Eat
NCTC	National Counterterrorism Center
NGO	Non Government Organization
NSA	National Security Agency
OSINT	Open Source Intelligence
PRT	Provincial Reconstruction Team
PSYOP	Psychological Operations
SECDEF	Secretary of Defense
SIGINT	Signals Intelligence
SOCINT	Sociocultural Intelligence
SOF	Special Operations Forces
TECHINT	Technical Intelligence
TRADOC	U.S. Army Training and Doctrine Command
TTIC	Terrorist Threat Investigation Center

THEORIES OF SOCIOCULTURAL INTELLIGENCE

I

Understanding Guerilla Warfare for Incorporation of Sociocultural Intelligence

1

The urban guerrilla is not afraid of dismantling and destroying the present Brazilian economic, political, and social system, for his aim is to help the rural guerrillas and to collaborate in the creation of a totally new and revolutionary social and political structure with the armed people in power.

(Marighella 1969, p. 1.)

Some of the most famous and studied revolutionists, warfare strategists, and militant leaders have written numerous publications that showcase them and their followers as individuals serving the people with whom they operate. It is apparent through their biographies, memoirs, and military manuals that these are individuals who continuously seek to identify social, political, military, religious, and economic strife within their areas of concern. These leaders and their manuals are examined here in an attempt to solidify a need for a new intelligence discipline known as Sociocultural Intelligence (SOCINT).

Virtually every manual written by revolutionists based on the art of guerilla warfare mentions the traits and characteristics of the individual guerilla, who can also be considered at times—depending on the political circumstances—a terrorist, insurgent, revolutionist, etc. To eliminate confusion, the term guerilla will not differentiate insurgents, terrorists, or revolutionists throughout this writing. A psychological profile of the guerilla will not be examined; however, the tactical characteristics of the individual will be identified in an attempt to justify greater needs for a formalized and official sociocultural intelligence discipline.

Marighella describes numerous characteristics of the guerilla in his *MiniManual for the Urban Guerilla*.

> to be a good walker, to be able to stand up against fatigue, hunger, rain, heat. To know how to hid and to be vigilant. To conquer the art of dissembling. Never to fear danger. To behave the same by day as by night. Not to act impetuously. To have unlimited patience. To remain calm and cool in the worst conditions and situations. Never to leave a track or trail. Not to get discouraged. (Marighella 1969, p. 2)

From the above-quoted descriptions, one may observe that the individual guerilla must be resourceful. Being resourceful is not necessarily described in the manual, but to obtain and maintain the individual characteristics Marighella describes, the guerilla must not rely on himself, as many could easily believe, but more so on the people for support.

The individual guerilla must utilize resources to obtain shelter or safe houses to hide, rest, and be treated for any medical needs. During his or her hiding or resupply activities, the guerilla must depend on the people to provide such necessities as the guerilla does not have an official business or government to rely on in acquiring them. While it is evident that the guerilla is needed to fight their cause, those surrounding them are of greatest importance. "The urban guerrilla must know how to live among the people and must be careful not to appear strange and separated from ordinary city life" (Marighella 1969, p. 2).

The art of being a guerilla is to act like a ghost. A ghost is rarely seen, yet can haunt an individual or individuals with ease. It does this tactically by disappearing immediately after its act. Like ghosts, the guerilla must be capable of moving with ease, blending in with the people, acting as a typical person in society. With this, they must also be capable of performing their mission and immediately after transform themselves away from the guerilla that they are.

Because of the guerilla's continuous activities to reach an end to their means, they serve as guerilla on a full-time basis. They are rarely capable of serving in any other professional capacity besides being a guerilla. Marighella continuously refers to the methodology of adopting a systematic approach to their activities.

Systematically, the guerilla must obtain data on intended targets. No person could ever obtain raw data and transform it into actionable intelligence by themselves. It is a process that utilizes numerous persons. Because of this, the guerilla's intelligence operations are dependent upon the people to be used as sources and assets for data acquisition.

Once intelligence is procured, the guerilla must be capable of acting on that intelligence. Guerillas' greatest tool is fear. In an attempt to promote fear, the guerilla conducts actions that result in death or serious bodily harm to their targets. Prior to being capable of instilling such fear, however, the guerilla must have the appropriate tactical tools to conduct such acts. They often rely on firearms, explosives, or any other means of device that may kill or maim an individual. One common tool Islamic extremists use today is a sword for beheadings.

However, procuring weapon systems and acting upon their intelligence does not end the guerillas in their operation. They must escape the scene in which they operated. To do so, they must find a means of travel. The guerilla can always depend on moving on foot. More conveniently, they can use some form of transportation that is motorized, such as a motorcycle, car, boat, or aircraft. At times they may purchase such means of travel, steal it, or rent it. Due to unprecedented investigations after the Oklahoma Bombing, Timothy McVeigh was identified as the "guerilla terrorist" because of a traffic stop that revealed he had rented the vehicle used for his attack. Luckily enough, his renting the vehicle provided adequate insight leading to a paper trail that assisted in his conviction. Understanding the systematic approaches laid out by individuals, such as Marighella a means to mitigate, intercept, and prevent atrocities caused by guerillas could be fulfilled. It is those networks and systems that sociocultural intelligence will identify and help understand, leading to such actionable measures in mitigation and destruction of guerilla movements.

Sociocultural Intelligence will be the lead in understanding networks and systems throughout geographical domains. Guerilla groups have time and time again been observed operating in small groups often referred to as cells. These cells comprise small teams of individuals ranging between 3 and 25 individuals, rarely much more. Each cell has an independent duty. Some serve strictly as the intelligence, logistics, or action arm (the action arm is the group that physically performs the act of killing, capturing, or maiming an individual or individuals.).

Every cell is to be construed as a network. Every network has a link to another network, making them a system. The more networks are connected, the larger the system. Sooner or later, the guerilla networks will have some form of association, formally or informally, to networks that are not part of the guerilla group. While the traditional intelligence disciplines, such as Human Intelligence, Signals Intelligence, and so forth focus on opposition group's networks, the discipline of sociocultural intelligence will focus on the informal and formal networks connected to the opposition group's network. It is their network of supporters which provide their greatest strength.

> Their strength lay in the support they received from the Irish people. In the final analysis it was the people who bore the enemy's reprisals. Whoever betrayed the cause, or gave up the fight, or suffered loss of spirit, it was seldom the people. (*The IRA Green Book* 1956, p. 1)

To identify strengths in guerilla Warfare, it is evident from numerous Manuals that social systems and Networks must be identified, understood, and evaluated in order to counter the guerilla movement. As previously mentioned, guerillas operate in small groups referred to as cells. Although the group's structures are known, it is crucial and possibly more important to understand how the people organize.

All people, no matter what their ethnicities, cultures, social status, or geographical domains live in some form of network. Not only that, people also create artificial networks to support their livelihood. Telephonic communication is an example of one such artificial network. Guerilla groups understand the importance of these networks possibly to a greater extent than recognized government entities.

The IRA Green Book states three major objectives for successful guerilla warfare operations:

(1) Drain the enemy's manpower and resources.
(2) Lead the resistance of the people to enemy occupation.
(3) Break down the enemy's administration.

It should be noted that without admitting it, the guerilla is in fact conducting human network warfare. The three objectives listed above can lead one to conclude that in order to meet the desired objectives, each objective network must be identified and understood for actionable means. Some of these networks not mentioned but inferred are Political, Military, Economic, Social, Infrastructure, and Religious (PMESI-R) structures, which are multiple networks encompassing one large system. Without the support of the people, the guerilla movement will falter. As the IRA Green Book states, "In fact, a guerrilla force will be unable to operate in an area where the people are hostile to its aims. And it must be remembered always that it is the people who will bear the brunt of the enemy's retaliatory measures" (IRA Green Book 1956, p. 16).

Communication, within any and all networks, throughout the PMESI-R principle is subjugated to information operations conducted from the guerilla group. This information operation is in competition with that which is conducted from their opposition, which is more often than not the government. It is crucial to conduct an information operation campaign for the guerilla, dispersing its message throughout the people to gain support, recruit, promote world public opinion, educate, lead in active and passive support, and continuously liaise. By doing such information campaigns, the guerillas build their muscle. Their muscle is the people.

Unlike disinformation or adverse propaganda machines, the guerillas must accurately describe and inform upon the situation. Although this information may be misinformation (information with unintentional inaccuracies), it must be based solely to socially condition the people about atrocities and grievances to build the support needed for continuous operations. Communication is crucial. Without it, no campaign can succeed, no matter which side one is on. Communication is a large system composed of multiple networks. Identifying the means and methods by which guerillas conduct their communications enables the disruption of the network. The utilization of runners, for example, is known to military strategists from reading guerilla manuals. A runner is strictly a messenger. Runner's communication is a method that goes as far back as man has been engaged in battles. It utilizes individuals to pass messages from leaders to subordinates. The message can be written or verbally passed. This is a means of communication that is overly difficult to intercept. Understanding this method and the means in which messages are trafficked enhances the abilities to intercept and break. This is something that coalition forces have failed in doing to date. One reason is possibly because an official sociocultural intelligence discipline fails to be applied.

During the War on Terror, specifically within Afghanistan, coalition forces became dependent on Signals Intelligence to intercept cellular phone communication. It has become known that opposition groups such as Taliban and Al Qaeda have marginalized the use of cellular phones among their high-level leaders and today are utilizing runners.

Communication, like virtually all other networks, is not unidimensional. Networks are normally always multidimensional, but their dimensions vary. The guerillas attempt to keep their networks simplistic in nature, but complex for their opposition to understand. Because of the inherent masculinity of warfare, women are seldom identified in guerilla operations. They serve as great nodes within their networks though, and are encouraged to be incorporated. When the IRA was at its weakest state, women played a crucial role in continuing operations to rebuild and socially condition the masses. In his *Guerilla Warfare* (1961) manual, Guevara fills the entire section 3 (titled "Organization of the Guerilla Front") with the utilization and incorporation of women within the guerilla outfit. Women have been observed on numerous occasions to assist the guerilla in achieving their objectives.

Pashtun culture in Afghanistan has a long history of utilizing women. Yet, the United States has displayed complete ignorance towards these women, due to lack of sociocultural understandings. In doing so, the United States has overlooked a major network when fighting the War on Terror in Afghanistan. An example of the importance of women in Pashtun culture can be seen in their authority. Within Pashtun culture, if a male in the household is killed, it is customary for the woman to determine the action to be taken. That action ranges from doing nothing at all to the extreme act of killing up to four males associated with the death of her male family member.

Further, women serve in numerous roles in guerilla warfare. They can fulfill the obligations of the action arm like the infamous Black Widows terrorist group that can be found predominantly in Chechnya. They often serve as support entities such as cooks, medics, and intelligence operatives. One of the greatest services a woman can provide in guerilla warfare according to Guevara is to serve as an educator and social worker. "When the fronts have been consolidated and a rear exists, the functions of the social worker also fall to women who investigate the various economic and social evils of the zone with a view to changing them as far as possible" (Guevara 1961, p. 33).

During guerilla operations, existing networks created by the state may crumble. In such cases, the guerilla often establish "underground" networks utilized as "life lines" for their movement. Pre-existing hospitals may be controlled by the nation-state limiting their use by guerilla fighters. Consequently, ad hoc hospitals and clinics must be established. Such establishments are often created in individuals' homes, in caves, or in dense vegetated areas or swamps difficult for security forces to patrol or attack, allowing the guerilla to have advanced warning to vacate the area.

These underground systems are not restricted to medical treatment facilities and can encompass any type of industry, including weapon manufacturing, such as the locations found in the North West Frontier Province and the Federally Administered Tribal Areas (FATA) in Pakistan. They can involve the manufacturing of clothing, such as footwear or ammunition carrier systems and backpacks, about which Guevara writes in *Guerilla Warfare* Guevara 1961, p. 36).

Because pre-existing networks may be crippled, observation of the guerillas must be taken to identify their moral, dress, health, equipment, etc. Such observations should reveal signs that identify inconsistencies between the guerilla's personal stature and the stature of the local indigenous persons. Such signs will help identify the likeliness of newly established networks created by the guerilla group. Because guerilla warfare is identified as warfare among the people, it is those networks that need identification, understanding, and disruption. Traditional intelligence disciplines too often overlook such networks as they are consumed with targeting the guerilla group in a lethal means. Understanding the consumption of the traditional intelligence disciplines and obtaining a greater appreciation of the guerilla movement with emphasis on the informal and formal networks associated with such, it is evident that a formalized and official intelligence discipline dedicated to understanding those networks mentioned must exist. This discipline is Sociocultural Intelligence.

Identification of SOCINT

Sociocultural Intelligence is a concept that officially fails to exist. Anthropologists continuously debate whether their profession and nation-states militaries and/or intelligence communities should collaborate data.[1] Numerous ethical elements have been established by anthropological associations throughout the world and their argument is mute when such a concept fails existence. If SOCINT were to officially exist, organizations such as the American Anthropological Association would have little ground to continue arguments related to the collaboration of information. Sociocultural intelligence is a needed crucial element within the US Intelligence Community (IC) and its practice has unofficially existed longer than the establishment of any nation-state.

> And Moses sent them to spy out the land of Canaan, and said unto them, Get you up this way southward, and go up into the mountain: And see the land, what it is; and the people that dwelleth therein, whether they be strong or weak, few or many; And what the land is that they dwell in, whether it be good or bad; and what cities they be that they dwell in, whether in tents, or in strong holds; And what the land is, whether it be fat or lean, whether there be wood therein, or not. And be ye of good courage, and bring of the fruit of the land. Now the time was the time of the first ripe grapes. (Numbers 13: 17–20)

Reading the aforementioned passage taken out of the Bible, one can obtain an historical sense of sociocultural intelligence. Some key attributes to understand historical elements within sociocultural intelligence based on the passage are observing and analyzing the land (geography, geology), the people (anthropology, psychology), the communities in which they live (economics, demography, criminology, political affairs), the infrastructure (archeology), and lastly the art of spying. Historically, these elements constitute portions of sociocultural intelligence. They are still the much-needed attributes within the social sciences to bring defining conceptualization to the discipline of sociocultural intelligence.

Today, the following elements of social studies should be included to ensure complete identification of the key attributes needed to grasp the first part of the term, that is, the sociocultural elements of sociocultural intelligence:

- geography
- anthropology
- psychology
- economics
- religion
- demography
- criminology
- political affairs
- archeology

The second half of the identification to define sociocultural intelligence is the term intelligence itself. According to military doctrine, the term intelligence relates to directing of collecting data that will then be analyzed and processed into a usable product to be distributed to those who need to know.[2]

Most recently, a newer terminology add-on has been created, "actionable intelligence," which simply means that the end product of data collected can be utilized or "actioned" by the end user for operations. The greatest action any user can have within any military organization or intelligence community is based upon one's situational awareness. When combining the key attributes of intelligence and the social sciences, you have what is now called sociocultural intelligence, abbreviated as SOCINT.

From this point out, the term sociocultural intelligence, or SOCINT, will mean the process of directing, collecting data related to any of the social sciences, analyzing, producing, and then disseminating such data for situational awareness in any operational environment. Like all other intelligence disciplines, SOCINT is unique and original for numerous reasons. One stands out, however: the discipline of collecting such data.

The uniqueness of SOCINT

Numerous intelligence disciplines exist, each being unique through its own function. SOCINT is no different. It is unique in its utilization and methodologies of data collection. Brief overviews of multiple primary intelligence disciplines are presented below to help understanding and, later, to differentiate the discipline of SOCINT from them. Data collection and utilization towards understanding are needed to better comprehend the importance of SOCINT.

The secretive world of intelligence and covert operations has a wide array of tools available that originate from the numerous methods of collecting intelligence. The United States gathers intelligence via several major collection tools:

- Imagery Intelligence, better known as (IMINT), is used to gather information by means of geospatial imaging and or photography.
- Signals Intelligence (SIGINT) is often used along with IMINT. Collection of information from SIGINT can be conducted through various means, a few are through electricity, communications, and radar.
- Measure and Signatures Intelligence (MASINT) is conducted through multiple sources such as Acoustical, Optical, Laser, and Infrared means.
- Technical Intelligence (TECHNINT) is used to identify advancements of scientific and technical information among nation-states.
- Open Sources Intelligence (OSINT) is the utilization of publicly available information through a vast array of sources, such as media, print, journals, books, etc. to assist in the collection efforts of intelligence production.

Once a good credible source of information is gathered, countering threats off that information can be conducted. This is considered to be Counter Intelligence or (CI). None of these six different sources of information should be considered true or affirmed sources of information until they are verified. In order to do this, humans should be used.

Using humans as sources of information is known as Human Intelligence or HUMINT. HUMINT is one of the seven major sources of collection of information, and used in virtually every country. Human Intelligence, arguably, is considered messy and very risky. Because of the risk involved in using humans, US leaders in the 1970s decided not to use them as often as they once did (mostly due to the Church and Pike Committees[3]). There is a great possibility that this is where the United States has failed in its intelligence world. Many intelligence professionals understand the need of HUMINT, but may fail to comprehend the needs for SOCINT.

Data collection within the function of SOCINT is unique from all other intelligence disciplines predominantly because collection efforts are limitless. The utilization of open source, face-to-face conversations, imagery, etc. are all methods of collecting the data needed to better understand a sociocultural environment. The greatest needs of understanding the collection efforts within SOCINT begins within the collection approach. The collection efforts for SOCINT should entail all sources of information, but should focus and dominate in the interaction of human elements within the geographic areas of concern. This approach must move from a broad range of research to a narrower research focus, based upon continued gap analysis of data throughout the collection phase of the intelligence cycle. Although collecting data is crucial within any intelligence function, more importantly is the understanding of the utilization of such data.

The incorporation of SOCINT

More often than not, SOCINT would be utilized for non-lethal operations. Like every other intelligence discipline, SOCINT should strive to enhance Effects Based Operations (EBO),[4] which require diligent and consistent study of the Area of Operation (AO) and understanding of systems and networks that should constitute the bulk of SOCINT. By understanding the human behavioral aspects of relationships as well as formal, informal, present, and emerging systems, we can provide ourselves with a better opportunity for 'success' by knowing who, what, where, when, why, and how to influence within the systems themselves.

A systems analysis approach within SOCINT in an attempt to accomplish goals, and desired end-states requires that all actions or thought through 'non-action' have linkage to the overall goal or resolution of nested plans of action. This systems approach should be based upon our understanding of links, nodes, and connecters that make up the multi-faceted networks whether the intended 'target' operates within the weakened state of the host nation's infrastructure, economic development, security forces, political figures, an insurgent leader or group, etc. By understanding that no one or nothing in a 'functioning system' is an isolated actor or action, we can develop an appreciation of how to develop functional, reliable systems as well as learn how to safely disrupt them, take them apart, or eliminate them through non-lethal or lethal means. The paradoxical approach to this view is that by understanding a system's approach, we can link people, projects, and programs of disjointed and dysfunctional systems into a coherent, integrated approach to building reliable and sustainable networks. This is the discipline of SOCINT. "Those skilled in war subdue the enemy's army without battle. They capture his cities without assaulting them and over-throw the state without protracted operations" (Griffith 1963).

The utilization and implementation of SOCINT for non-lethal targeting should act through an appreciation as well as an understanding of the human element. Geographic topography/key physical terrain play a role in the 'how' systems have adapted in order to operate. However in the targeting process, topography may not be as important as the systems that are emplaced and operated by the individuals and groups who keep them functioning.

It has become readily apparent that our past and current approach in dealing with sociocultural elements within the United States government continuously fails because it lacks an understanding of sociocultural networks within organizations or simply ignores the formal and informal networks and systems within an area of operation, which inevitably leads to our inability to influence towards our own projected end-state.

Government entities assuming intelligence responsibilities have failed to define the underlying threat within the functional areas of social networks. Observations of newly developed fusion cells located within the United States and abroad will identify that the primary focus and synchronization of analysis occurs when all parties understand functionally the breadth of the enemy network. This is what creates the environment that allows for the sociocultural information/context to be integrated usefully. Incorporating the sociocultural information provides situational understanding and predictability in anticipating overpressure or second and third order of effects possibilities. This implies recommending that SOCINT be incorporated into planning and executing as a critical component to understanding what the current actions will mean in the future environment.

The United States government as a whole has demonstrated a lack of understanding for a non-lethal targeting approach. This is predominantly due to the lack of implementing a formalized SOCINT discipline into the national intelligence community. Too often, those who target tend to focus on a lethal means of operation or strike. When such targeting operations are conducted, induced negative perception, turmoil, and difficulties into the population that they are competing in often occurs.[5] These outcomes negatively impact the organization or entity and/or the AO that they are attempting to influence or persuade. It is evident that such operations can rarely exist within the United States for Homeland Security purposes hence greater focus on non-lethal operations needs to exist and through SOCINT success of the non-lethal operation becomes greater.

While fighting Counterinsurgency (COIN) operations, it is the non-lethal operations that change areas in favor of Coalition Force (CF) elements. SOCINT should not be thought of simply as a tool for war fighting. It is an art needed to be officially recognized because of its value for multiple uses such as law enforcement operations and business. The case studies below will provide historical examples of the unofficial utilization and implementation of SOCINT.

The historical implementation of SOCINT

Countries and militaries throughout history have always sought out understandings of sociocultural areas. People such as Christopher Columbus, a knighted naval explorer for the Spanish Monarch who was granted title of "Admiral of the Ocean Sea" for his explorations of foreign lands, and Sir Thomas Edward (T.E.) Lawrence, better known as Sir Lawrence of Arabia, a prominent soldier for Great Britain due to his embed throughout the Arabian peninsula during the First World War, were both prominent figures involved with SOCINT. These are arguably the most prominent unofficial SOCINT operatives throughout time. They performed their governmental duties and provided a mass knowledge of sociocultural data for later use. Further, it is a concept that has been utilized throughout the world since biblical times. Although these are two individuals serving nation-states in the performance of SOCINT, nation-states have utilized full organizations to continue such practice.

Germany

Leaders within Germany prior to World War II, while planning what would become a second world war, conducted after-action reviews based on World War I. They recognized the need of multiple area factors to assist in their overall campaign plan of world conquer. With Italy on their side to assist the efforts in Europe, and with Japan to assist in the Pacific and East Asia, they needed at a minimum one more large land mass influencer.

Two area targets were identified: Africa and the Middle East. Great Britain and France dominated the continent of Africa when this planning occurred in the early 1920s. Knowing that one specific country would most likely not side with the communists in the region, the German Thule Society, which later became the German Social Party, decided that, instead of targeting a country as a whole, it would target specific people within numerous countries.

In 1928, the German Thule Society went to Egypt and spoke with Islamic leader Mufti Hassan Al Banna about geopolitical advancements the western world was achieving behind the backs of everyone else. Because of some

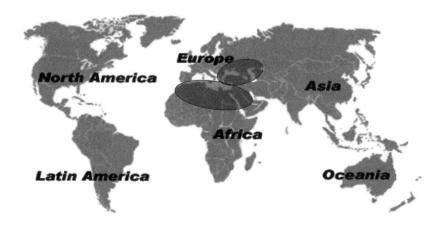

Map 1.1 World War II areas of operations conducted via the Egyptian Muslim Brotherhood

social and political indifference between the numerous entities within fraternal orders predominantly stemming from Great Britain, the Germans formulated a plan to bring Islamists together to spy and fight against British domination within the region. Based on numerous principles of many secret fraternal societies, the Germans assisted in the creation of the Egyptian Muslim Brotherhood in 1928.

The Brotherhood, as it is often referred to today, was responsible for continuing the social conditioning of Muslims throughout the Middle East. They also conducted recruitment for military operations in support of their socialist brothers. Arguably one of the largest "SS" divisions throughout World War II was the Waffen SS Division, which consisted predominantly of Muslims throughout the Middle East and more specifically of recruits from Baghdad following their creation of the Baath Party.

This Division of Muslims operated mostly in and around Bosnia. It was another of these groups of highly trained militants that socially conditioned individuals through Information Operations (IO) to fight to their deaths based on similar causes believed by socialists. While this Division of Muslim fighters was set to assist the Germans in world domination, it was not the only fighting entity that was created.

Several Muslim militant organizations were produced from the Muslim Brotherhood that remained throughout Africa and the Middle East. These smaller factions operated as small units that conducted harassment operations against western allies throughout the war. As the war descended after time, the factions of the militant arms of the Brotherhood remained and still do today. They are responsible for gathering fighters from across the Islamic global community that defeated the Russians in Afghanistan, advertising and exacerbating the concept of "jihad."

Today, this radicalized Muslim organization continues its operations globally, a direct reflection of the incredible Psychological and Informational Operation (PSYOP and IO) campaigns conducted by the Germans prior to the onset of World War II. Neither, the PSYOP nor the IO campaigns would have been successful if it weren't for the utilization of SOCINT to gain sound situational awareness of the area desired to be influenced.

Vietnam

During the Vietnam War, the United States began fighting against not necessarily a country state, but rather against a people within a country state. This

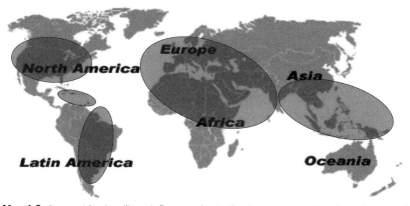

Map 1.2 Current Islamic militant influences due to the German operations through the establishment of the Egyptian Muslim Brotherhood

concept of warfare alluded to minimal situational awareness of the battle space. This was revolutionary warfare, better known today as counterinsurgency. Fighting such a war through a conventional means is virtually impossible and to date no country has ever truly defeated an insurgency. "There was no substitute for being immersed in the history, politics, and society of a region, in this case Indochina. The best analytic records were generally registered by those officers who had had considerable such exposure" Robert S. McNamara (US Secretary of Defense Ret.).

Some of the greatest of Generals within the United States military fought without truly understanding the Human Terrain during the Vietnam War. They lacked sociocultural understandings of a place most Americans never heard of, or even knew existed until years after the involvement in the war. Even when government leadership along with military Generals thought they were beginning to understand the human terrain, they never truly did.

One of the greatest steps in achieving a true understanding of the sociocultural dimensions within the Vietnam War started with the initiation of Military Assistance and Advisory Group (MAAG), which later became known as Military Advisor Corp Vietnam Studies and Observation Group (MACV-SOG). MAAG and its later offshoot initially served as advisors to the French in their efforts during what was then considered the Indochina War. They advised predominantly on political, military, and economic issues throughout the region.

No person would be considered a successful MAAG operative if he or she sat behind a desk and simply read historical and anthropological data related to the people in Indochina. This knowledge would be proven minuscule to those they advise, that is, the military assets who fought their adversary daily. It was imperative that MAAG operatives be just that: operatives.

MAAG operatives were highly skilled individuals with great talent to embed with the indigenous allied forces. Most came from some form of Special Operations background throughout all branches of the US Armed Forces. They continuously embedded with indigenous people to learn everything they could to identify the needs, concerns, and credible actions that could be taken to win the "hearts and minds" of the local populace. Thus, these advisors had the most credible first-hand understanding of the people and could arguably be considered the US Military's Vietnam SOCINT operatives. This was not the first time, nor would it be the last, when the United States Department of Defense unofficially conducted SOCINT.

Without arguing success in Vietnam, argument can be made that success within the MAAG and MACV-SOG programs prevented additional loss of life during the war. In reality, very few people in the United States knew anything about the culture, different religions, or languages spoken in the area of Vietnam. Because of such a lack of knowledge, the United States lost thousands of American lives and millions of dollars.

The main goal of the United States when entering the Vietnam War was to stop the spread of Communism. That goal was never accomplished partially due to lack of knowledge of the enemy, failure to obtain situational awareness, and minimal utilization of SOCINT. Stopping the spread of communism not only failed in Vietnam, it also failed right next door to the United States greatly because of neglecting the unofficial SOCINT utilization.

Cuba

The United State was adamant about keeping and maintaining a great distance from communism during the Cold War. When Fidel Castro became the leader of Cuba, the government of the United States became extremely concerned because of his ties with Russia (the United States's number one enemy during the Cold War). The United States reacted with desperate measures to rid Cuba from the dictator. They did this with virtually complete ignorance of sociocultural understandings of Cuba.

Numerous attempts were made by the US government to assassinate Castro, all of which failed. One attempt called for setting a revolt against him.

Operators from the United States and South America were placed into Cuba in an attempt to gain supporters to revolt against Castro himself. In order for this revolt to be successful, local Cubans were needed to conform to the plan led by the American government.

Little was known about the patriotism of Cuba and love for Castro by his people. Because of the people and love for their leader, obtaining support to revolt against him became impossible. The plan to start a revolution failed because the United States government underestimated Cuba's strength. The US government had little knowledge of the people, the culture, and the Cuban leadership's ability to maintain strength and unity within its country. This operation led by the United States government could easily be argued as the prime reason why the 13-day "Cuban missile crisis" occurred, here again, lack of SOCINT. Years later the United States would rebound from its ignorance of necessity for SOCINT within its own borders.

Inside the United States

In 1994, the US Department of Education along with the US Department of Defense collectively researched educational needs within the United States. The concept was twofold: (1) add more teachers within the United States in areas of low-income households in an attempt to increase educational opportunity, and (2) assist poverty or close to poverty stricken areas through quality educational systems in an attempt to build economic growth. A second order of effect was to reduce crime. The program introduced was called the Troops to Teachers program.

Sociocultural intelligence played a vital role in the Troops to Teacher concept's success within the program. While performing the discipline of

Map 1.3 Example of initial area assessment

Map 1.4 Example of Secondary Area Assessment after the introduction of the Troops to Teachers Program within the United States

SOCINT, multiple factors were utilized: crime rates, income, single parent ratios, national primary education testing, SAT and ACT scores, and more. Once all data was compiled, it was easy to map out areas throughout the United States that called for critical educational assistance through the Troops to Teachers program.

As indicated by maps 1.3 and 1.4, the initial assessment had less areas of concern; however, the areas were so large that the geographical area mass outweighed the current areas of needs after the implementation of the Troops to Teachers Program. It is evident that this case study is very simple and possibly lacks additional information. The key point, though, is that through the implementation of a tie (Troops to Teacher Program) into the overall network (the educational system throughout the United States), change was implemented that proved successful. Without looking at any statistical evidence such as test scores, crime rates, or economic enhancements within the study, map 1.4 shows success through the reduction of land mass in need of educational programs such as the Troops to Teachers element.

The Troops to Teachers program became a proven concept due to continued research on crime rates, test scores, employment, economics, etc. The United States government with assistance of First Lady Laura Bush recognized such success and allocated resources for continuation through the 2001 No Child Left Behind Act. This would be the eye opening situational awareness for decision makers within the Department of Education and Department of Defense. The network at play would be the educational systems throughout the United States.

SOCINT is a proven necessity for all means of National Security, including Homeland Defense, as demonstrated through the incorporation of the Troops to Teachers Program.

The need for SOCINT today

Through the observation of historical uses of an unofficial SOCINT, it is evident that

1. SOCINT is not a new concept.
2. SOCINT is a proven principle of an intelligence function to provide situational awareness that better informs decision makers with options of action plans.
3. When SOCINT efforts exist, success is likely and when sociocultural intelligence is lacking, success is rarely achieved.
4. SOCINT needs to be formalized in an attempt to officially train SOCINT operatives and promote better understanding of areas of concern to mitigate unreasonable acts based on ignorance of understanding sociocultural elements throughout such operational environments.

The intelligence function supports decision makers and their staffs through current and relevant collected analyzed data products, focusing on identified interests and ongoing threat situations in the organization's area of responsibility, including support to air base operability/defense (as applicable), base agencies, tenant organizations, corporations, and transient units. The world today confronts terrorist threats and rogue regimes such as Iran, Russia, China, Venezuela, North Korea, etc. Intelligence support to counterinsurgency operations should act no different from any other operation it is intended for, including homeland security. Addressing the needs of SOCINT, rogue regimes, terrorism, and insurgencies should be conducted with the same principle, no matter the circumstance.

Since terrorist acts are criminal acts and insurgencies often depend on terrorist tactics, criminal records are a major source of SOCINT data. Decision makers must work through established law enforcement liaison channels because the collection, retention, and dissemination regulated by law enforcement channels are restricted. Few intelligence operatives are trained in obtaining criminal records unless they serve in military investigation offices of the U.S. Army (CID), Navy (NCIS), Air Force (AFOSI), and HQ US Marine Corps, Criminal Investigations Division, Federal Bureau of Investigations (FBI), etc. Criminology is a portion of the SOCINT function, but few intelligence operatives are trained in collecting such data, increasing the need of making SOCINT an official intelligence function.

The geographic combatant commander, through the commander's J-2 Joint Intelligence Center and the Chief Intelligence Security Officer (CISO) and in consultation with DIA, CIA, embassy staff, country team, and applicable host-nation authorities, obtains intelligence and counterintelligence specific to the operational area, and issues intelligence and counterintelligence reports, advisories, and assessments to the units within the combatant command's control or operating within the combatant command's area of responsibility (AOR). This network is the backbone for communicating intelligence and counterintelligence information, advisories, and warning of terrorist/insurgency threat throughout the region. Unfortunately, none of these representative organizations or entities has a sociocultural element officially designated within. This hinders positive effects based operations even when such operations are non-kinetic and intended to show good faith.

Immediately after it invaded Afghanistan following the terrorist attacks of September 11, 2001, the United States began dropping pallets of Meals Ready to Eat (MREs) out of cargo aircraft to help starving Afghans. Although this was intended to be a gesture of good faith, many Afghans were offended by this operation and in fact took it as a slap in the face. Afghanistan is considered a Muslim country, yet MREs are mostly filled with pork products, a meat considered "haram" (forbidden) by Muslims. Even with a social science cell operating out of the United States Pentagon, military decision makers failed to have situational awareness of the area of concern. This could have been mitigated if an official SOCINT element had been established within the intelligence community.

DOD Directive 2000.12 tasked the secretaries of the military departments to ensure that a capability exists to collect, receive, evaluate for a service perspective, and disseminate all relevant data on terrorist activities, trends, and indicators of imminent attack. Threat analysis is an essential step in forming predictive analysis. Country threat assessments and information about terrorist/insurgency organizations, biographies, and incidents are shared in these databases and disseminated throughout the commands and services. Unfortunately, even with such directives in effect, the data presumed to be collected and analyzed does very little with predictive analysis outside the tactical level. Operationally and strategically, sociocultural indicators have proven the greatest means of predicting future outcomes within areas of concern. Because such directives within the national intelligence community fail existence pertaining SOCINT, future attacks or secondary "Cold Wars" will reoccur with time. More worrisome will be the reaction of the United States government to such attacks in light of the ignorance stemming from non-existent formalized SOCINT.

To focus the threat analysis, intelligence and counterintelligence offers priority information requirements for identifying potential targets. Many information requirements exist. Those pertaining specifically to sociocultural intelligence are:

1) religious, political, and ethnic affiliations
2) recruiting methods, locations, and targets; i.e., students
3) important dates
4) transportation
5) medical support availability
6) means and methods of communicating to the public

Religious, political, and ethnic affiliations

Religion, politics, and ethnicities are topics that Americans as a whole have been socially conditioned to never discuss in social gatherings. Because of their culture, many Americans are completely ignorant about such principles, including our own government leaders.

In the past and most likely in the future, we will continue to see insulting mistakes made towards such principles, such as sending women diplomats and or their staffers into Muslim countries without publicly wearing, at a minimum, some form of shawl to cover their heads out of respect for the Muslim society they are visiting. Such principle as our leaders sitting with their legs crossed, showing the soles of their shoes is disrespectful in many countries. Identifying people as equal in many ethnically or tribally diverse nation-states often causes increased hostilities towards the United States even though we are engrained to believe all are created equal. It is small acts like these that contribute to the rest of the world viewing the United States as an arrogant society. With the incorporation of SOCINT in an official intelligence function, such views could be greatly reduced as understandings of religion, politics, and ethnicities grow. "All men are created equal; this does not mean after their creation they will remain equal to others" (Author Unknown).

Recruiting methods, locations, and targets

Individuals who turn to organized crime, such as the mafia, gangs, and or terrorist groups are often labeled with some form of psychological dysfunction. Although numerous authors have attempted to psychologically profile terrorists, my personal endeavors speaking with such persons show that these authors are less than fifty percent accurate. Psychological profiles are important to understand when accurately described. However, more important is to understand the historical, social dynamics that have allowed these persons to be psychologically molded into who they are. To be capable of understanding such social synergies, a mass compare and contrast of the top terrorist producing countries needs to be conducted. Understanding these social synergies could be used in an attempt to mitigate future acts of terrorism via the introduction or termination of ties within the social network nodes. Such compare and contrast surveys would be impossible to complete without trained sociocultural intelligence operatives.

Important dates

Immediately after 9–11, the United States Intelligence Community made immediate yet poorly analyzed emphasis on terrorist attack dates. Looking at a calendar and researching whether a terrorist attack had occurred on that date, a gambler would almost always win if his bet was on "a terrorist attack occurred on this date." This does not mean that dates lack importance, rather quite opposite, but they must be understood for different reasons from those we initially believed in after 9–11. Important dates mostly stem from a religious or political standpoint, based upon the cultural environment in the area of interest, and can initiate certain behaviors and activities within populations. One example is the celebration of St. Patrick's Day in the United States. Many Americans celebrate this Irish Catholic holiday and believe that going to Ireland at that time would be great. What they do not realize is that, although St. Patrick's Day is celebrated in Ireland, the festivities are minimal compared to that in the United States. Although the utilization and formulization of SOCINT is not intended to identify when and where we should go to party, it is partially intended to assist in understanding why specific dates are significant to some and not to others.

Transportation

Continuing with specific elements to be identified with the incorporation of SOCINT is the research and understanding of infrastructure, first dealing with transportation. One needs to understand the means of transportation used within communities, as well as why and what would happen if such means were taken away. Keeping in mind that SOCINT is based on sociocultural understandings, ties and nodes must be thoroughly identified and understood for manipulation to obtain desired effects. Based upon the type of culture identified in the area of concern, be it an agricultural, industrial, or technical culture, transportation plays a significant role. The culture identified will determine the transportation needs.

Medical support availability

One of the greatest needs throughout the world is basic medical assistance. Many countries face medical dilemmas. When advanced countries observe the medical negligence in an area of need, more often than not the advanced state becomes dumbfounded. Basic education and implementation of proper sanitation is often all that is needed to mitigate most medical negligence. Sociocultural intelligence operatives with minimal medical training, using medical sources and assets, could identify needs of populations to better their conditions, which would improve decision-making processes.

Means and methods of communicating

Proper decision-making processes often fail to occur simply because of miscommunication. Communication is crucial in identifying and understanding a society. Oftentimes, horrific incidents in one's life are caused by miscommunication, such as car accidents, divorce, interpersonal violence, being laid off from work, etc. Communication stems from multiple means whether it be verbally spoken, written, or conducted through some form of signaling means. Simple hand gestures are forms of communication and, pending the geographic location, one hand signal can mean something very different from the same hand signal used somewhere else. The need to identify and understand communication is crucial to obtain desired effects within areas of interest. The incorporation of SOCINT is a tool that should focus on such communications.

Identifying those intelligence requirements utilized to identify targets and knowing that non-trained sociocultural operatives perform such duties, shows that multiple gaps of information exist within the overall intelligence end product. If SOCINT were to be formalized and recognized as an official function of the intelligence elements, such gaps of information in understanding the who, what, when, how, where, and why would be reduced. Such additional data would enhance decision makers' situational awareness, bettering their abilities to succeed. Consequently, Effects Based Operations could be better understood, including why intended targets reacted to the initial action the way they did. More so, the decision makers would better predict what the intended targets reaction would be prior to implementing such actions. SOCINT is a tool that could be used for National Security across all fronts of securing the United States and its national interests. SOCINT is a discipline that must be officially recognized and implemented inside the intelligence community.

Notes

1. American Anthropological Association Executive Board Statement on the Human Terrain System Project (2007). http://www.aaanet.org/issues/policy-advocacy/Statement-on-HTS.cfm (accessed February 24, 2009).
2. Numerous Military publications exist that define the term "Intelligence." Some of these publications are Joint Publication 2–0, U.S. Army Field Manual 2–0, Marine Corp Doctrinal Publication 2, etc. All of them have very similar terminology to define "intelligence" which allows such formulization to conclude this very broad definition.
3. The Church and Pike Committees were Democrat-led initiatives following fears in the United States, including from individuals in the US government, that originated from knowing that intelligence organizations such as the NSA and the CIA were spying on Americans. Some intelligence professionals believe that these two Congressional Committees ruined the United States Human Intelligence capabilities.
4. Effects Based Operations as a whole is a US military operations process that incorporates specified means to achieve a desired state within a specified Area of Concern or Area of Operation.
5. MG (Ret.) Robert H. Scales provided insight to the Senate Armed Services Committee related to Military Operations throughout the War on Terror. His message was clear and direct, informing government leadership about the impact civilian casualties cause and the blow back received among US military representatives operating abroad. It is assumed that his message was intended to reduce "collateral damage" and increase precision strikes.

2

Current Research on Sociocultural Intelligence

Chapter Outline

Counterinsurgency: the people's wars

Many professionals fail to understand when, where, and why terrorism initially began. Arguments have been raised as to the numerous past events that may have fueled terrorism today, such as the Crusades. Many historical documents help understand how modern day terrorism tactics have evolved. No matter the argument, the tactics utilized by terrorists and insurgencies lead people to believe that such operations are to be considered irregular warfare. Disappointingly, virtually all of these writings lack a deeper appreciation of the people and the sociocultural networks that promote such activities.

Through actions and counteractions preceding 9–11, there was much in-depth research based upon intelligence principles and dealing with counterinsurgency and terrorism operations. Such actions have promoted malfunctions and malfeasance within the intelligence community. In an attempt to gain a greater appreciation of modern research pertaining intelligence and counterinsurgency, including relations within the sociocultural needs, a brief background introduction to modern day insurgencies and the intelligence community must be included. This aims to promote critical thinking as to where the United States stands today in understanding operational environments and intelligence needs specifically through SOCINT.

The American Revolution

Throughout history, the Presidents of the United States have been granted "executive power." Along with this executive power, the President has the right to instigate secret actions, better known as "covert operations." The President has at hand numerous groups of individuals to perform these actions. When a President implements his rights to conduct such actions, he does not need to inform any other means of government, except for those directly involved. Because of this executive power, secrecy is easily enforced.

Understandably, the United States during the time of the American Revolutionary War did not have a president, but leaders made decisions. Without any official political appointments into a government, a social network existed and continuously grew that allowed an insurgency to take place within North America to fight the British. It could be claimed that Osama Bin Laden studied our first elected President, George Washington, and his social network of "insurgents." Washington understood the need and implementation of clandestine activities and Bin Laden also preached such activities in his "Al Qaeda Manual."

Clandestine operations are conducted with team of three to five, set in groups known as cells. They operate with the principle of compartmentalization, which was used by our forefathers, as can be seen in the secret meetings that took place to form the Continental Congress. Historian and writer Alexander Rose exemplifies compartmentalization in his book, *Washington's Spies: the Story of America's first Spy Ring*.[1] It is the same compartmentalization used by terrorists today, in turn ensuring that secrecy remains within the different operating cells. History thus identifies organizational structures within a specific culture from our past, which assists in identifying the related elements we face today when it comes to terrorism and insurgencies.

The French Revolution

Following the American Revolution, other countries fought their own government. One of those countries was the one time Continental Army's ally,

France. Although this happened in the past, it is obvious that something—some group or someone—was key in facilitating the world's explosion of insurgencies. Just saying that the United States Revolution was the facilitating element is not enough, and understanding what was going on at the time in the world is necessary and crucial in predictive analysis for strategic national security matters.

Before the 1800s, most of Europe was ruled by kings or queens whose power was hereditary. A vote never took place to allow the people of those countries the opportunity to decide who would be their leader. After the American Revolutionary War, however, Europeans could see the strength Americans had gained by unifying against a monarch. Today, understanding the historical political elements within revolutionary/insurgency operations is part of the function within sociocultural intelligence.

The French people wanted change, but had no popular vote to enact it. A clandestine method was needed, and a political club of radical revolutionaries, known as the Jacobins,[2] came to existence. Although one of their goals was to rule and dominate the government, the Jacobins did not want to see the king of France gone. They specifically wanted to limit his royal powers. It is important to identify the political systems in existence during this time as well as the incorporation of a newly developed network and its implementation into the larger system to promote the desired effects, which could be construed as effects based operations.

The Jacobins ruled France in the years 1793 and 1794, a time referred to as the Reign of Terror, because of their violent tactics and secrecy. By the year 1798, the word "terror" was used to identify any act conducted by those trying to achieve political successes through means of intimidation and violence. Any person conducting such acts was a terrorist. Since 1798, the word terror has resumed its negative connotations. Because of this, many professionals in the field of terrorism believe the French Revolution is where terrorism started.

It is now important to understand why it continues and what can be done to prevent terrorism, insurgencies, and any other threat towards National Security. We need not only to identifying the macro elements of the who, what, why, where, when, and how, but also the micro elements, such as migration patterns, economics, social networks, media, etc., which are crucial especially in times of increased irregular warfare.

Traditionally trained intelligence operatives fail appreciation, understanding, and initiative to conduct such research to fill intelligence gaps of information. This only emphasizes the need for an official sociocultural intelligence function within the intelligence community.

Grave mistakes had been made when identifying today's warfare operations as irregular or unconventional.[3] They are grave because people continuously die and an end state fails to appear along the horizon of hope. From a historical point of view, today's warfare is very regular. Throughout history, armies have sought to ambush their enemies, create new means to cause mass havoc and destruction to promote the greatest psychological impacts on the local populace. Rules of warfare through treaties such as the Geneva Convention have provided individuals with a false sense of hope that warfare could be clean and the loss of life limited. Such treaties fail to understand the deep roots of war and the principle behind it. Bluntly put, war is a tool used to force masses of persons into submission; it historically has been conducted by any means possible to reach the overarching goal of submission upon others. A a select handful of organizations commit to laws of warfare, yet a great majority of people do not. The minority of conformers will lose in the end simply because of their ignorance of the world around them.

Reliance on technical intelligence

The goal behind the official incorporation of SOCINT is to prevent such ignorance around those involved in decision-making processes within national security due to the enhanced counter insurgency and counter terrorist operations assumed in today's elements of warfare. A great amount of research has recently been conducted about the need for SOCINT within academia, the intelligence community, the US Department of Defense, and outside privatized organizations. Much of this research was done because of the lack of understanding as to why the United States has failed to reach victory in Iraq and Afghanistan. In trying to reach such understanding, it is important to identify that multiple reasons exist and not just one. Once the multiple reasons were identified, many professionals throughout the national security elements indicated some key intriguing aspects towards today's warfare and the failures that exist in conducting operations.

Technical intelligence has become the forefront of intelligence functions, especially since the technological race that took place during the Cold War. Because the Church and Pike committees that took place during the Carter Administration attacked the CIA, NSA, and human intelligence within the United States, leaders reduced and almost destroyed any HUMINT abilities barring interrogations, and focused predominantly on technical intelligence disciplines.

Commanders today refuse to respond to time sensitive single source human intelligence unless they can obtain a SIGINT platform overhead of the intended target for fear of the negative social conditioning of human intelligence that began during the Cold War and continues even today. The greatest and most successful Irregular Warfare operations are predominantly the result of acting upon time sensitive human intelligence simply because terrorists and insurgents don't often use cell phones or other technical means of communications. If an appreciation of the communication networks (be it person to person, third party, or technical communications) existed through a trained SOCINT team, decision makers would be forced to adjust their concept of operations to better their tactical advantage. [4]

While technical intelligence has been ongoing since World War I, the reliance on such has proven to be a grave mistake in today's wars. Identifying leaders and maneuver elements in mass armies allows technical intelligence to appear as a crucial device. Unfortunately, counterinsurgency lacks state leaders, state armies, and mass movements as those faced during World War I, World War II, and greatly throughout the Korean War. Simply put, technical intelligence and the reliance of such only induces failure during Irregular Warfare operations because of their failures to identify the systems and networks, migration, media, communications, and other tools and principles that dominate the means of insurgency advancements. [5]

Analysts in today's intelligence system

Some would argue that analysts have become the "Good Will Huntings" of the intelligence community. This reference is based upon the thought that too many intelligence analysts fail to ever leave their environmentally safe offices, and simply read a lot without ever experiencing the true operational environment. These individuals are book smart. What a majority of these analysts lack is the true sense of what life is like, based upon the geographical areas for which they are responsible. They are undereducated in identifying the Essential Elements of Friendly Information (EEFI's) that is or should be identified within Commanders Critical Information Requirements (CCIR's). [6]

They maybe ignorant to the lifestyle changes within agriculture-based societies between summers and winter months (this argument can also be made for herding, industrial, technical, etc. cultures). They are clueless when it comes to identifying proper dialog, not just through language, but through nonverbal communications and written dialect because of false assumptions of literacy rates throughout the world. Serve with the Department of the Army overseas and you may hear "these people are idiots, they can't even read or write." Who is the real idiot considering that print media and billboards continue to be produced for psychological and informational operations? If you know the locals can't read and write, then it becomes obvious where the ignorance truly lies. It is not just military members who express their undereducated thoughts and actions, such mentalities are also demonstrated throughout the State Department, Homeland Security, local and state law enforcement entities, etc. The list of sociocultural ignorance is limitless.

Too often, reading and writing, then re-reading and re-writing creates inaccuracies. Analysts need to stop reading and instead physically identify with the geographic elements for which they are responsible. This is crucial mostly because of the forever changing sociocultural dynamics within geographic regions. Because analysts fail to get out of their comfort zones, today, due to the confines of remaining on a base, most intelligence operatives within the intelligence community are absolutely clueless as to what reality is abroad. When writing reports such as their intelligence preparation of the battlefield (IPB) documentation, they overlook the cultural elements that should be identified in the cultural intelligence preparation of the battlefield (CIPB) benchmarks for understandings.[7] More often than not, such understandings are overlooked simply because CIPB fails to exist today in the minds of leaders.

Because cultures continuously evolve and change, history books only serve as a baseline of understanding.[8] Although these writings present valuable information, including understandings of pride, tradition, and history itself among a people, advanced and continuous research must be conducted through updated literature and personal experiences. The mandatory reading of T.E. Lawrence for many within the IC who operate throughout the Middle East, makes it evident that we are behind simply because no modern day mandated readings exist. The Middle East has changed dramatically since T.E. Lawrence's adventures with the British Army. If an analyst went to a Middle Eastern country such as Dubai with only an educational understanding from T.E. Lawrence's writings, he would be dumbfounded.

The guillotine of perception

An identified example occurred, and argument continued within the Department of Defense with regards to the local views of the Afghan National Police. Most government officials and military members within the United States claim the Afghan National Police are corrupt and not wanted among the Afghan people. This is partially true, however the inaccuracies are overwhelming. While working in Afghanistan and speaking to the local populace, the existence of a pecking order can be identified among the locals as to whom they would like to see come assist them when faced with violence from opposition/Anti-Afghan forces. The order of preference starts with the Afghan National Police or the Afghan Border Police pending the location, followed by the Afghan conventional Army, the Afghan Commando's, the United States Special Forces, and then the US conventional forces. The issues of inaccuracy or partial truth stem from ignorance. Although American and coalition forces believe corruption is heavy within the Afghan National Police, they must understand that corruption is actually a partially accepted element within Afghan culture.

Many decision makers may not like the simple idea of "getting out from behind one's desk and start seeing for one's self attitude," yet it is crucial for future operations and for how the United States should conduct such operations to ultimately reach success. More importantly, analysts would better understand the thinking and processing of the locals, the realities behind what they believe to be, and the importance of briefing ground truth to leadership to better safeguard their own brothers and sisters of arms. It is evident that arguments would be made from decision makers about the realities of local views, but again, these are individuals who have never spoken with a local person to truly grasp their surroundings during their tours of duty.

With that in mind, we must understand how we view ourselves to break the attitudes within, then identify and appreciate the realities of how we view the indigenous persons around which we operate. We need to realize our ignorance and prejudices, as well as understand how the indigenous persons view us to try to promote social change and cooperation by fixing such local perceptions with positive interaction and events. Lastly, we must be willing to understand how the locals view themselves, which will promote a greater local situational awareness throughout the geographical areas in which operations exist.

The ugly arrogant American perception will persist unless we start seeing through the eyes of others and not just our own. As Dr. McFate argues, we must begin to incorporate more ethnocentrism into our operations and analysis.[9] She argues that without incorporating an ethnocentric approach to intelligence, we will ultimately fail. Intelligence is a process set to assist us better in understanding the elements. We must stop viewing it as strictly data. Through strict means of reliance on technological intelligence, we will never understand the environment, rather simply know the information that pertains to the data collected about the environment. This is greatly induced from lack of critical thinking and the inability of persons to visualize their areas of responsibility.

Tools to observe

Because too many in leadership positions lack the time to read long, drawn out reports, sociocultural information must be analyzed and produced through literature, but also through some means of visual delivery mechanism. Recent computer advancements have made possible tools ranging from simple processing, such as the production of charts or graphs utilizing EXCEL spreadsheet type systems, to more complex systems, such as ANTHROPAC, ANALYST NOTEBOOK, or CRIMELINK along with other classified systems for link diagrams that can be utilized to visualize the nodes and ties within social networks. In addition, geospatial systems promote enhanced observation of locations of interest or concern, such as GOOGLE EARTH and ARCGIS. While visualizing data is needed, it must be re-emphasized that the aforementioned principles should strictly be utilized to assist in the visualization of information, and not to conduct the thinking of the analyst. Such tools should never replace or supersede the necessities of individual critical thinking processing.

With the assistance of information technology, not only will qualitative aspects of data result, but quantitative elements will also be identified. To stress the importance of SOCINT, let's note that keeping an updated and accurate sociocultural understanding within a centralized informational data bank of the battle space can improve winning the battle of hearts and minds. Quantitatively, the sociocultural data will present numbers and figures to assist the updates within the decision maker's playbook, to identify what has worked and what has failed in their previous efforts.[10] This reduces the likeliness of continuing repetitive operational mistakes. When such mistakes continue, they ultimately result in the loss of life throughout the operational environment due to increased violence and hostilities that supplant all previous efforts and outcomes.

Selling the concept

Because the United States is a technologically driven society, the utilization of such principles will be needed to sell the concept of SOCINT into an official intelligence function. Some other principles, however, may hinder the sale of SOCINT, such as the need to physically go out and be with the local population. The US military is still one of the toughest fighting militaries in the world, yet it may no longer be willing to take the risks needed to defeat threats. Force protection has become an oxymoronic catch phrase. The amount of force protection on soldiers weighs them down, making it difficult to trek through austere mountainous terrain where the enemy hides. Vehicles are weighed down and too large and bulky to maneuver on the dirt roads throughout many of the locations where operations occur.

We fear injury and death so much that we induce greater probabilities of such without even realizing it. Most of those in decision-making positions who do realize the realities of our over emphasis towards force protection might conclude that the easiest is to simply remain on secured compounds and never leave to face the enemy, let alone interact with the people. If this is the position of over 80% of deployed military members serving overseas, victory will never exist because 20% of deployed persons will never constitute the force posture needed to fulfill all necessary actions in a COIN fight.

Needless to say, leadership has socially conditioned their own colleagues to fear injury or loss of life within the ranks; they also fear failing. A roadblock thus exists within the SOCINT concept. If you cannot freely get outside the secured locations and are held to the same rules of operation as a traditional military member, SOCINT will never exist and even if it did, it would never be capable of producing the knowledge needed to make a significant impact. With this in mind, it is imperative that SOCINT be a function within the intelligence community based on principles of independent and highly trained operatives that need little to no support for months to years at a time from allied elements. They must become dependent of the locals where they operate.

SOCINT operatives could never be part of, nor controlled by, the conventional military. They must be independent, but be utilized and accessible by any and all ground force commanders during times of war or military operations other than war. Still, emphasis must be reiterated with the principle that SOCINT teams cannot be controlled or directed by any outside entity to include military units. Too often, the intelligence community changes its structure due to malpractice and malfeasance within. Changing the intelligence structure is not needed at all during these times, implementing additional tools instead will hone success from within. To better understand failures within the intelligence community due to structural changes, let's observe the evolution of the intelligence community.

Changes in the IC

Some of the greatest and most dramatic changes to the US intelligence community happened after an investigation of the September 11, 2001 attacks took place. One must understand that the investigation was not conducted by individuals in any intelligence career, but mostly by politicians, most of whom were attorneys by trade. The recommendations from the findings were published for the world to see and to be implemented. Many of these recommended changes were made to please and comfort the people of this country. However, the most dramatic recommendations may prove to cause more chaos to the intelligence community and may eventually backfire.

In the year 1947, President Truman created the Central Intelligence Agency (CIA). This organization replaced the Office of Strategic Services (OSS), which was extremely active as America's espionage agency throughout World War II. Former members were used to create the CIA as we know it today. The CIA has been active and operational since its creation. The agency is strictly an intelligence agency and not a law enforcement organization. The CIA actively investigates and conducts operations against sabotage, espionage, subversion, arms proliferation, and many others. These operations are conducted through intelligence gathering, covert actions, clandestine services, propaganda, and numerous other means of measures that better the security of United States national interests. If the function of SOCINT is to exist, it must fall under a very similar principle as the CIA. This means SOCINT possibly must fall within the CIA itself as another internal element.

One person oversaw all activity through the CIA. The individual who oversaw the entire intelligence community, known as the Director of Central Intelligence, was also head of the CIA. As of the third week of December

2004, however, this person no longer oversaw the entire intelligence community, but only the CIA. The overseer of the intelligence community is now a body of individuals known as the National Security Council, which is led by the Director of National Intelligence. This implemented change will soon enough prove to be a drastic mistake because it has failed to change the means in which we conduct intelligence operations and has not increased the understanding of societies and cultures so needed in today's American government.

People such as Frank Church and Otis Pike are just two individuals who were so ignorant and frightened by government secrets they had to take their own team of government officials to court between 1975 and 1976. They went to court to ensure secrets would no longer be kept from Congress by the CIA, allowing way too many people to know what is going on, which in turn, may allow leaks of information out to the public and later our enemies. Because of the Church Committee, the old saying "loose lips sink ships" has been proven to hold a tremendous amount of truth. To make things worse, by letting too many individuals to know information they truly do not need to know about, the government now allows individuals to oversee the intelligence community.

None of these secretive aspects matter when it comes to SOCINT. All sociocultural data that gets collected, processed, analyzed, and produced into an informational delivery mechanism should remain unclassified so long as all sources, assets, and methodologies of obtaining the data remain excluded from the final report. Confidence in the SOCINT teams must be held to the highest of standards to mitigate any need to identify sources and assets used for information procurement. With this identified, multiple organizations will either want data from SOCINT operatives or will decide against such data out of animosity between the numerous elements within the intelligence community.

Following 9–11, the government of the United States recommended the implementation of a new agency, which was introduced into the intelligence community as the Department of Homeland Security (DHS). This new department was a sure "crowd pleaser" to the people of the country. The name sounds incredible, and because some are more uninformed than others, many feel that the Department of Homeland Security is a new organization that will save the country from every bad regime known to the United States.

The Department of Homeland Security will not save the world, but rather may possibly hurt the world we live in. Numerous federal law enforcement organizations such as the Federal Aviation Air Marshal Service, the Secret Service, Border Protection, Customs, and many others now are part of the DHS. These different groups hold many jobs protecting and serving while virtually none of them have a proactive intelligence role assisting in defeating the true enemy to the Western World, which is terrorism. Within DHS, a sociocultural intelligence element must exist because of its value in identifying sociocultural networks throughout America, which can identify key areas of interest outside simple crime rate evaluation. Because individual profile is assumed to be illegal, area identification through sociocultural intelligence must exist.

Continuing with the argument that restructuring the intelligence community is worthless and instead should incorporate new intelligence tools such as SOCINT, let's mention the creation of another intelligence agency, the National Counterintelligence Center. This new organization was developed because of the powers of "Executive Orders" the president can use. President George W. Bush used his executive powers appropriately by creating such an organization. The problem that comes with creating such an organization, however, is that now the government has one more organization that must be controlled and monitored. Not only must it be controlled and monitored, it must also be fully understood culturally within. This is something that the United States Department of Defense has failed to even identify among itself.

The National Counterintelligence Center has been charged with being the primary organization within the United States government for analyzing and integrating all intelligence pertaining to terrorism and counterterrorism, excepting purely domestic and counterterrorism information as well as conducting strategic operational planning for counterterrorism activities. Are there not organizations that have those same responsibilities already in such groups as the CIA, FBI, and State Counter Terrorism offices? These different organizations mentioned do indeed have specialists who conduct such operations and will continue to do so. The National Counterintelligence Center will be walking over or taking the same steps such organizations as the FBI and CIA take to investigate, analyze, and disseminate regarding terrorism issues.

When too many people get involved in an investigation, sloppiness occurs and the opportunity for the persons being investigated stopping all activities becomes likely. This happens because many enemies have just as many informants as do our own investigative intelligence agencies. A more appropriate principle that the President could have made was to have such an organization as the National Counterterrorism Center (NCTC) be a "branch" of the CIA or another already in place element within the IC. When this department was created the Director of Central Intelligence (DCI) was to oversee the NCTC. Having the NCTC ran, owned, and operated by the CIA would have made sense. Because of the newly developed National Intelligence Center, the principle that the NCTC be ran by the CIA has been foiled.

The NCTC is its own entity in the intelligence community. Leaders of the government must understand that this new organization is not a law enforcement organization, rather strictly an intelligence organization dealing with security issues relating to terrorism and national interests. It fails to identify anything and, importantly enough, it has failed to produce any sociocultural information pertaining to indigenous persons who commit such acts that threaten the National Security of the United States.

Not only will the NCTC step on the toes of other organizations and fail to produce anything of value, but others will do such harm as well. The Terrorist Threat Integration Center (TTIC) was created on May 1, 2003. This organization is claimed to be an "all source agency," meaning it will have complete access to all intelligence information available to the US government, including SOCINT from SOCINT if it were ever to exist. Because of the information it has access to, it will also be responsible with providing a terrorist threat assessment to government leadership.

By observing the role and tasking of the TTIC, any person with knowledge regarding the United States Intelligence Community should be able to understand the argument that this organization will most likely do the same job as many other organizations already conduct. This organization was designed to provide a bridge between the agencies dealing with only domestic terrorism issues (such as the Department of Homeland Security and Federal Bureau of Investigations) and those who deal predominantly with international issues (such as the CIA and Department of State). This organization, much like the National Counterterrorism Center, will soon reveal its inadequacy to provide the people with the job it is intended to do. It will fail because it has no intelligence collectors within. Everyone is culled from other organizations to work on temporary duty assignments, thus creating a new culture each time people enter that specific work environment—causing greater chaos within.

The CIA and FBI have made numerous claims that they are completely undermanned with analysts. The Terrorist Threat Integration Center supposedly will have approximately five hundred analysts working twenty-four hours a day, seven days a week. Rightly so, many individuals will find this hard to believe, since prestigious agencies such as the FBI and CIA continuously fail to maintain and recruit candidates for analytical positions.

To better the need of the analytical career fields inside, the United States government should have recruited personnel to fulfill such positions in already needful organizations, such as the FBI and CIA. This could result in a serious issue with operational security and communications security in the intelligence community. To provide some salt to our own intelligence community's wounds, we shall not forget that recent publications have already identified the need for analysts to physically leave their desks and go operational to better understand the environment in which they conduct analysis. The majority of these writings fully support the implementation and concept of SOCINT.

The patriot act and SOCINT

Security issues will always arise regarding any threat towards national security. One newly developed recommendation has already caused chaos to many American citizens. Today, the agency responsible for all domestic terrorism issues is the FBI. During the Revolutionary War, British soldiers oftentimes entered homes of individuals and searched for any contraband that would associate the owners and their families with the American Revolutionists. They would at times find contraband and, when they did not, would at times produce a piece that truly did not belong to the owners so the British soldiers could convict and punish anyway. Because of this, the writers of the Constitution ensured the residents of America that such actions would never happen again and produced the Fourth Amendment.

Because of this amendment, federal, state, and local law enforcement officials must obtain a warrant to gain authorization for "search and seizure" through a judge. This means that those law enforcement officials cannot write their own "search warrant" like the British soldiers did. This has been changed through the Patriot Act.

Today, because of the Patriot Act, federal law enforcement officials, such as the FBI, can legally enter an individual's place of general abode and conduct a search for paraphernalia regarding terrorism, terrorist activities, or financial activities regarding terrorism. This sounds like a good time to bring the phrase "No Harm No Foul" into the equation meaning that if the person did nothing wrong, then they have nothing to worry about relating to terrorism.

When the federal authorities enter the individual's house and find nothing pertaining to terrorism, but find other illegal paraphernalia, they can be arrested for that contraband instead. When the public cried out about this possible violation of privacy, no one listened to what our forefathers intended when they produced the Fourth Amendment of the US Constitution. With the incorporation of SOCINT, greater understandings and societal profiles can be made which would reduce the amount of unnecessary breaches of the fourth amendment among individual persons conducted by the FBI and its fellow law enforcement agencies.

Internal overreaction

Terrorists have won the battle they chose to fight against the United States. They attacked the country on September 11, 2001. They were able to cause mass destruction, implement fear, and intimidate members of our government, which resulted in poor policy decisions and hindered the nation's economy. Each time the United States is attacked or placed in some form of jeopardy, the government reacts. It oftentimes reacts without thinking in a sound manner. Way too often, restructuring of the intelligence community takes place simply because of failure to understand the systems and networks already at play within the IC.

Taking away the Office of Strategic Services and creating the CIA did not stop the Russians from placing nuclear weapons in Cuba, causing the Cuban Missile Crisis in October 1962. Renaming the United States Intelligence Board to the National Foreign Intelligence Board during the Carter administration did not stop Timothy McVeigh from blowing up the Oklahoma City Federal Building on April 19, 1995. Allowing individuals such as Frank Church to lead the Senate in investigative allegations of the CIA illegally collecting intelligence on United States Citizens in the 1970s did not prevent the World Trade Center from being bombed in 1993. Lastly, the 1996 Intelligence Reform Act failed to prevent hijackers from taking over aircrafts and crashing them into the World Trade Center, the Pentagon, and an isolated field in Pennsylvania on September 11, 2001.

The 9–11 Commission and the rest of the leaders inside the United States should have learned that the above-mentioned actions relating to the intelligence community had failed to prevent foreign and domestic enemies from hampering national security. The changes recommended and implemented since 9–11 will be as useful as the ones that took place in the intelligence community since the independence of this nation. Changes will not result in positive means, however implementation of additional tools such as SOCINT to what already exists, will.

The United States intelligence community is not the only organization needing assessment when introducing and implementing a new principle of intelligence function such as SOCINT. Because the United States was built on the principle of "We the People," support of the people must exist for such implementations. Currently, many people fail to support a concept such as SOCINT. Academia and professional associations fear such a concept due to their own lines of work of interacting with the international community and fear closeness to the government based on international perceptions. One such organization that stands out is the American Anthropological Association.

External overreaction

The American Anthropological Association (AAA) comprises members who perform the duties, contribute, and/or support such persons related to the practice of anthropology. Those with membership predominantly come from the United States or were educated in the United States. The organization is one of the oldest and largest professional systems related to the field of anthropology. According to its official website, AAA was designed and organized to

> to promote the science of anthropology, to stimulate and coordinate the efforts of American anthropologists, to foster local and other societies devoted to anthropology, to serve as a bond among American anthropologists and anthropologic[al] organizations present and prospective, and to publish and encourage the publication of matter pertaining to anthropology. (http://dev. aaanet.org/about/)

In 2007, the AAA publicized on their web page a statement pertaining their views towards the US military's re-introduction of a sociocultural entity called Human Terrain System. The "American Anthropological Association Executive Board Statement on the Human Terrain System (HTS) Project," as it is called, encourages fellow anthropologists to clearly stay away from HTS as it fully expresses its distaste towards the HTS component.[11] Understanding what the HTS truly is and why it is important will present great argument towards AAA's statement towards the HTS itself.

The HTS was built based on historical approaches of embedding advisors into foreign lands to better understand the people, which in turn would assist military commanders in their decision-making process. Without question, every time such a concept has been implemented within any military organization, an enhanced understanding of the battle space occurred. When understanding the full scope of an operational environment, such as a commander's battle space, decision making becomes clearer and facilitates greater successes in accomplishing missions and limiting the amount of loss of life.

If the AAA was truly as ethical as they claim to be through their bylaws and historical statement of formulization, they would not oppose the US Army's HTS, but rather promote such a principle since HTS conducts open source and unclassified data production by their studies across Iraq and Afghanistan in an attempt to bring peace and prosperity throughout these regions via understanding local populations. The work the HTS fulfills is not intended to be utilized for lethal targeting operations, but the complete opposite. The HTS information is to be used to assist in the non-lethal operations to influence the operational environment and promote safer, healthier geographic domains for all persons within, including but not limited to local indigenous and US military personnel.

Many anthropologists within the HTS have been threatened by their academic institutions to be fully released from their institutions. They have been threatened to be terminated and lose any and all anthropological association affiliations. Marc Tyrell discusses it in his article *Why Dr. Johnny Won't Go To War: Anthropology and the Global War on Terror,* with relevant arguments about the ethics involved with the science of anthropology.[12] He makes marginal argument based on past anthropologists who simply made "rules" to the science itself and identified who could associate with whom if involved in such science. Unfortunately, the argument made is weak simply because the multiple organizations within the anthropological function were authorized to create such organizations due to those military men and women before them who partook in the anthropological explorations of foreign lands that prepared yesterday's intelligence and created today's boundaries.

While public organizations are wonderful concepts to promote individual and collective thought, they should remain open to the world around them. It is apparent that members and AAA affiliates who oppose the HTS concept within today's military present greater threats towards others than the HTS can ever establish. The bylaws of the AAA may appear as though they are encouraging and reasonable to ensure ethics remain within the organization, but so does the code of conduct of the Ku Klux Klan, which states:

> We, the members of the Traditional Christian Knights, Citizens and probationers of the Invisible Empire, in order to ensure unity of organization, to guarantee an effective form of government, to perpetuate our great institution through patriotic and fraternal achievements, to preserve forever its holy principles; to continue and make vital its spiritual purposes; to achieve its laudable objects; to obtain its lofty ideals; to consummate its mission and promote effectively all things set forth in our Imperial Proclamation, do declare these by-laws as the Code of Conduct for our Order and all things thereof, in lieu of the Original pre-script of the Ku Klux Klan. These laws are hereby set forth as the Supreme Law of this Society, and we pledge our voice, our loyalty, our Manhood/Womanhood, and our Sacred Honor to enforce the same. In our endeavor toward the faithful fulfillment of this, our honorable mission, we solemnly invoke the blessings of Almighty God, through his son, Jesus Christ, Our Lord, on behalf of our Country, our Homes, Our Race, and each other, now and unto generations yet unborn. NON SILBA SED ANTHAR!"[13]

As a principle, when such elements interfere or attempt to interfere in such social change, every aspect of need, risk vs. reward, ethical dilemmas, etc. must be observed and fully understood. By observing organizational codes of conduct or bylaws, one must investigate deeper into the truth of the specified organizations truest of intentions. Historically speaking, change continues but when change is self-induced, it may often cause more hindrance or destruction to organizations such as the Intelligence Community. Sometimes, instead of complete overhaul and change, simple implementation of new ideas, systems, functions is all that is needed to better networks at hand. The introduction and understanding of an ethically sound SOCINT function into the intelligence community is one of those ideas that can become a successful entity within.

Notes

1. Compartmentalization is an organizational structure often utilized by terrorist organizations. While the organizational structure is not strictly utilized by terrorist, some other unique organizations, specifically throughout elite government entities, also utilize the principle of compartmentalization. It is utilized rather than a traditional hierarchical system in an attempt to protect its members from compromise and association with other members. Often times, organizational members may never know who their fellow counterparts are.

2. For an excellent recount of the French Revolution, specifically to obtain an understanding of the buildup which led to the Revolution itself, it is recommended to read *Citizens: A Chronicle of the French Revolution* (1990) written by Simon Schama, Vintage Books. Hopkinton, MA.

3. The article, Ethno-psychological Characteristics and Terror-Producing Countries: Linking Uncertainty Avoidance to Terrorist Acts in the 1970s is an excellent article written about the cultural elements that produce terrorist environments. Unfortunately, the authors continuously refer to the principles as "ethno-psychological" elements; this terminology is misleading because the formal and informal elements (the cultural environment) throughout these geographical domains are what influence the psychological principles within the individual actors. While terminology may appear debatable, this provides an excellent foundation for understanding sociocultural elements that could be included in SOCINT priorities of information within an intelligence collection plan. Wiedenhaefer, R. (2007). Ethno-psychological Characteristics and Terror-Producing Countries: Linking Uncertainty Avoidance to Terrorist Acts in the 1970s. Studies in Conflict & Terrorism, Vol. 30. Issue 9, p. 801–823.

4. Ralph Peters makes great cases against today's United States Intelligence Community. He points the over reliance on technical intelligence collection tools and the lacking of the human collector. He articulates the importance of understanding the systems and networks within geographical areas of concern and the inability to gain the awareness needed if such is understood without human interaction to appreciate such. He mostly, and possibly unknowingly, argues for the need for SOCINT and not necessarily HUMINT. His writing about this specific topic could be found in the July 2005 issue of the Armed Forces Journal titled *The Case for Human Intelligence: Our Addiction to Technology is our Greatest Weakness* pp. 24–26.

5. The 2005 Joint Center for Operational Analysis. Quarterly Bulletin. Vol. 7. Issue 4 (pp. 44–59) has a document written by Montgomery McFate titled, Anthropology and Counterinsurgency: the Strange Story of their Curious Relationship. Many military leaders once argued the importance of technological advancements to be and remain a superpower to protect national security. Today, because of insurgency warfare and the United States fighting their counterinsurgency efforts, original thought of technology is quickly being re-looked at. Today's counterinsurgency war has made understanding the people in which operations occur more relevant. This exemplifies the focus on Anthropology and Counterinsurgency: The Strange Story of their Curious Relationship.

6. Garra, in his works titled *Focusing Intelligence: Part 1,* provides great understanding of Commanders Critical Information Requirements (CCIR). He provides a decent attempt to identify and understand how CCIR's are transformed into Priority Intelligence Requirements (PIR), Friendly Force Information Requirements (FFIR), and Essential Elements of Friendly Information (EEFI). The greatest downfall behind this article is the extraordinary negligence to identify EEFI, which is the predominant bulk of SOCINT. This could be considered disastrous because it is the typical thought process with most military decision makers being EEFI always is in the back of their heads where in today's wartime environments argument can be made that it may have to be in the very front of their minds in order to win the "hearts and minds' of the people which is crucial in fighting insurgencies.

7. *Culture Matters: Better Decision Making Through Increased Awareness* is a very interesting paper that emphasizes the needs for a technical tool to be developed in an attempt to better understand what the authors (Davis and Fu) call Cultural Intelligence Preparation of the Battle space (CIPB). It somewhat contradicts the theory that emphasis on technical intelligence must be down sized and a greater emphasis of cultural intelligence must be developed.

8. Ronfeldt provides an incredible argument demonstrating a need for continued focus in understanding societies based off societal evolution. The greatest impact within this argument is the demonstration that evolution makes us need a continual focus in understanding societies and cultures in an attempt to limit misunderstandings in how we deal with the world around us. For full understanding of this thought, it is suggested to read his document titled, *In Search of How Societies Work: Tribes, The First and Forever Form.*

9. McFate initiates this paper with some minor background pertaining intelligence failures. The paper stresses the concept of "Ethnocentrism," which she defines as the ability to see the world through "their/others eyes." This is a principle that the United States has failed to neither understand nor accept. As this War on Terror continues one can only be hopeful decision makers do understand and accept such a concept. Lastly she identifies intelligence as an understanding and not just strictly information which is how so many view it. Those who use intelligence should never forget that it is a product of information analyzed and processed to better provide a greater understanding. To obtain a greater sense of this principle read "Far More Difficult than Counting Tanks and Planes" found in the *American Intelligence Journal, vol. 23, pp. 16–22.*

10. *Quantifying Human Terrain* (Eldridge and Neboshynsky) is a thesis paper written to identify the abilities to quantify social aspects within a specified area of interest. This concept utilized geospatial data and network analysis to build centralized "Human Terrain" data. Most importantly, this thesis identifies Human Terrain as a principle that retrieves data, analyzes such, and builds the analyzed data into a product. This is the technical element within the product of SOCINT.

11. The AAA made an incredibly horrible attempt to oppose the US Army's Human Terrain System which has been presented throughout this statement. Judgments have been made pertaining to what the authors claim to be "ethical" elements within AAA. It is obvious that these statements have been made without ever truly investigating the HTS program, identifying the US Intelligence Communities Ethical Values, nor read the classic book *Art of War* by Sun Tsu. No commander has a desire to kill when opportunities to manipulate systems can occur through nonlethal means. Unfortunately this statement was written in a fashion to make people within the anthropological field to believe differently.

12. Tyrell, M. (2007). *Why Dr. Johnny Won't Go To War: Anthropology and the Global War on Terror.* Small Wars Journal Excerpt. Vol. 7.

13. Understanding ideologies of groups is crucial while working any counterterrorism or counterinsurgency operation. Some group's ideologies may appear to be simplistic and harmless until greater in-depth research is discovered about their truest motivations. While on paper, organizations such as the Ku Klux Klan may appear harmless, the average individual knows otherwise.

Professional Practice in Sociocultural Intelligence

Understanding how we view ourselves: the exercise

US military has utilized SOCINT principles throughout its history. It did so during World War I, World War II, Korea, Vietnam, and even today some type of social and cultural advisory system has been recreated and reproduced to improve the military decision-making process. When wars end, so do the sociocultural advisory systems. A need for an ongoing principle of SOCINT exists.

An exercise was presented that determined a need for SOCINT. The identification of a need was presented as well as the first phase, or at least a portion of the first phase, of SOCINT that entails the principle of "how we view ourselves." This was achieved strictly by observing members representing the intelligence community during a moderated dialog.

Without a doubt, many professional soldiers, politicians, academics, along with others, such as the media, would attempt to argue the need for a SOCINT entity. While the Department of the Army's Human Terrain System (HTS) claims it is not an intelligence function, it does fall under the US Army's Training and Doctrine Command (TRADOC) G-2 (Intelligence). Because of this and without continued argument of the HTS and it being intelligence or not, for the sake of this exercise and understanding where the HTS falls in the Department of the Army, it was considered an intelligence function and a concept of SOCINT. The topic of the conversation was built around an article titled, *All Our Eggs in a Broken Basket: How the Human Terrain System is Undermining Sustainable Military Cultural Competence* (Connable 2009, pp. 57–64).

The focal point of this exercise was having participants to a blog on a social networking site who worked in the intelligence practice read the aforementioned article and share their comments related to the concept of HTS. Although the social networking site blog is an unclassified forum, its name will be excluded along with that of all participants due to national security and the nature of their organizations, locations, and operations in which they are employed. Exclusion of such identifiers cannot be stressed enough for this academic experiment.

The exercise had three categories of participants: strategic intelligence influencers, operational intelligence influencers, and tactical intelligence influencers. In this case, the strategic intelligence participants were identified as those in positions to influence policy. Operational intelligence participants were those who operated overseas or stateside to provide direct support to those fighting the war on terror abroad on a tactical level. Lastly, tactical level intelligence participants were those directly involved in the ground level War on Terror in places such as Iraq or Afghanistan (but not limited to these areas)—such participants are often referred to as the "grunts" of the war fight.

Through observing the participation to the forum of such intelligence operatives, this exercise showed minimal understandings and appreciations for highly trained SOCINT operatives based strictly on the Department of the Army's HTS. One of the points to be identified among participants was the difference of thought between tactical, operational, and strategic intelligence operatives. Such differences are crucial for those with interest in SOCINT as they reveal a need to assess how we view ourselves. Another point was to identify a true need for SOCINT through passive interviewing and observation among those willing to participate.

It would be hypocritical however if operatives and advisors within SOCINT identified that a need for change became evident, yet change failed to exist. The ultimate goal of SOCINT is to promote situational awareness and methodologies for effects-based operations within nonlethal targeting, which will induce change. Such principles should be utilized to promote similar practices internally and externally if such a principle were ever to exist.

To prove there is a need for SOCINT within the internal systems and networks identified throughout the intelligence community, this exercise was led by Human Subjects operating within the intelligence community. The findings will be used not only to identify such principles, but to also to conduct critical thinking to promote greater knowledge, relationships, and perceptions through implementation of ties within the pre-existing intelligence community.

All Our Eggs in a Broken Basket: How the Human Terrain System is Undermining Sustainable Military Cultural Competence, was written by a Marine Major who articulated a dislike for the HTS. It should be noted that the author of the article is a trained Foreign Area Officer (FAO) and intelligence operative who has served throughout the Middle East, including Iraq. Most FAOs are interrelated within the strategic elements more so than within the tactical and operational environments—even though their work is demonstrated on a tactical level. MAJ Connable never articulated throughout the article whether he has ever served with or among the HTS about whom he wrote.

MAJ Connable's use of such terms such as "assumption" and multiple references to previous DOD statements related to the HTS program would have one believe his dislike stems strictly from being a trained FAO and Intelligence Officer without ever serving with or beside an Human Terrain Team who serve as the field operators within the HTS program. People serving as FAO and intelligence officer as he did often feel that, in their position, they are capable of performing the function of a SOCINT element, such as the HTS. Their doctrines along with others such as PSYOP, Civil Affairs, etc., do present their tasks of understanding some elements within the sociocultural environment. This does not mean however that they are the experts in the field, but rather that they are the next closest thing to being experts because no other position is specifically designed to understand such elements within an area of operation.

Without a doubt, HTS is a concept that needs to be adjusted within the system itself. Notwithstanding professionals such as MAJ Connable who attempt to defend their employment tasking, many fail to believe similarly outside the strategic elements. Through passive observations upon a system, it should be noted that a split exists between tactical and strategic intelligence operatives. During the dialog triggered by the article written by MAJ Connable, an overwhelming number of tactical operatives showed great support for a SOCINT function and very few showed any negative support towards such a principle.

Twenty-eight persons contributed to this exercise. Of the twenty-eight participants, six replied with discussion based completely off topic expressing comments related to responsibilities of other organizations. These are construed as "side" conversations and do not hinder nor support the findings of this exercise. However, these six respondents were excluded from the original twenty-eight participants, leaving a new total of twenty-two participants.

Out of twenty-two participants in this exercise set to identify how we view ourselves and to show a need for some system of SOCINT practice to be officially introduced into the intelligence functions, fourteen identified a desire for such implementation. All tactical intelligence persons identified (totaling eleven) within this exercise were in favor of a SOCINT function. Two operational-level operatives and one strategic intelligence operative also showed desires for SOCINT. This means that over 64% of participants were in favor of SOCINT.

Five of the twenty two participants showed a dislike towards any concept of SOCINT. Of these five, all were identified in the strategic intelligence functions. Only 23% of participants were against SOCINT. Lastly, three participants were identified as being neutral in this exercise. Two of the three were identified as operational and one was identified as strategic operatives. With three out of twenty-two identified as neutral, neutral participants totaled 13%.

Argument can be made that the participants were lopsided in position being strategic, operational, or tactical; however, they were not. The blog is a concept that allows several hundred intelligence representatives to partake in professional dialog as each individual wishes. Normally, the discussions are overwhelmingly dominated by strategic level based participants with a few operational members and a minimal amount of tactical representatives. One crucial observation made about this exercise alone was that when tactical operatives were adamant towards their views and perceptions to needed entities or life-threatening experiences, they were quick to voice their opinion. Contrary to this, the strategic representatives loved to chime in on conversation about anything they have the least amount of experience in. When they were completely clueless to the realities around them, they immediately shut down and refused to participate.

Of the responses, the 23% of participants with negative views towards a SOCINT principles identified other organizations' responsibilities deemed required to conduct such SOCINT. These members quoted field manuals and handbooks related to external fields, such as Civil Affairs and PSYOP. None of the tactical participants relied on books, manuals, etc. for their responses. Instead, they relied on personal experiences. They never argued what a person or entity should or should not be doing in the performance of their duties, rather excepted that no matter the task of who should be doing what, "what" was not being conducted. In this case, the "what" was the SOCINT needed to better assist in the day-to-day operations.

While strategic operatives may believe they know what is needed for the war fighter, that is, the tactical operative, at least in the case of a needed SOCINT, they did not know realities other than what they have read, which is more often than not guidelines of hopes and dreams. To demonstrate the seriousness in identifying how we view ourselves, the six participants who were taken out of the equation of the original twenty eight because of off subject conversation were identified as strategic operatives. This is important to note because, as mentioned earlier, few strategic operatives actually participated in the exercise. Reality is, if the strategic persons would have stayed on discussion topic, the numbers between tactical participants and strategic participants would have been equal.

Identified are two separate entities with their own communications and methodologies of understanding and articulation. Within the intelligence community and without identification of the separate intelligence organizations, multiple cultures and social parameters exist. While most dialogs on this specific forum is conducted by strategic operatives, this exercise proves that when the strategic operatives fail to understand a need for social change based on real world practices, they either protest the concept of thought or they simply move to another subject with which they are more comfortable. This is not as evident on those partaking the tactical elements.

Tactical operatives express their thoughts and ideas almost always based upon what they have experienced and not strictly on what they had read. Although this exercise alone is not enough to demonstrate the importance to conduct passive polling, interviews, and or surveys among our own intelligence community to resolve problems, it does express that a lot can be learned in understanding how we view ourselves as an intelligence community.

4 Case Study: Afghanistan

The following case study has been developed from multiple sources, most of which came from local indigenous persons throughout Afghanistan. Their identities have been altered for their protection. The information for this case study was obtained through ongoing research and physical operations that lasted from October 2001 to November 2008.

The people

Afghanistan is a country with a very diverse population, with many ethnic groups, including Pashtuns, Tajiks, Hazaras, Nuristanis, Uzbeks, Turkmen, Baluchis, Pashais, and many others. Each group has its own particularities, be it in dress, grooming, customs, courtesies, etc. People living within the borders and nearing lands of Afghanistan are good by nature. The actions of some individuals, like those working closely or actually within the Taliban, should not lead one to consider the entire population as enemy.

Considering that the word Taliban means "student," how could every member of the Taliban be considered the enemy? Our own ignorance of labeling individuals has misinformed us of the truest of enemy. Intelligence reports, news media, and publications often lead readers to believe that all members of the Taliban are combatants. Such written products rarely point fingers at organizations such as HIG, HIQ, LeT, etc. Many reasons exist as to why this happens, including laziness; however the real reason is because today the United States truly does not know the enemy or the people with and against whom we operate in Afghanistan. Now is the time to learn and understand those around whom we operate to resolve the crisis and swiftly limit any further unnecessary collateral damage.

The intelligence community takes on numerous roles and responsibilities. One of those roles is deciphering who is an enemy and who is not. This is a very simplistic task that is overly complicated in nature. Understanding the people cannot be performed through technological intelligence instruments, such as those upon which the United States has become reliant. To understand any individual let alone an entire society, human interaction is needed. The discipline of SOCINT is human based. The sole purpose of such a discipline is to understand the sociocultural parameters that lay inside geographic areas of concern.

Reading fact books with thousands of references about societies and cultures written by academics does not provide the true sense of feeling, warmth, understanding, etc. of the human sociocultural parameters. We must be willing and capable to listen to life stories to gain the greatest understanding as to what a person's world is like. If we lack opportunities to listen to such storytelling, then the next greatest tool is to read their stories. To better understand the impact that a formalized and official SOCINT discipline may have on national security, let's look at the story of Mahmood.

Mahmood has a great amount of life experiences from which we as Westerners can learn. He is a young man with great passion and strength. He has been through hell and yet, he has found a way to cope and continues to strive. Today, Mahmood works with his best friend whom he refers to as his "cousin" Mohammed. His story was originally written in 2008 as research in sociocultural dynamics then used to assist US Government organizations in understanding the Afghan people.[1] It is included here to provide an opportunity to learn about a small geographical area of

Afghanistan and the typical ongoing life of survival of many Afghans. The following description of Mohammed's shop will help visualize Mahmood's environment and understand several key elements of SOCINT, such as local wedding customs, smuggling operations, family, love, religion, and much much more.

Mohammed's shop

Mohammed has a small "everything you want" type shop in the city of Jalalabad. The shop is about four feet wide by about eight feet long. The lights are powered by a small red generator that runs on gas, an overly priced commodity in Afghanistan. This generator sits outside of the shop. Air conditioning is nonexistent; no fans, only sweat beads keep one cool during the scorching days.

Mohammed's shop is what many would refer to as a small shack. On the outside, beautiful, brightly colored Afghan carpets lay on the floor. Alongside the carpets lay local Afghan Shalwar Kameez, better known as "Man Jammies" (partoog or shalwar are the trousers, the kameez or khat is the long shirt, if it has no collars then it may be a kurta worn by the men). Hanging above the carpets and Man Jammies are pakol, the hats that Ahmed Shah Masood wore, the famous Northern Alliance commander who was killed by an explosive just before the horrific attacks of September 11, 2001, made so popular here in Afghanistan. Hanging alongside these two small wooden shacks that are part of Mohammad's shop above the men's wardrobes are beautifully designed and overly bright colored scarves for women. Some modern Afghan dresses can also be found. Most noticeable is a man who works a 1950s vintage sewing machine. He is the store tailor. While he is only 35 years of age, his physical attributes make him seem older than fifty.

Around the shop is a group of local Afghan men, including Mohammed himself, lying on six-foot-stacked mattresses in the peak of the 120° heat during the summer months in an attempt to stay cool. A large red plastic tarp is draped above the main office space. Two smaller wooden storage areas outside are also utilized to try to gain some shade from the blistering rays of the daily sun.

Every month, except during Ramadan,[2] valued customers are often offered "Chai" (Afghan Green tea mostly purchased from North Korea and China). A small propane burner heats the water for the loose tea and is also used to cook a mixture of tomatoes, onions, okra, and possibly some beans that will be later served with rice and a small steel bowl of cooked goat. All food is eaten with the right hand and always served with the locally made "nan,"[3] the customary flat bread served virtually with every meal. The goat is served in small individual bowls with red or brown oil that is most likely colored from the spices. A Westerner could easily construe the red colored oil as blood from the meat, but blood cannot be consumed by Muslims in any form cooked or uncooked. Therefore draining the blood from all slaughtered animals is required. The piece of meat served is about the size of a fist and in the middle of it is the bone.

When customers are scarce, all those working in Mohammed's shop lay still to conserve the energy that is rapidly drained from them by the sun and lack of potable water. The store looks inert until one of the workers sees a customer. Mohammed and his team of businessmen then jump up and provide the traditional Pashtun embrace of friendship. They wrap their arms around one another with great smiles, grip their hands together around the friend's back, and instill a small squeeze that expresses their happiness.

Mohammed owns this small shop where one can buy everything from illegally reproduced movies on DVD, phones, electronic devices, clothing, cricket bats, gems, and jewelry. Mohammed works there with his brother, uncle, a tailor, and his trusted jeweler, Mahmood.

Each person who works with Mohammed is business oriented and knows how to wine and dine a customer. Such a business approach makes one want to come back just to learn from their experiences living in Afghanistan under Taliban rule and, today, under the newly appointed Afghan government.

All those working with Mohammed have incredible stories, some too unimaginable and scary for anyone not living in Afghanistan to fathom. This is just the beginning, no one will know how their stories will unfold, but hopefully this will exemplify what they have already been through.

Mahmood

"I go through Pakistan and into India like a thief. I have no passport, no visa, and I must bribe my way past police checkpoints and Taliban illegal checkpoints." So says Mahmood, the jeweler who works in Mohammed's shop.

Mahmood has been to Afghan prison four separate times under Taliban rule. He has been tortured and scarred. He is not even thirty years old.

He shares his home with fifteen other people, all living in only five rooms. He sleeps on the floor with his spouse with only a blanket, one pillow, and no mattress so his seven-month-old child can sleep soundly in the one bed that is considered "his." Food is cooked on a propane burner or in a small wood oven surrounded by clay. There is no running water inside the house. Water is pumped from the outside well then carried inside in buckets for daily use.

Mahmood's house is a one-storey white building. It has one aqua blue door and no windows. The outside is surrounded by a four foot wall made of mud and stone. Don't be fooled by the mud wall though, it is strong enough to not allow a .50 Cal machine gun to penetrate.[4] Everything in Afghanistan is strong: the people, the homes, the families, and the will to survive. These walls start out as stone walls that are plastered in mud; the mud is touched up every six months or at least once a year. The mud keeps the houses very cool in the extreme summers and warm in the icy winters.

Mahmood understands his beliefs and values, and has found his way to balance everything evenly. Although he does not believe women should be forced to wear the traditional Burkha, as the Taliban once mandated, the women in his family must do so for other non-Islamic reasons. The Burkha is a covering garment worn by women in countries such as Saudi Arabia, Pakistan, Afghanistan, and numerous other Arabized locations. Colors vary based on location and personal family status. Here, it is light blue. This garment covers the entire body from head to toe with only a small mesh screen in the front of the face to view the outside world. It is a hot covering that causes many women to trip while walking the streets.

As mentioned, Mahmood does not force the women in his family to wear the Burkha for Islamic purposes, but he does so for security. Mahmood has worked for the United States government as a laborer in the past. He fears that many Afghans want to kill him because of his close relations with Americans. He also fears that women in his family will become targets if his relations with the United States are discovered. This is why they must wear the Burkha; it may protect them from those who want to kill.

Mahmood comes from Laghman province, one of the leading gem mining areas in all of Afghanistan. His family is very powerful in Laghman. His father is the tribal Malik (leader). His family has been involved in the gem industry for over five generations. Because of the Taliban rule and bandits, he and his family moved to Jalalabad, which is located in Nangahar Province south of Laghman. Once they moved to safer Jalalabad, Mahmood soon began to work as a laborer with the United States. This is how he first met his good friend, his "cousin" Mohammed.

Like many Afghans, Mahmood did not find working as a laborer appealing for very long, but he saved enough money to open his own jewelry shop in downtown Jalalabad. Business was difficult because people in Afghanistan have very little money. They often can't afford wheat, one of their prized food sources, which is used to make nan. There was no way Mahmood would be capable of earning enough money to support his family so long as his fellow Afghans continued to die of malnutrition and starvation. All his struggles were resolved one day after seeing his "cousin" for the first time after almost a full year.

Americans tend to view time as money, and the more time that goes by without working, the less money is earned. In Afghanistan, time is simply time. One may sit and wait for good to come. The term most often heard about this concept is "Enshallah" which means, "God willing." On this specific day for Mahmood, God was indeed willing.

Mohammed had walked into Mahmood's store in Jalalabad not knowing who owned the place. He looked at Mahmood with disbelief, because he had never had any inkling that his old friend knew anything about gems or jewelry. The two embraced and sat for a while, chatting about family, friends, and their past. As time progressed and after plenty of hot tea, Mohammed asked Mahmood if he could fix a piece of gold jewelry he would like to wear around his neck. This took no time to fix for the expert jeweler. In fact, the greatest amount of time was spent in the socialization between the customer and his service provider. Business is nothing to rush in Afghanistan, instead good relations are essential to build and maintain. This is the way most business is conducted throughout Afghanistan.

During the conversation prior to the work that was later conducted, Mohammed informed Mahmood that he still worked for the Americans. He was no longer working as a laborer as he had saved enough money to open his own business to serve Americans' essential needs, such as cellular phones, DVDs, tobacco products, etc. Thus, he had built a small shop on an American base. After Mohammed saw the excellent work on his piece of jewelry, Mahmood asked if he might need a jeweler to work in his shop. Mohammed, being the savvy businessman that he is, knew that one of the greatest ways to boost economic growth was to increase the number of products offered for sale and desired by the Americans.

Jewels are a hot commodity in American culture. People often buy jewelry for their loved ones as a sign of love and appreciation. American service members make extra money for serving in combat locations. They had the money, and Mohammed knew what they wanted, and in this case it was gems. Both Mohammed and Mahmood were originally from Laghman Province and knew numerous mining experts in that region. They could work together and get the best gems for the best price using both networks simultaneously. Immediately, Mohammed had another worker in his small shop serving the Americans needs.

Prior to working for Mohammed, Mahmood conducted drastic business operations for survival purposes for him and his family. More often than not, he would travel through mountainous terrain into Laghman and other provinces throughout Afghanistan to purchase his gems. He would travel through Taliban-controlled areas, encounter bandits, drive on dirt roads known to have Improvised Explosive Devices (IEDs), encounter troubles, and risk his life for his family. All of this was done simply to ensure that those who lived under the same roof as he had enough food and potable water.

Mahmood traveled extensively between Afghanistan, Pakistan, and India for his gem business. These business trips could easily be construed as the most dangerous times of his life. He faced the horrors of Taliban, mining bandits, corrupt police, and war. Mahmood is not a thief, he is not an extremist, and he is not a militant. He is a survivor. What follows are just a few of his unbelievable experiences across one of the deadliest regions on earth.

Travels through hell

Mahmood is about five feet five inches tall and weighs short of one hundred and fifty pounds. He has olive skin, black hair, a trimmed yet shaggy beard, and green eyes. Mahmood told about his trips to India to sell his gems with a smile to disguise the fears he faced on every journey. He traveled from the city of Jalalabad through one of the world's deadliest border crossings known to mankind. It's called Torkham Gate.

Torkham Gate is arguably the largest land border in all of Afghanistan. Thousands of large trucks filled with supplies for the Afghans cross daily. These are known as "Jingle Trucks" because of their decorations in bright colors and dangling metal steel beads. Most of the supplies they carry are sources of food, such as cooking oil and wheat. In addition to the Jingle Trucks, white and yellow taxis with up to twelve passengers each flow nonstop through this border crossing. Most of the passengers are internationally displaced persons (IDPs) from years of war within Afghanistan and the North West Provinces of Pakistan due to Taliban and Al Qaeda elements.

Standing at the gates of Torkham are also women wearing light blue Burkhas and children dressed in beautiful colored clothes. Little boys wear their tan, white, and light blue man jammies (Shalwar Kameez). Girls wear their long pants and shirts, similar in design as the boys' man jammies. The girls' clothes are brightly colored in combinations of green, red, pink, yellow, and purple. Depending on their age, some girls wear colorful head scarves. More often than not girls who are just short of puberty do not wear head-scarves. These girls do not enjoy the luxuries of so many American children. Many lack any formalized education and often can be observed as serving their siblings in motherly roles.

In Torkham Gate and throughout most of Afghanistan, it is common to see young girls between the ages of six through twelve holding babies in their arms. They serve as the family's day care and nurture their siblings. They do not beg for food, candy, or toys. The police and border guards on both sides of the borders would beat them if they saw such unruly behavior. If such items were to be handed out, they would be the first to swarm like a thousand bees understanding and even possibly accepting the beatings that such actions may incur.

Across from Torkham Gate, in Pakistan, is the famous Khyber Pass. Khyber is a historically rich area crossed by some of the world's most famous warriors, including Alexander the Great, Genghis Khan, soldiers of the British Empire, and many others. It is considered the "passage into Asia." Khyber Pass, like most "passes" bordering Afghanistan, lay in the valleys of mountainous terrain. These mountains' snow caps, which remain for about half of the year, form the main water sources for the indigenous people.

Mahmood always begins his travel early, immediately after "Morning Prayer," which he normally says at around four in the morning (Afghanistan is an Islamic country, therefore prayers are said five times a day). The sun just begins to rise as Mahmood kisses his wife, who still lies silently asleep. Like all good fathers in the world, he tucks the blanket that keeps his seven-month-old daughter warm before kissing her with love. Next, he walks out to the business district of Jalalabad where he finds his taxi.

The taxi has no air conditioning and will soon feel like an oven in the midday heat. The white and yellow station wagon taxi takes him to the edge of Pakistan. Once at Torkham Gate, he then walks across the border where thousands of people opposite of him wait to enter into Afghanistan. He then finds another taxi, which he takes to Takal village, the "University Town of Peshawar" in Pakistan.

This journey can take up to three days depending on which areas his cab driver chooses to ignore due to violence throughout Pakistan. In police bribes alone, he must pay anywhere between 2,000–5,000 Pakistan Rupees and a carton of cigarettes. Mahmood tells me the story, recalling a time when he stopped in a village for rest and food.

He had discovered the village was controlled by the Taliban, probably Mangals Bagh's men. While seeking food and water, he had been forced along with everyone else in the shopping district to gather in the middle of the street. Taliban all around had accused a man of being a thief. In front of all bystanders, they cut off the thief's hand, held it in the air as it dripped with blood, and yelled over the screaming voice of the man recently brutalized, "anyone caught stealing will be dealt with according to Islam. We will cut off their hands and leave those mutilated for Allah to see when they perish into hell."[5]

Knowing the violence in Pakistan, Mahmood always looks to move fast and keeps on his journey to India. From his rest stop in Pakistan he jumps onto a bus filled with people also heading into India with luggage, woven items, and carpets strapped to the roof. Mahmood's fears do not leave him once in India though. Gangsters and thieves abound, but Mahmood is street smart.

As soon as he gets into India, Mahmood finds a hotel to use as his safe house. In the United States, this hotel would not even earn a one star rating. It is a shanty place, host to cockroaches, bugs, and rodents. There is no restaurant in the lobby. At the entrance is a small office with a sliding glass window. Mahmood asks for a room and the receptionist hands him a key. The building is only a few stories high, without an elevator. Once in his room, Mahmood hides his precious gems, then leaves to "shop around" the nearby jewelry stores. This is where he will make the greatest profit for himself, his wife, and his little girl, Shiasta.

Mahmood does not purchase anything from the jewelers. He looks at their products through their glass casings and identifies gems similar in size, color, clarity, and quality. He asks about prices. He finds the highest prices offered, and then approaches the dealer he is most comfortable with about his own deals.

More often than not, Mahmood brings Indian jewelers into his game with ease. He never shows what he has to offer, but instead invites a jeweler to his office, which is his hotel room. The jeweler meets him later in the evenings once the store is closed. But first, he must show that he has the money to pay for what Mahmood has to offer. Mahmood then lays out a cloth rag filled with thousands of dollars worth of merchandise. The gems glisten, bright and of high quality. The Indian customer likes what he sees and the two begin to negotiate. After time and appeasement from the two parties, the new customer leaves, and Mahmood immediately changes room for fear his customer may betray him and inform his "friends."

The feared "friends" are thieves, bandits, and Indian equivalent Mafiosi. They have robbed him in the past. They have beaten him and left him on the streets at night, putting him at further risk of attack. What Mahmood has are stones from war torn Afghanistan worth thousands on the world market. He does not have low-quality merchandise as he is very selective. He has rubies and lapis from Bamyan Province; tourmaline, garnet, jade and onyx from Laghman and Nangahar; topaz and quartz from Konar. The selection is plentiful, the quality is impeccable.

Mahmood completes his mission to sell his merchandise and begins his journey back to his family. Only when he steps into his home and embraces Shiasta does he know he is safe.

The above story exemplifies just one of the many journeys Mahmood had to accomplish to survive the harsh living conditions in Afghanistan before he started working with Mohammed.

Muggers, thieves, killers, all the types of individuals any sane person would want to ignore abound around eastern Afghanistan and western Pakistan. Those most feared are the Taliban, an ideologically motivated Islamic insurgency organization. Today they are an opportunistic group that feeds off the poor and helpless. Their leaders are typical narcissists who continually use skewed Islamic theology to implement their own laws of fear and intimidation among the locals. There are now numerous factions of the Taliban, who often fight one another to enhance their power.

Paying for crime

Before the United States intervened in the atrocities that the Taliban continually implemented among the people for over twenty years, Taliban ruthlessly controlled everyone by fear. They would conduct public beheadings in the Jalalabad soccer stadium, which later became part of Governor Sherzai's compound. They would pull people out in the middle of the streets and chop off their hands for punishment, tried without due process. They would throw hundreds of people into the Nangahar prison daily for the most ridiculous of Taliban implemented laws. Today, women are still placed into prison for running away from prearranged marriages so they can be with the ones they truly love.

Mahmood knows all too well about life in Nangahar prison during Taliban rule. "Jail is like home, we called it our guest house. Everyone went to jail when the Taliban ruled here." The "everyone" Mahmood speaks of refers to individuals from 14 to 90 years of age—men, women, and children. Crimes to be punished via time spent in Taliban-controlled prison ranged from murder, thievery, rape, to extremes, such as missing one of the five daily prayer as mandated by Sharia (Islamic Law), wearing too baggy "man jammies", styling hair (having a "Christian Haircut"), not paying taxes to Taliban, and trimming one's beard. For women, such laws included traveling unescorted by a male, showing any part of skin which meant their required Burkhas were too short and a man might see their ankles, being raped by another man, or refusing to marry.

The process of being charged of a crime was very simple. Taliban had their own Islamic Police force that would travel throughout the city of Jalalabad searching for individuals in violation of their own implemented laws. Amir Belmaroof was in charge of this special Taliban police force. His men would snatch an individual off the streets, take him to Nangahar prison, torture him through beatings, and force him to confess a crime he knew he did not commit. This was known as their military court martial. Once a confession was presented, they would then send the prisoner to face the Taliban judge. The judge would decide the fate of the prisoner depending on the crime committed and confessed to via torturous beatings. Depending on the prisoner's own personal wealth, the punishment would be very little or very severe, ranging from beheadings to large cash payment and giving away a young female child based on the severity of the crime. Such children would be then placed into the international sex slave market or be raped and abused.

Jailed by the Taliban

In his case, Mahmood never had a lot of money. His family was powerful in Laghman, but his journeys among the Taliban began when he moved to Jalalabad as a teen. At the age of sixteen, Mahmood fell in love. He knew this young girl through his family. One day, he put on his finest white Shalwar

Kameez and his newly handmade black vest, known as a "vaskat." Normally men in Afghanistan wear sandals on their feet when outside. This day was special though, and to get to Bibi, his first love and later on wife, he had to travel via motorcycle. So Mahmood wore black leather boots to protect his feet, but more importantly to show off the little bit of economic wealth he had gained.

Driving his red Suzuki motorcycle through the Taliban-controlled streets of Jalalabad, he suddenly remembered he had forgotten his camera and money. So halfway through, he turned around to head back home to pick up his belongings. He retrieved his camera and money and, on his way back, his first encounter with the horrors of Taliban began.

Taliban had noticed that the red motorcycle had driven by them twice already and decided not allow him to go by a third time. They forced him off his motorcycle, inspected his hair, his clothing, and quickly interrogated him. They asked him where he was going and who his father was. He informed them that his father used to work for Shah Massood, the onetime King of Afghanistan, as a Colonel in the Afghan Army. This was the first mistake Mahmood made. From that little bit of information about his father's past work, he would from here on out be construed as a Communist, which the Taliban hated due to the Russian war in Afghanistan.

Taliban grabbed Mahmood by the collar. They took all his money, his camera, and he never saw his Suzuki again. They threw him into the back of a pickup truck and hauled him off to Nangahar prison. He had not done anything wrong. He had no drugs on him, was not intoxicated, never hurt anyone, nothing. Yes his father did work as a Colonel in the Army, but that was not illegal and it was not Mahmood who had the Army connection anyway. So why was he arrested? Because of his clothes.

Mahmood was wearing the traditional Afghan "man jammies." He was told that they were too loose. The pants of the Shalwar Kameez are very baggy to begin with. They reached to his ankles like most traditional "man jammies." According to the Taliban, they were too baggy. The reality was that the Taliban in the area were threatened by Mahmood's father, believing he was a spy for the Afghan Communist Party.

At less than five feet tall and not weighing more than one hundred plus pounds, Mahmood at age sixteen, took the first serious beating of his life, which came from a complete stranger armed with an AK-47 machine gun. This beating occurred in a small five by five mud walled room inside Nangahar Prison.

It was winter in Jalalabad. A cold winter season that kept the dark prison damp and frigid. There was no toilet in the room, no bed, no blankets, nothing other than a small steel ring welded to the ground. Above the ceiling was another steel ring. Feces from the previous victim lie on the ground in the corner of the room. Mahmood was scared knowing the stories of Nangahar prison, and waited in silence and in the cold, shackled to the floor.

The AK-47 toting guard walked into the room, a wooden club in his hand and the AK slung across his back. His beard was thick and long, his hair covered by a black turban. He unlocked the chain that restrained Mahmood via the steel ring in the middle of the floor. He then grabbed the chain still attached to Mahmood's ankle and connected it to the ring above his head. Another Taliban guard walked into the room and the two guards began to pull all the slack out of the chain. They continually pulled the chain through the loop in the ceiling until Mahmood swayed upside down in mid air. He did not squirm nor tried to resist. He knew there was nothing he could do, but endure what was about to happen.

Mahmood closed his eyes and thought about the love of his life for strength and courage. The sound of a loud smack cracked through the room's air. It was the club striking the back of Mahmood. He screamed in pain and realized that this was the worst thing he could do. His abusers began to yell at him. Through the yelling, another loud smack broke through the air. This time it was Mahmood's ribs. The guards began to hit him repeatedly, and blood started to flow out Mahmood's mouth.

This beating continued on and off for three consecutive days. When beatings did not occur, Mahmood was forced to pray with a Mullah along with the other prisoners in the courtyard five times a day. Many could not even stand due to the pain and agony they had been through the night before. They would listen to Islamic extremists rhetoric used as an attempt to socially condition the prisoners to join the Taliban. For three days, Mahmood was not served one ounce of food or water, and received no medical treatment. His lips bled from dehydration. For three days, Mahmood endured the most brutal form of brainwashing. On the evening of the third day, his Uncle came to free him. Mahmood's guards informed him that he had paid for his sins and was released.

Being freed was overly confusing to Mahmood. He never knew what he did wrong to go to prison in the first place. His uncle embraced him, and took him to his car. They drove to Mahmood's home. Waiting for Mahmood was his entire family excited and saddened by this experience. As he walked in, he saw Bibi, who was also waiting for him. This is when Mahmood knew for sure he would one day marry Bibi.

It was not long after his first encounter with the Taliban police that Mahmood decided he had to earn wealth so Bibi's father would allow him to marry his daughter. As he turned seventeen, he decided to follow the five generations of gem traders by creating his own jewelry business in the city of Jalalabad. His store was small with no lights other than a portable lamp plugged into a generator. His jewelry and gems lay in a small glass case. He would continually develop his skills by designing and creating his own jewelry.

Soon after he opened his shop, he began to receive customers. Some of his most dependable customers were Taliban themselves. They were dependable because they came to his shop; they were not the greatest customers though. Mahmood was forced to sell his merchandise to Taliban at very low costs, which at times made him lose large sums of money. They never were his friends and acted more as a nuisance. They would continually threaten him and take items at will.

Within a few short months of working in his newly established jewelry store, Mahmood faced the second most terrorizing time of his life. He was working on his generator behind his store. Without realizing the time or hearing the call to prayer because of his work, he missed his mid afternoon prayer. Taliban Islamic Police were in the area checking all store owners to ensure no store was open and no workers was around as they were all forced to go to the local Mosque.

Amir Belmaroof, the Special Taliban Police commander, saw Mahmood behind his store working on the generator. He immediately grabbed the seventeen-year-old Mahmood, stood him up and angrily asked why he was not at the Mosque. Mahmood was scared like all other locals when being face to face with Taliban members such as Amir Belmaroof. He did not know what to say and immediately froze.

Amir barked orders to his fellow Taliban nearby and ordered Mahmood to be detained. Again, they threw him in the back of the Taliban police pickup truck, continuously chastising him for his non-Islamic behaviors of failing to adhere to the "Salat."

Salat is one of the five pillars of Islam. It means that Muslims must pray five times daily. The prayers should be performed immediately upon "Fajar" at dawn's awakening, "Zuhar" at true noon, "Asasr" before dinner, "Maghrib" at sunset, and "Isha" at dusk. During the Taliban rule, individuals were forced to perform their duties of Salat through attending the Mosque. It was "Non Islamic" to perform Salat by yourself. For this, Mahmood was arrested.

Mahmood knew all too well what was about to take place in his prison room. What he did not know was whether he would be killed as a "Kafir" (non-believer). The Koranic Sura 4:89 states, "They but wish that ye should reject Faith, as they do, and thus be on the same footing (as they): But take not friends from their ranks until they flee in the way of Allah (From what is forbidden). But if they turn renegades, seize them and slay them wherever ye find them." According to Islamic extremists, such as the Taliban, this Sura provides the rights of such groups to kill non-believers, those that leave Islam, and those that believe in nothing at all.

However, Mahmood does believe in Islam. He is a good Muslim who knows right from wrong. He was caught up in the moment attempting to fix his generator behind his store. Because of his negligence, according to the Taliban that day, he paid restitution through three consecutive days of beatings similar to the ones he had received only a few months ago. He was hung upside down and beaten with a wooden club, only this time, a new punishing tool was used.

When being beaten consecutively for hours on end, the human body goes numb for short periods of time. Prisoners of war often pass out during advanced beatings then come through again due to the continuation of such painful torture. Mahmood never passed out. He claims to never have cried during this period in prison until right before he was released. The lead guard grabbed the chains that were connected to Mahmood's ankles and released them, dropping Mahmood four feet from the air down to the floor. Before allowing Mahmood to get to his feet, the guard grabbed his hand and wove a thin wooden dowel between his fingers. He then placed Mahmood's hand flat on the floor and began to stomp his hand repetitively four to six times until his fingers were completely shattered. The guards, laughing at a young man who was only 17 years old, then walked out of the room.

In the following hour, Mahmood's family returned to the prison to gain his release. His father could not go and a woman could not travel without an escort through the streets of Taliban-ruled Jalalabad. His uncles were the ones who came to retrieve Mahmood, a dangerous mission in itself for his family.

Anytime someone went to Nangahar Prison, it was considered dangerous. A person must dress perfectly, males must ensure their beards were not trimmed, their hair must not be groomed, the women must be escorted and have their Burkhas cover them appropriately in accordance with the Taliban's likings. About six months after his second release from prison, Mahmood found out how un-Islamic Taliban rules really were.

Young men do not grow beards overnight. At seventeen, Mahmood noticed a few hairs on his chin and decided to shave them off. He was still trying to impress his soon to be wife and looking good was important to him—as to many boys his age.

Mahmood found out that his friend had recently been sent to Nangahar Prison. He had not shaved his facial stubble in a few days, as it takes time to grow back. He decided to visit his friend to provide him comfort and food because he knew firsthand what life was like without food and extensive torture in this prison. As he went through the main doors, a guard noticed the hair stubble on his chin. It was evident that Mahmood had shaved it off a few days before.

The guard asked Mahmood if he had shaved his beard. Mahmood answered that he was a young teenager and that facial hair was not yet growing at this time in his life. The guard knew otherwise. Because Mahmood informed the guard that he was only there to visit a friend, the guard allowed the two to see one another, for three days straight. This time, rather than being beaten into submission, the guards played the interrogator "good cop bad cop" game with the two friends.

Guards would question one and, based upon the answer, would beat the other. In this case, Mahmood would be questioned and his friend would be slapped by the guards in the face. Mahmood would try to answer the questions based on what the guards desired to hear. He could not bear to see the blood continue to spray off the face of his friend. No matter how Mahmood answered though, he would never please his guards. Such interrogations lasted hours on end. The two friends would embrace one another in comfort as soon as the guards left the room. Before long, guards would return and repeat everything over and over again, but this time with Mahmood taking the beatings and his friend answering the questions.

Mahmood thus spent three days in prison for visiting his friend. It was his friend's family who came to the prison to earn the release of them both. Prison officials would not inform family members of their sons, daughters, mothers, or fathers being kept in prison sometimes for days, week, months, years, and at times would never tell anyone at all. This is why Mahmood's mother and father never attempted to gain the release of their son. They just were never informed.

One can easily argue that Mahmood was thrown into jail on his third trip because he just wanted to visit his friend. The reality is that it was because he did not grow out his beard. Islamic extremists believe that all men should wear a beard because of the Hadith. The Hadith is the second most sacred book in Islam which outlines the life of the Prophet Mohammed. Numerous passages in the Hadith such as number 498 states, "trim closely the moustache, and let the beard flow (Grow)." Hadith number 500 states "Act against contrary to the polytheists, trim closely the moustache and grow the beard." There are numerous other scripts in the Hadith that mention the Islamic importance of the beard.

Mahmood, just before his eighteenth birthday finally had the beginnings of what could be construed as a good beard. Of course it was not the "one fist" length that the Taliban required as per additional Hadith passages, but it was scraggily and unclean. This scruffiness did not appeal to him, and he thought his love Bibi would not like the way he looked. He decided to trim his beard.

The things men do for women sometimes is, well let's just say, a bit crazy. Mahmood did everything to impress Bibi and her family. The one thing he shouldn't have done was trim the shag on his face. The day he decided to shave would be the last time Mahmood made the mistake of not adhering to Taliban law.

Taliban Special Islamic Enforcement Police ran by Amir Belmaroof saw Mahmood the day he decided to trim his beard to look presentable for his love. As soon as they saw him, they snatched him off the street and sent him to Nangahar Prison. He would spend four days there. Only one day would he drink anything at all—a small cup of Chai (tea). He was offered some food, but he feared it was poisoned and refused to eat. He went through the same style of torture as he did from the first and second trips to prison. His family (uncle) was informed that he was in prison on the second day. He attempted to gain his release and was denied. The third day, his family brought him food, but it never reached him. On the fourth day, they finally earned his release. He was beaten so badly that he could not walk. He stayed home lying in bed for two consecutive days. It was not until he saw Bibi that he regained enough strength to get up and walk for the first time since his release.

Mahmood did everything in his power to remain safe from Taliban from this point on. His safety was through Taliban compliance. He complied with everything they wished. He grew his beard, he prayed five times a day, he would assemble when called to the streets to watch public executions, and he would hide at night in his home without ever leaving until the security of the sunlight. He lived like a prisoner in his own life through the restraints of the Taliban for three consecutive years.

A taste of freedom

It was not until the year 2001 when Mahmood, like so many other Afghans, gained a sense of freedom. It was exactly October of 2001 when Mahmood knew he would be freed. He remembers the first day he heard music on the radio. This was the first sign that something had changed in Afghanistan. He could not understand what it was until he heard bombs and gunfire out in the distance of his home. He clearly remembers sitting with his entire family around a small radio and listening to Pakistani news that claimed the United States had invaded Afghanistan. He remembered hearing similar sounds as a young child when the Russians had invaded Afghanistan. Only this time it was the Americans, not the Russians.

Mahmood also remembered the stories his father told about the amount of support the Americans provided to the Afghans. He knew that it was the Americans who assisted in the Afghan "Jihad" to fight off the Russians. Mahmood felt the first ounce of freedom the day he heard the bombs in the distance. Till today, he states that was never so happy as the day the Americans came. This was the day he knew that he would finally be able to love Bibi, the day he knew he could marry her.

Within days of Mahmood learning of the United States invading Afghanistan to gain its freedom from Taliban rule, he told his mother for the first time that he was in love. He told her as she was washing clothes that he loved Bibi and wanted to marry her. "Mom" stopped everything she was doing, dropped the clothes she was handwashing in the metal bucket, grabbed Mahmood and embraced him with joy. The Afghan people, specifically those of Pashtun ethnicity, cherish love and marriage.

Within a day, "mom" informed her husband of Mahmood's dreams to marry Bibi. Afghan culture prevents the groom-to-be from asking a father, be his own or the bride's, for permission to marry. The groom-to-be's mother informs the groom's father, then it is the decision of the groom's father to decide whether he wants his son to marry a specific girl. In Mahmood's case, Dad agreed that the two should be married.

The same day "dad" found out about of his son's desires, he walked to Bibi's home to speak with her father. The two talked for over an hour about topics ranging from health, friends, and the most recent US operations in Afghanistan. The two agreed about the happiness both families felt towards the Americans' intervention to rid the country of Taliban control. As the conversation progressed, Dad asked Bibi's father what he thought about Mahmood marrying his daughter.

Afghan culture dictates that the father of the bride is the ultimate decision maker who will decide whether a man and woman will marry. In this case, Bibi's father believed Mahmood was a good man, but that the two were just simply too young to marry. He informed Dad to ask Mahmood to wait just a little longer to ensure that Taliban were no longer in control of the country. Within weeks, both families saw the expedited successful operations of the United States military. The two fathers met again and agreed to the marriage.

During the time of Mahmood's original conversation to marry Bibi, the Holy Month of Ramazan (Pashtun pronunciation of Ramadan) was occurring. It is a time of peace, purity, cleansing, and forgiveness. It is the time the Archangel Gabriel descended from Heaven to give the revelations to the Prophet Mohammed that allowed completion of script for the Holy Koran. Immediately after Ramazan, the celebration of Eid Ul Fitr begins. Eid Ul Fitr translated from Arabic to English literally means the "Celebration to break the fast." It is a time of celebration, brotherhood, moral victory, fellowship, and unity. Large family gatherings occur with feasts. It only made sense to allow the two to marry after the Holy months and immediately after Eid Ul Fitr, especially knowing that the Afghans and Americans joined as one in unity to achieve moral victory over the Taliban who for over twenty years deprived the Afghan people freedom.

Dad paid, as all fathers do in Afghanistan, a large sum of money to the bride's family only days before the marriage occurred. This bride price is called "Haq Mehar," which is more of a security for the girl and proof that the boy and his family will be able to support her. It is the only thing she will have if the marriage fails. Payments of Haq Mehar do not have to be paid through money but can be made in gold, gems, or property. Marriage is not a sacrament in Islam; it is only a contract that states so on the Nikah Nama (Certification of Marriage). Usually, the more important a girl's family is, the higher the Mehar (bride price). Mahmood's father paid a total of an equivalent of four thousand US dollars to Bibi's family and promised to pay for all food eaten during the wedding celebration and her wedding dress. Mahmood's family also promised to pay for Bibi's fathers wedding Shalwar Kameez.

The Afghan wedding

Afghan weddings are very popular celebratory events. Unlike in the United States where brides and grooms must decide on the number of guest who will attend the wedding, in Afghanistan, families invite all their friends and loved ones. This means that, instead of just the husband and wife, all members of the family living in the home of the guests, children, grandparents, etc. are invited as well. Many Afghan homes house up to twenty people under one roof. And so over two thousand people attended Mahmood and Bibi's wedding.

American weddings last on average several hours and traditionally consist of attending a ceremony in a religious place of worship followed by a celebration in another venue. In Afghanistan, the traditional wedding lasts over two days. On the first day, generally large crowds of attendees gather around the entire area of the groom's home while the bride's friends and family do the same at her house. Mahmood wore his nicest Shalwar Kameez and Bibi wore an emerald green gown, the color of fertility. Afghan women often wear either the green dress or at times may be found wearing red, the color of happiness and good luck. Pre-Islamic culture is evident in the colors; the white gowns are a new addition since the past 40 years, though they are not typical at all as wedding gowns. The bride and groom do not get to see one another as it is bad luck.

The celebration lasts through the night and into the morning. The morning of Mahmood's "Nikah" (wedding) several Malik's (tribal elders) and a Mullah (religious leader) went to Mahmood's home. As they entered his home, the Mullah asked Mahmood if he was ready for marriage. Mahmood stated the obvious, nervous "yes." The Mullah instructed Mahmood to cleanse himself and prepare for his journey of marriage.

Mahmood cleansed himself from head to toe and put on a newly suited white Shalwar Kameez. He and his entourage drove to the home of Bibi and entered through a crowd of her friends and family. Over two thousand people lined the streets around her home in Jalalabad. Without seeing his soon to be wife, Mahmood stood in a room while Bibi stood in the adjacent room in her home. The Mullah read a page out of the Holy Koran to the two of them loud enough so they both could hear the Sura (Koranic passage). He completed his reading and asked Mahmood if he wanted to marry Bibi. Mahmood said "yes." The Mullah then turned the corner of the wall to face into the room Bibi stood and asked her the same question. She too said "yes" and the two were married.

Unlike American wedding ceremonies, there was no "You may now kiss the bride." The two still did not get to see one another. Mahmood left Bibi's home as a swarm of people clapped and smiled in happiness upon the completion of the wedding ceremony. As he disappeared in the crowd, Bibi then walked out of the room and into a crowd of women in her home. The wedding celebration segregated men from women following Afghan and Islamic customs. Both men and women told stories promoting happiness and much laughter throughout the day and the night. Food and music was there for all to enjoy. Mahmood left at the end of the evening with his family, leaving his new wife behind in her own family's home.

The following morning, Mahmood went to retrieve his wife. He got into his father's car. Following him in twenty other vehicles were numerous friends and family members. All the vehicles were filled with beautiful Afghan roses. Mahmood went to Bibi and took her hand then led her from her parent's home to his father's vehicle. The two sat in the back together and went to Mahmood's home.

Afghan groom's families often treat a son's wife as a burden, Mahmood's mother and family, however, embraced Bibi as their own daughter. They treat her with respect and love her as one of their own. This is not always the case in Afghanistan. Women are often abused by son's mothers, fathers, and their husbands. Mahmood who has morals and respect for all of mankind loves his wife and treats her as his angel.

The cost of the wedding was difficult to meet for Mahmood's family. Mahmood knew he had to find a way to pay back the money that caused his family serious economic throwback.

Taking on new responsibilities

Earning money in the early months of a newly freed Afghanistan was not easy. Today, millions of malnourished people starve daily due to lack of economic growth. Mahmood would not allow his family to starve. He worked in his jewelry shop extended hours. He worked simultaneously during the heat of the day for the Americans as a laborer. It took Mahmood several years to earn enough money to give back to his family to assist them for the payments made. They never asked for the money and did not want his repayment.

Mahmood took it upon himself from that day forward to care for his family's needs to include his mother, father, brothers, and grandparents. Seven years later, Mahmood extended his family once more.

In February 2008, Shiasta was born. Her name means beautiful in Pashto. Shiasta was born in Nangahar hospital. Before the Afghan Mujahedeen and the United States forces freed Afghanistan from Taliban rule, Nangahar hospital was used to support and treat Taliban members. Women could not go to the hospital to deliver their children and were expected to deliver in their homes where, more often than not, no midwife was available. Women delivering children during that time often died in childbirth. Today, Nangahar Hospital has changed and women can safely deliver their babies.

Still, out of fear of Taliban influence, men are hesitant to go to the hospital to watch their child's birth. Bibi had Mahmood's father drive her and "mom" to the hospital. The two women stayed in the hospital for two days, receiving care from experienced and trained medical staff that was much better than those working during Taliban rule. On the third day, at approximately 10:00 am, Mahmood heard the door of his house open. He watched his father, "mom," Bibi, and Shiasta walk through the door. He watched his mother and Bibi in their light blue Burkhas walk into the home suddenly lit by the outside sunlight as the door opened. He states it was like watching Allah open his gates to heaven. Shiasta was wrapped in a dark green blanket. He could only stare at her in amazement.

It was not until the second day Shiasta was home that Mahmood finally held his daughter. He had been too shy before then to do so. He believes the first time he saw her changed his life. The time he actually held her is the time he knew that he would do everything to make sure she would be "happy and safe." If you ever see Mahmood and ask him how his family is, he smiles and say they are all "good." If you ever ask Mahmood "how is Shiasta?" He smiles from ear to ear, his green eyes brighten, and his cheeks glow, he will even at times chuckle in happiness replying she is "Great!" Mahmood will never allow Shiasta to be in harm's way.

Mahmood knows many stories of men giving away their young female daughters. One reason is opium farming. Farmers grow opium to provide their families with enough money to live. When eradication efforts exist, they often times have their crops cut or burned down, which mean they lose their income. The Taliban or Narco-Terrorists provide them the seeds to grow opium and when they fail to grow they are punished and must repay for the seeds that were provided.

I once met an older Afghan man on the edge of his opium field, his hands smashed against his face. He was wailing in tears, mourning. He had been forced to repay Taliban for the loss of this opium fields, but had no money to give and so had to hand his youngest daughter who was only six years old over to the Taliban. She would most likely be used as a sex slave through the illegal human trafficking industry between Pakistan and Afghanistan. This is a common experience for many fathers in Afghanistan.

Mahmood understands that this is one of the many ways the Taliban continue to instill fear into the communities of Afghanistan. He knows it is not Islamic, and what they do is evil. Mahmood vows that under no circumstance would he ever allow anyone to take his Shiasta away from him. He swears he would have to be killed before such a thing would happen to him.

Mahmood has been through hell and back like most Afghans and Pashtuns alike. He experienced brutality and torture at a very young age. He is brave and strong, and admits he would never be who he is though without his family and closest trusted friends.

Learning through listening

From a SOCINT standpoint, a lot can be learned from an individual like Mahmood. The notes needed to write the aforementioned life of Mahmood took only a few short hours. Engaging in dialog with local indigenous persons no matter the location, and having them trust with whom they are speaking is essential. Most people throughout the world love to talk about their life and the lives of those around them. Those who fail to live in technologically based cultures rely on storytelling for entertainment. Speaking with locals such as Mahmood is crucial to gain a local perspective about the past and current environment in which operations exist.

Mahmood, in only a few short hours presented insight to the gem trade in Afghanistan and the traditional Afghan wedding. This is specifically important to understand and recognize as the Taliban continuously fulfill their own Information Operation (IO) campaign making statements that wedding parties have been bombed. By understanding the time lines as to when Afghan weddings should or should not occur and the magnitude of mass movements of individuals into an area, analysts can recognize weddings more effectively, which will better inform as to when operations should and should not occur in an attempt to reduce civilian collateral damage.

Speaking to others to verify such stories is also necessary. Mahmood knows of the horrors related to the opium industry. He verified the process of Taliban and or Narco-terrorists providing seeds to farmers, needs to repay, and consequences that can result by not repaying such seeds.

Greater insights about the religious beliefs that can be found throughout a region have also been better understood. Numerous views and extremes related to the religious practices allows a better understanding towards the people along with expectations and requirements. These religious practices assist decision makers in knowing when, how, what, where, and who to speak to during specific times of the year or even specific times of the day to build relations. This shows respect towards others' beliefs and assists in rapport building.

All of these mentioned factors are just a handful of the successes a formalized SOCINT discipline can bring to the table in fighting unconventional or asymmetric threats. Speaking with the locals and placing oneself in their perspective by living with them and knowing all there is to know about them will and has assisted decision makers in the past while operating abroad and will continue to assist if honed appropriately even within the borders of the United States. SOCINT is an intelligence discipline which has unlimited value internally and externally in dealing with national security.

Notes

1. The author of this book was on assignment in Afghanistan working as a social scientist throughout the year 2008. During this time, he encountered Mahmood and was authorized by Mahmood himself to write his story. Mahmood understands the necessity for this writing to demonstrate what life was like prior to the US invasion in 2001 and how life has changed for many Afghans since.

2. Ramadan is the ninth month of the Muslim calendar. It is during this month that Muslims observe the Fast of Ramadan. Lasting for the entire month, Muslims fast during the daylight hours and in the evening eat small meals and visit with friends and family. It is a time of worship and contemplation. A time to strengthen family and community ties.

   a. Muslims believe that it was during the month of Ramadan that the Prophet Muhammad received the Holy Quran.

   b. The good that is acquired through the fast can be destroyed by five things:

      i. the telling of a lie

      ii. slander

      iii. denouncing someone behind his back

      iv. a false oath

      v. greed or covetousness

    c. These are considered offensive at all times, but are most offensive during the Fast of Ramadan.

    d. On the evening of the 27th day of the month, Muslims celebrate the *Laylat-al-Qadr* (the Night of Power). It is believed that on this night Muhammad first received the revelation of the Holy Quran. And according to the Quran, this is when God determines the course of the world for the following year.

    e. When the fast ends (the first day of the month of Shawwal) it is celebrated for three days in a holiday called Id-al-Fitr (the Feast of Fast Breaking). Gifts are exchanged. Friends and family gather to pray in congregation and for large meals. In some cities fairs are held to celebrate the end of the Fast of Ramadan.

    f. During Ramadan, it is highly recommended to reach out to the communities and seek the needs they may have. It is also worthy to stop by in the evenings or invite Muslims to one's home to eat a small dinner meal to break their day time fast. Money is not worth giving rather, assistance.

    g. Due to fasting during the day, many Muslims especially the elderly may be very weak due to lack of sustenance. Slow down convoys for people crossing roads, offensive actions should be carefully monitored as people may move slower than normal and not react at the pace desired by CF.

3. Nan is flat bread eaten virtually with every meal in Afghanistan and nearing locations such as Pakistan. It is made from wheat. This bread is very similar to pita bread.

4. United States Special Operatives conducted research to identify what size caliber would be capable of penetrating these walls found all over Afghanistan. During an early period, the author had an opportunity to witness such testing. The walls are made of mud, then are lined with large stones, and filled with more mud. With time, these walls become very dense and virtually impenetrable.

5. Taliban and other Islamic extremists continuously interpret the Suras found in the Koran to suit their needs. Most of the Suras they interpret are not in nature as articulated by these extremists.

ETHICS IN SOCIOCULTURAL INTELLIGENCE II

Understanding Ethics within Sociocultural Intelligence 5

The ethical realities of understanding ourselves internally

The terms "Ethics" and "Morals" have long been a subject of debate, and still are as we use a philosophical approach to differentiate between the two. Neither terms are about simplistic understandings of lying, cheating, and or stealing. Further, this is not an attempt to find one definition for each term, rather an attempt to identify similarities between the two, and the necessity of both ethics and morals within the intelligence community with a focus on SOCINT. Three authors, Ronald Howard, Thomas Plante, and Immanuel Kant have articulated philosophical approaches towards a greater good, all of which can and should be incorporated into a SOCINT discipline.

> Always do the right thing even when you think no one is looking. (Author Unknown)

Authors often times write very differently about topics of interests. The aforementioned authors wrote different books using different terminology for the very similar purposes of educating individuals in theory and philosophy with regard to morals, ethics, and "the greater good." Of note, all mentioned authors made very similar arguments as to the necessity of ensuring that individuals maintain ethical principles. The key in truly understanding the importance of ethics within any intelligence discipline lies in the critical thinking and analysis needed for decision making. This is a necessary element specifically for those serving the United States in any function of the government.

No matter one's personal thoughts or opinions on ethics and morals, no matter the continuing debates, and no matter the profession, some form of honorary system of philosophical thoughts and actions is necessary for the greater good.[1] Because this is an opinionated principle, right or wrong, focus will remain based upon such a concept. Noted among the aforementioned experts who studied and wrote about "morals" and "ethics," is that the terms have too many similarities to debate considering their overall meanings and philosophical conceptualization. Because of this, the terms "morals" and "ethics" will be used interchangeably.

Depending on who you are, what you do, and what you believe in, the concept of "the greater good" is also a debatable subject. Fortunately, the "greater good" is not debatable within the United States Intelligence Community. The overarching goal behind the total system of the US Intelligence Community is based upon the "greater good" of this nation.

One man's terrorist is another man's freedom fighter. (David Horowitz)

Although one individual without sound morals or ethics can manipulate a system, he cannot break the system itself. The United States is a large system built with thousands of networks within. If the United States society upholds the motto "In God We Trust," the large-scale system can never break and will remain strong because of the moral and ethical values implemented based on an existing faith in God. Recognizing SOCINT as a discipline that should officially exist to promote situational awareness entails presuming that part of this awareness includes "how we view ourselves, how we view others, how others view us, and how others view themselves." Identification of ethical dilemmas within the United States "systems" must be presented first. This approach serves as the rationale to implement clear, concise critical thinking and analysis that will later be used to assist in the ethical decision-making process.

Ethics, morals, the "greater good"—all work interchangeably to secure the freedoms and the protection of national security from enemies foreign and domestic. They constitute principles that act as guides for everyone who resides within the borders of the United States. For the Americans who live abroad, these principles are meant to serve as guidelines for them to act as ambassadors, ensuring they represent America as a respectful, sincere, and caring nation for all. Principles are often times written as guidelines within organizations that are meant to promote ethical behaviors. More often than not, these guidelines are considered codes of behavior. Immanuel Kant states eloquently that,

> On the other hand, if adversity and hopeless sorrow have completely taken away the relish for life; if the unfortunate one, strong in mind, indignant at his fate rather then desponding or dejected, wishes for death, and yet preserves his life without loving it-not from inclination or fear, but from duty-then his maxim has a moral worth." (Kant 2005, p. 14)

Military and civilians alike, during times of war, reveal personality traits seldom witnessed by others. It has been reported that after the Vietnam War, people such as Senator John Kerry made claims that American service members were "animals" and that his counterparts "cut off ears, heads, and raped individuals."[2] Many "hippies" in the United States made similar claims during that period. This led some people to ask whether or not individuals lose their moral or ethical codes during times of war. After observing service members serving abroad in combat and later upon their return home (including the author of this book who deployed to five different combat zones), the answer to such a question is "absolutely not." Individuals who enter a war do not lose any moral codes so long as they went into the war with their own strong moral and ethical values and maintained their organization's understandings of such codes.

War does bring the worst out in many people. However, this does not mean that their morals are lost. As children, we are taught our own morals and values. Morals are individual beliefs and actions deemed acceptable. Individual morals and values vary greatly. We try to uphold whatever morals and values we have at the highest level at all times. This does not mean that we are perfect though. Far from it. As individuals enter a war, their imperfections oftentimes come out. Lack of respect towards adversaries becomes more prevalent. Respect is one of the greatest traits that maintain high levels of ethics and morals. Respecting yourself, your co-workers, your organization, your enemies' organizations, and your individual enemy can be construed as one of the greatest keys to survivability. With respect should come concern for what is around, which should enhance an individual's situational awareness. As Plante states,

> Respect means treating others with esteem, consideration, and honor. Respect involves treating others with attention and acknowledging that they have rights and needs as well. Respect means being considerate and appreciative of others. Respect means treating others as you'd want to be treated. (Plante 2004, p. 93)

The United States as a whole has evolved to become a society that loves to label people, and people thrive on previous accomplishments. Retired representatives within the Department of Defense have taken selective positions of authority within the civilian elements of the DOD. Many of these individuals are retired officers mentally holding onto their previous ranks of Colonels and above. They fail to accept that they are no longer officers in the military. They also fail to accept that many of their co-workers never served in the military and, more often than not, could not care less as to their previous rank. These individuals are similar to the middle-aged man who still thrives on his accomplishments of being an all state quarterback in high school. Again, no one cares. Their demonstration of elitism allows a disrespectful perception among others. What they, the others, do care about is what the person can now do successfully and morally. Reality is that many of these individuals lack moral and ethical values because they believe they still are what they no longer are or never truly were. Because of such narcissist mentalities due to the lack of ethical principles of respect towards others, their inability to make proper decisions becomes apparent. This often happens because of a lack of integrity as paid managers and as superficial leaders. As Plante says, "Integrity is the foundation for living an ethical life" (Plante 2004, p. 61).

Those in leadership positions who lack such ethical stature must understand that they affect the lives of others with every unethical decision they make. Because narcissists are in many positions of authority within leadership among government elements, they often induce nepotism and bring friends into the ranks of sub-leadership. More often than not, the narcissists have close systems of contacts that also emulate the lead narcissist's mentality. When such individuals are brought into the larger system of responsibility through the nepotistic system created from the top, the behaviors and negative actions taken below result in psychological abuse of power, low group morale, poor work quality, and results in a disgruntled work force. These reactions within the greater system can easily be mitigated with simple social conditioning of the leadership referencing the "Golden Rule." No matter one's religion, the "Golden Rule" exists. Howard (2008) expresses in his writings (p.57) different levels or "metals" of the Golden Rule:

1. Golden Rule: Do unto others as you would have them do unto you.
2. Platinum Rule: Do unto others as they would have you do unto them.
3. Diamond Rule: Do unto others as the Buddha or Muhammad or Jesus would do unto you.
4. Silver Rule: Do not do unto others as you would not have them do unto you.
5. Brass Rule: Do unto others as they do unto you.
6. Aluminum Rule: Do not let others do to you what you would not do unto them.
7. Lead Rule: Undo others who undo you.
8. Iron Rule: Do unto others before they do unto you.

The four principles or views within the discipline of SOCINT (how we view ourselves, how we view others, how others view themselves, and how others view us) will greatly enhance the views of others so long as conscious decisions to emulate the "Golden Rule" as often as possible continues within the national security spectrum.

The ethical realities of understanding ourselves externally

Virtually all religions teach some form of moral code based on actions that we, as individuals, should not do. Often times these types of moral codes are construed as "negative ethics" (Howard 2008, p. 53), one of them being "thou shall not kill." Killing an individual during a time of war becomes virtually inevitable. What many fail to realize and come to grips with is that killing an individual who is trying to kill you might not be good, but is necessary for one's survival. This can also be construed as a "necessary evil." The person involved in the act of killing another must decide whether the action is morally justified. Military members often have difficulty dealing with this.

Vietnam veterans had a horrible time dealing with such a process. Having an appropriate understanding towards ethics and morals would enhance the speed and recovery in the decision-making process needed to determine necessary evils. The majority of those involved in intelligence activities rarely face a "shoot or don't shoot" situation, however they do face dilemmas that require a similar decision-making process and entail informing action arms about processed data used for military operations that could take and/or change the lives of others.

Vietnam veterans needed psychological support after the war, just like many veterans from other wars. They came to be viewed as outcasts of the American society because they could not cope with civilian life as they used to know it. The American society could very well be construed as the outcast to the rest of the world during that time though.

A great deal of the American society failed to greet these veterans with open arms and acceptance. This caused Vietnam veterans much difficulty and tremendous amounts of animosity. During this time, a system (the veterans) within the United States was injected with some form of disruptive tie (e.g., opponents to the war, people who isolated the veterans) to cause the havoc and social distraught experienced by the brave men and women who once served. The social network was manipulated and socially conditioned a large group of individuals to act a certain way. Be it morally or ethically justified or not, the social structure manipulation or persuasion process worked.

Because we continue to "remain numb to critical issues, ignorant of our biases, and guided by decisions by age old ruts," (Howard 2008, p. 93) national security elements continue to decline in nature of success. If an ethical basis promoting proper decision making for intelligence collection within sociocultural entities were permitted, sociocultural manipulation in favor of national security would enhance nonlethal operations in favor of goals and outcomes related to the United States nationally and internationally.

It is true that many veterans feel guilt, anger, and possibly frustration due to their actions during war. In spite of such feelings, perception from others oftentimes looks as if these individuals had no morals or values. It is not because of the war that these feelings remain strong, it is because of the life they must begin after the war. Oftentimes society fails to accept these veterans. Work becomes difficult to find. Finding oneself again also becomes difficult. Veterans need acceptance. A mental social process must occur for this society of individuals to enter back into the larger system of the American society.

The mental process more often than not tends to lean towards moral principles that promote healthy decisions. Although it may appear that this may relate more to psychology, which is partially the case, this also relates to the sociocultural dynamics that can enhance the recovery and reintegration into the overall network. If a sociocultural entity were available to promote empathy, the Golden Rule, and situational awareness to the total network, enhancements of concern from the total population would most likely increase the speed of recovery of others (Plante 2004, pp. 114–115).

Because of the turmoil veterans witnessed, their faith in God often becomes stronger. Since morals are greatly induced through spiritual faith, it would only make sense to claim that their morals actually increase rather than decrease. After World War II and Vietnam, many veterans became so close to God that they were ordained as priests or ministers.[3] If any statistics were conducted regarding faith, which goes hand in hand with morals, it would be interesting to see how many veterans became closer to their God during or after their encounters with war. Although it would be wonderful to hear strictly success stories of integration back into civil societies among veterans, it would not help to truly understand how morals and ethics play such crucial roles in decision making.

After World War II, veterans throughout the United States had a seriously difficult time transforming back into "normal civilians." Their frustrations led them to bond together. Veterans on the west coast of the United States found a way to deal with their frustrations. Gangs were formed and were badly perceived by those not affiliated with them. Many think that veterans formed the infamous Hells Angels Motorcycle Club, and although the actual club was not formed by such persons, the principle behind the club was. Again this exemplifies the power of identification and implementation of social systems and nonlethal targeting to promote some form of change within a larger system. What many of these veterans unknowingly promoted are the five prerequisites to build ethical muscle that Plante describes (Plante 2004, p. 126):

1. a desire
2. agreement with the concept
3. models
4. feedback
5. support

In fact, veterans did have a great deal to do with forming a group similar to the Hell's Angels. A motorcycle club known as the "Pissed Off Bastards of Bloomington"[4] was formed by World War II veterans on the west coast of the United States. Later, other outlaw motorcycle clubs, such as the Banditos, the Hells Angels, the Outlaws, and the Pagans were also formed. The aforementioned make up the five main "one per centers" (those that are considered outlawed). Many other veterans have formed motorcycle clubs that try hard to fit into society and do well for those in need, such as "Rolling Thunder." The mention of motorcycle clubs in this discussion is used solely to show that, like all people, veterans need some form of societal acceptance and to provide simple ideas that can be used to incorporate social network manipulation through SOCINT.

As a society within the United States, you would think that politicians and those within the National Security Council would have ethical obligations to see such transformations exist among such a population. This also provides the opportunity to understand that oftentimes war does not ruin an individuals' morals, but that it is the systems they work for or among and the systems that they must re-integrate that create the pressure that takes their morals away. The society consists of multiple networks and systems, including those for which they once worked. It is crucial to note that networks and systems play a key role in listening and acting based on the information obtained and analyzed that relates to the needs of those requiring the nonlethal targeting or engagement for social manipulation.

Many United States war veterans must understand that they volunteered to call for service, with the exception of those who were drafted. Anytime individuals volunteer for service, they are subject to defend the Constitution and freedom of the United States. Oftentimes they can be called to face war. Before any one person volunteers for military duty they must understand this. They also must understand and face reality that coping with such hardships becomes a necessary means to re-enter the civilian life.

> There is one end, however, which may be assumed to be actually such to all rational beings (so far as imperatives apply to them, viz. as dependant beings) and therefore, one purpose which they do not merely may have, but which we may with certainty assume that they all actually have by a natural necessity, and this is happiness. (Kant 2005, p. 32)

Those who understandably lose morals are those who become innocent victims from war. Either way, losing morals from these people is still inexcusable. Many individuals have sympathy for those who lose loved ones during times of war; this is a possible mistake as empathy may be the necessary medicine. Rather than showing sympathy, it would behoove those individuals to show empathy. Feeling sorry for a person does not alleviate an individual's pain or suffering. Showing sympathy oftentimes presents the assumption to the victim that vengeance becomes acceptable. On the other hand, empathy provides an individual with the opportunity to express himself and to be heard. More often than not, being listened to is all that it takes for the negative to turn into the positive.

The ethical realities of understanding others

Many victims from terrorism take action because of the loss of a loved one. It is presumed that one terrorist group known as the "Black Widows" from Chechnya conduct operations due to their losing loved ones. The "Black Widows" are predominantly females from Chechnya who either lost a husband or father to the Russians or a group supporting the Russians. There are many arguments whether the acts taken by the "Black Widows" are immoral. For some, the "Black Widows" assume the responsibility of fighting the war their loved ones no longer can fight. Because of this, the "Black Widows" believe they are fighting a moral cause.

> There is an imperative which commands a certain conduct immediately, without having as its condition any other purpose to be attained by it. This imperative is Categorical. It concerns not the matter of the action, or its intended result, but its form and the principle of which it is itself a result; and what is essentially good in it consists in the mental disposition, let the consequence be what it may. This imperative may be called that of Morality. (Kant 2005, p.33)

The "Black Widows" are a terrorist organization. Much like the "Black Widows," other terrorists fail to view themselves as terrorists, but instead view themselves as "Freedom Fighters." Terrorists in groups such as Al Qaeda are no different. Al Qaeda understands how the United States gained its independence from Great Britain. Many countries believe the United States gained its independence by utilizing tactics of unconventional warfare that were deemed inappropriate, unethical, and immoral. United States history has been an excuse to such groups as Al Qaeda to conduct terrorist operations. The public views terrorist operations as unethical.

Terrorists view themselves as soldiers. Muslim extremists view themselves as soldiers for God. Any one person who views himself or herself as a soldier for God will never view their actions as unethical or immoral. The Irish Catholics opposing British law signed the 1916 Proclamation that states, "so long as God is on our side we will be victorious in our cause." Terrorists continuously claiming faith in God produce documents such as this. American currency has "In God We Trust" written on it. Does this mean that all United States wartime actions are morally acceptable? The answer directly depends on the individual who is interpreting the cause of such military action and who is deciding what is morally acceptable and what is not.

War is not the reason why individuals lose their morals. Rather, they lose their morals because of decisions based on the means in which the director of action processes information, and in turn determining an outcome based on personal moral and ethical principles for their own so-called greater good. Oftentimes individuals have already lost their morals before they enter a war or had none or very little moral values in the first place. Society also played a factor in those who presumably lost morals during such times. It is up to the individual to decide what moral codes they want to live by. Most importantly, excuses cannot be made for those who appear to have lost morals during times of war.

Without ethics, morals, and a concept such as "the greater good," decision making and thought processing can be faltered. For those working within the intelligence community, decisions and thoughts can never intentionally be faltered because the lives of fellow Americans are always at risk. It is unfortunate, but as humans we learn from numerous elements and one of these elements is learning from those we look up to.

Ethical realities to understanding how others view us: the why of Afghanistan

America has been recently seen negatively around the world and within. A lot of this perception results from American actions following the Al Qaeda attacks that occurred on September 11, 2001. Acts such as the invasion of Iraq, questionable interrogation techniques, unanswerable questions as to why continued forays in Afghanistan, etc. All are actions that allow others around the globe to wonder whether the United States still believes in what its forefathers envisioned and believed about mankind. All of these acts occurred initially from some form of thought process that occurred and/or was approved by American leadership.

Freedom must be presupposed as a property of the will of all rational beings.
(Kant 2005, p. 66)

No matter one's opinion on the War on Terror, these actions are questionable, not just because of any set rule violations, but more so because of the ethical dilemmas that have become apparent. Because these actions have already occurred and been rectified, or are still occurring if solutions to resolve the issues were not achieved, we need to examine the question of why.

Questioning or, at a minimum, discussing the "why," will present ethical elements that begin with the American leadership and the Intelligence Community—those we should look up to. Why do the war efforts in Afghanistan still continue? Had previous wars in Afghanistan been studied to identify the flaws of former occupiers, such as the Russians, Alexander the Great, the British, or Genghis Khan, might mistakes not be repeated? Why has a Joint, Combined, or Interagency strategic plan still not been produced with benchmarks and timelines to identify and promote steps needed to achieve victory more than eight years into the war? Why did the United States leave the people of Afghanistan after promising so much once the Russians left and without ever following through with the promises? Although some may believe these types of questions about Afghanistan have nothing to do with ethics, indeed they do.

Ethically, leaving the people of Afghanistan after they defeated our number one enemy during the Cold War, Russia, after they sacrificed so much and after we failed to follow through with our promises make us out to be liars. The Afghans as a whole, specifically the Pashtuns, have a culture of honor that is hard for any American to fathom unless one has spent time inside Afghanistan. The world knows what we did during the Russian Afghan War by assisting the Afghans in their efforts. Many Afghans know of our walking away from them immediately after the retreat of the Russians. We had an obligation following what the Afghan people had done, not just for themselves, but for the United States national security by defeating a communist super power during that time. Bluntly put, we betrayed the Afghan people.

We not only betrayed the Afghan people, we betrayed our own people too. The men and women serving within the United States military have been put into harm's way and continue to be placed into the austere environment of Afghanistan. The initial actions of invading Afghanistan were to rid it of Taliban control and to search and destroy Al Qaeda, but this is only theory. No one truly knows why the War on Terror was brought into the country of Afghanistan. Not one terrorist on 9–11 was an Afghan or from any of the main ethnicities that can be found in Afghanistan. They were Arabs. Howard states that research has been conducted and such "shows that it takes three to four weeks of daily repetition to create a habit" (Howard 2008, p.152). Unfortunately, the years of immoral deception and blatant lies expressed about the War on Terror have perfected the hatred among the world's population.

If the United States was true about the attempts to capture or kill Osama Bin Laden, knowing that he was in Afghanistan and not in the tribal areas of western Pakistan, then why was the city of Kabul one of the first places the US forces inserted into Afghanistan? It was historically known that Osama Bin Laden had a base in the southern province of Kandahar, nowhere near Kabul. What was more known was that Taliban had a greater base and foundation in western Pakistan tribal regions, so why even go into Afghanistan at all? This current affair is mentioned because it has become apparent that we have lost our ability to conduct ethically sound critical thinking and analysis. Everything the United States has done to date in Afghanistan is complete mirror imaging as to what the Russians had done except in reverse order.

The Russians sent in Conventional forces first whereas the United States sent in their elite Joint Special Operators.[5] The Russians later sent in their Spetznas, as the United States almost two years into the War in Afghanistan sent in their conventional forces. Studying the Russians activities and then observing what the United States has done to date, a person can find multiple examples as mentioned. Reversing a process of military tactics and strategy is not enough to better the odds in defeating a system of people who have never been defeated by any super power throughout history. The decision makers within the government who relied on their intelligence representatives, in which both parties lacked critical thinking as their efforts were hindered by unethical logic, continued to place their men and women serving at risk.

Unless a person be a fly on the wall located in the Oval Office of the White House, we will never know why activities in Afghanistan started they way they did, nor will we understand why they continue as they do. The issue is about understanding "why," through a philosophical approach, considering that the discussion inside the Oval Office on this topic will most likely never be released. The only means of getting answers is through a sociocultural perspective via incorporation of ethical philosophy. To bring this disastrous issue to better light, Howard discusses Orwell's book, *Politics and the English Language*:

> Destroying villages and killing the defenseless, Orwell noted, had become 'paci-
> fication;' imprisonment without trial, 'elimination of unreliable elements.' Orwell
> would probably not be surprised that killing innocents has become 'collateral

damage;' killing our own, 'friendly fire.' His comment on politicians who utter tired phraseology still rings true: 'The appropriate noises are still coming out of his larynx but his brain is not involved.' (Nor, of course, is his heart.) (Howard 2008, p. 20)

A hypothetical question of "can we win in Afghanistan?" needs no answer because in truth, the answer is not "yes" or "no." Rather, due to the current cultural environment within the intelligence community and throughout the national security elements within the United States, the answer is, "it's impossible." Most intellectuals will say that nothing is impossible. Unfortunately, winning a war in Afghanistan today via the operational environment in our own systems and networks with the current elements of multiple unethical systems is just that: impossible.

How is it that the United States, the world's strongest superpower cannot defeat the people within such an underdeveloped country like Afghanistan? Maybe it is the fighting spirit of the Pashtu people, maybe it is the corrupt Afghan government that the US put in place, or maybe the Pakistani involvement is the partial cause. All these issues may be a part of the equation, but in reality these factors are so minuscule they just don't matter. What does matter are the needs of ethical enhancements of the intelligence operatives and decision makers who lead this War on Terror along with the willingness for leaders to act upon such information.

People may ask themselves, what is it that matters to win in Afghanistan? Only one thing matters, and it's not about winning or losing, it's about learning to accept what is the only thing acceptable: ethical common sense. Common sense is not very common though, nor are moral obligatory commitments. Approximately eight years into US military engagement in Afghanistan, a person would believe that by now, we have it all figured out. Many people do have Afghanistan figured out, however those who matter are absolutely clueless and ignorant to what will work and what will continue to fail in Afghanistan.

The decision makers high in the food chain of the United States government express their ignorance daily when it comes to Afghanistan. They refuse to accept that war inside Afghanistan was initiated by non-Afghans. Remember that there was not one Afghan on any of the aircrafts that caused the horrific havoc inside the United States on that sunny day of September 2001. These US government men and women are intelligent people though, and it is unfair for them to claim their ignorance. What is worthy is the identification of their lack of ethical responsibilities where they have allowed personal interests to get the best of them.

The personal interests are tied to the country of Saudi Arabia. A very well-known fact is that most of the money that comes from a nation-state supporting Sunni Islamic Terrorist comes from the country of Saudi Arabia. Saudi Arabia is one of the wealthiest countries in the world because of its oil industry, and the United States is one of the most oil-dependant countries in the world. Many of America's elite, which includes a plethora of politicians, rely on this dependency as they have ties to the Saudi government. But instead, Saudi Arabia plays a business continuing its money-making not just through oil, but also through one of the oldest money making industries in the world, which is war. Saudi Arabia plays both sides of the War on Terror: the United States and the Terrorists. If our politicians had had the ethical fortitude to do the right thing when they thought no one was watching, they would have broken ties with Saudi Arabia and, instead of invading Afghanistan, possibly would have invaded Saudi Arabia considering that the majority of terrorists on 9–11 were from Saudi Arabia or had connections to Saudi Arabia. Needless to say, this did not happen.

Fighting that occurs in Afghanistan mostly stems within the Pashtun dominated regions because the Pashtun people have for centuries fought invaders of their lands. Are we invaders? As an American, it is overly easy for us to say we are engaged in our activities because of 9–11. Remember though, not one Afghan was on any aircraft that day. So the question still exists, are we invaders? Articulation can easily be made that we indeed are the true invaders of Afghanistan, much like the Russians were throughout the 1980s, and because of this, our appearance as a nation-state allows others to look at us as the bully on the block who ultimately always gets put in their place.

Now that we are in Afghanistan and that the lives of approximately one thousand Americans have been lost, how do we leave and hold our heads high? Is there a way to appease both the American people, who are apparently tired of the war in Afghanistan, and the Afghan people, on whom we have made some positive impact? Like many other wars, no one wins and no one loses. A negotiation takes place, then both sides reach an agreement and become obligated "morally," "ethically," maybe even for "the greater good" to adhere to the results of these negotiations and peace treaties. Unfortunately, in Afghanistan you do not find only one side fighting against the Coalition Forces, but if you were to look for one and find it crucial to identify and initiate such actions, then the group would be Hezb Islami.

Hezb Islami is known to be violent. Gullbidine Hekmatyar, the founder of Hezb Islami captured some young Soviet soldiers and had the words *Allah Akbar* carved into their backs and, for some, into their chests.[6] Those Russian captives were supposedly trade goods. As horrible as the actions of Hezb Islami may sound, Hekmatyar was willing to double deal Mullah Mohamed Omar (a leader of Taliban) in 2001, badly, with promises of tens of thousands of men and guns that never materialized. Hezb Islami took the money and failed to deliver. According to virtually every opposition group in Afghanistan along with the United States, no one in his organization is trustworthy.

We would need to identify an organization that is willing to negotiate, one that has very limited or no ties with outside influences. Countries like Saudi Arabia or Pakistan could not be mediators in this event (because we know these two countries have played both sides throughout the war). It is virtually impossible to find such a country or internationally recognized organization to serve as a neutral mediator because throughout this whole ordeal of post 9–11 war, most globally recognized political elements and nongovernment organizations have profited.

The United States does not need to trust anyone, nor do they need to rely on anyone to serve as a mediator so long as they are capable of being open minded and maintain a moral standpoint to come through with any and all promises. Related to promises, Howard writes, "we then rationalize—time has erased the obligation, circumstances have changed, we didn't explicitly promise anyway but however clever our thinking, it doesn't erase compromise" (Howard 2008, p. 123). What we need to do is be willing to sit at a table with such a group and sign a peace agreement. Once we do this, it will be that much easier to keep an eye on the surrogates when or if they fail to keep their end of the bargain.

Because of the influence Hezb Islami has over the Pashtus, violence could be expected to drop to a minimum of 60 percent throughout the country. They predominantly act on the eastern provinces of Afghanistan. If they can reduce that amount of violence, the United States and the remaining Coalition would then be capable of fulfilling their obligations elsewhere. Such an activity as negotiating with insurgents like Hezb Islami and reaching a compromise would show the local Afghan populace that the United States is willing to provide them opportunities to secure their own areas. And that is Counter Insurgency 101. Such an activity is what the people want. They do not want to see the Taliban rule again, they do not want to see Arabs in their country, and they do not want to see continued activities with the Pakistani ISI. They only want to see security in their nation so people can go on with their lives. This is the moral and ethical responsibility that must be aimed for within the United States government.

So how do we win in Afghanistan? We identify our own flaws within our own systems in place and ensure that leaders are held accountable for the ethical flaws that they have demonstrated. We start negotiating with the people of Afghanistan. We negotiate and we allow them to secure themselves the way they deem suitable and not as we believe they should. Once that is accomplished, we concentrate efforts elsewhere in the country. We keep an eye on those we negotiated with and we assist them in their economic struggles. This may sound very easy and appealing, however it is not easy at all and for many in leadership positions, it is not appealing at all either.

Such a concept would force an entire nation (the United States) to admit to ethical flaws and irresponsible actions. The only way this could ever be accomplished is through social change within the National Security apparatuses. Social change will never happen though unless a neutral non-government entity who understands SOCINT conducts an all out SOCINT operation. This operation would be used to identify and analyze everything it can about our own network of National Security in an attempt to promote social change through reasonable effects based operations. The operation must be ethically conducted without any possible interferences of persuasion for accurate critical thinking and decision making throughout the entire SOCINT process.

The process of SOCINT can be achieved and can be so ethically. Importantly, the SOCINT process must initiate internally within the United States government in an attempt to resolve and fix a very broken machine. The initiators for such a process must be those in leadership within National Security and the Intelligence Community as a whole, which in turn shall provide the necessary impartial analyzed data production for responsible ethical decisions, which determine appropriate non-lethal action or inaction. As a whole, in today's multitude of global crises, the United States faces grave danger of losing everything its forefathers ever fought for. Such losses have been created internally within our own sociocultural systems induced by the elitist mind. Through the utilization and implementation of ethical principles laid out by authors such as Ronald Howard, Thomas Plante, and Immanuel Kant, the United States as a whole can return to its greatness.

Notes

1. While the United States and many Western nations lack formalized honorary systems, some countries do instill such a system among their people. While these honorary systems may not be originated by the country as a whole, but rather by a specific ethnicity within the society of the country, often times the majority of ethnic groups will utilize such a system to maintain some form of honor code. One such code is known as Pashtunwali, which originated from the Pashtun people and which is today recognized by most ethnic groups within Afghanistan, who at a minimum abide by an honorary code extremely similar to this original one. While working in Afghanistan and interviewing hundreds of locals indigenous persons, I developed understanding of Pashtunwali. The following outline of Pashtunwali was written utilizing field notes obtained from interviewing Pashtuns while working in Afghanistan:

Pashtunwali: The code of conduct for Pashtuns

Pashtunwali is an oral tradition that consists of general principles and practices (tsali) that are applied to specific cases. What is most distinctive about the use of customary law is its insistence on using community members or respected outsiders chosen by the disputants as fact finders and decision makers.

1. *Pirs:* Local charismatic religious leaders played important roles in politics historically because they and their disciples crossed tribal lines and could act as counterweights to the landowning tribal khans who tended to dominate Pashtun clans and lineages.
2. Pashtunwali is more than just customary laws, it is a way of life that stresses honor above all else, including the acquisition of money, property, as well as punishment to include even death.
3. Pashtunwali is all about being, maintaining, and preserving one's self honor and honor of the family, clan, and tribe.
4. Pashtun tribes that have remained in the hills and deserts continue to draw a sharp distinction between themselves and their tax-free, blood feuding way of life (*nang*) and those Pashtuns who live under state control (*qalang*).
5. Three Major Institutions of Pashtunwali:
   a. *Badal* (revenge) is the means of enforcement by which an individual seeks personal justice for wrongs done against him or his kin group. It is this right and expectation of retaliation that lies at the heart of the Pashtunwali as a non-state legal system. "Kill one of our people and we will kill one of yours; hit me and I will hit you back." While the community may recognize that acts such as theft, homicide, or rape are wrong, it does not take collective responsibility for judging or punishing people who commit such acts.
   b. *Melmastia* (hospitality) sets out the rights and obligations of hosts and guests. The Pashtunwali demands that guests be welcomed without question and be given the best of whatever the host has to offer. In addition to shelter, food, and rest, the code of hospitality demands that guests receive absolute protection as well. This solves two problems. First, it allows for

travel in rural regions outside the cash economy where one cannot buy food or rent a room in an inn or caravansary. Second (and as important), it solves the problem of how to ensure one's personal security in a world where there is no overarching legal authority to preserve the peace. In the case of Navy Seal Marcus Luttrell, who survived not only captivity but was also kept safe, it was thanks to an elder Pashtun who honored Melmastia within Pashtunwali.

    c. *Nanawati* (sanctuary) is a right to seek protection, request pardon, or demand help from a more powerful person or kin group by a weaker one. In its best known form, someone leaves his own community looking for permanent protection. A fleeing couple that has eloped against the wishes of their parents or a man avoiding a blood feud are common supplicants. The institution of sanctuary recognizes that although equality of rights and obligations is an ideal, it is one that is not always possible to achieve. Because the supplicant must declare his weakness and lack of autonomy, the request for nanawati occurs only in extreme cases. Nanawati may also take the form of asking pardon for a wrong done to a person. This may be done to preempt retaliation by admitting a wrong or as part of a settlement in which the losing party is forced to ask for the victim's pardon in order to bring an end to the dispute. The latter is an inducement to settlement because a victim's kin may fear that agreeing to accept settlement will make them look weak.

6. In addition it valorizes the accumulation of personal honor (*ghayrat*) and defense against insults by outsiders to the honor of the group or its women (*namus*).

7. *Jirga*: Where men meet as equals to discuss problems or resolve disputes, is the forum in which such decision making normally occurred. This is very similar to a *Shura* where elders meet from numerous tribes yet the major differences lie in that the *Jirga* is not always stemming from multiple tribes and more often than not occurs within the tribe but, even more so, on the VILLAGE level. Also, one may find younger men attending and participating in the *Jirga*.

8. Any attack on a woman, physical or verbal, is seen as an attack on a man's (father's, brother's, or husband's) honor. Such attacks must be revenged.

9. It is women's opinion that is often decisive in raising and lowering a man's position.

10. Taking an oath before God: this is a very serious matter among Pashtuns. The demand for an oath is, at minimum, an attack on a man's honor because it implies you are accusing him of being a liar. Indeed a man with a great deal of prestige may refuse to take such an oath for this reason unless the issue at hand is critical and there is no way to avoid it. On the other hand, because the role of honor is so serious, it is generally assumed that a man will tell the truth in taking an oath because it would be better to be dead than alive in dishonor.

2. While John Kerry may or may have not stated some of these accusations of his fellow military counterparts he encountered during his service throughout the Vietnam War, such claims were made by numerous news agencies during the 2004 Presidential race such as Fox News, ACSA.net, The National Review, along with many others.

3. Interviews and discussion among numerous Catholic Priests have shown that many individuals serving in times of war often resort back to religious beliefs upon their return home from conflicts.

4. Outlaw Motorcycle Gangs have played an integral part in North American Society. From their inception as noncriminal enterprises to today's romantic mysteries of illegal and or illicit behaviors, they have changed with time. Not all motorcycle gangs are involved with illegal or illicit activities, nor are all individuals associated with "1%'ers." One of the most educational pieces of information to better understand Outlaw Motorcycle Gangs is written through the Mid Atlantic Greater Lakes Organized Crime Enforcement Network (MAGLOCLEN).

5. To obtain a greater sense of Russian tactics while fighting the Afghans during Russian Afghan War, it is encouraged to read Les Grau's book *Bear Went over the Mountain*.

6. Information about the violent nature among Hezb Islami Gullbidine (HIG), specifically, Gullbidine Hekmatyar was discovered through interviews of numerous local indigenous persons throughout the provinces of Nangahar and Konar Afghanistan over the course of an approximate one-year period of social science work conducted in the year 2008.

6 Current Research in Understanding Ethics within Sociocultural Intelligence

The ethical intelligence reality check

For months afterwards we did not have a clear understanding of the enemy we were dealing with, and our every effort was focused on preventing further attacks that would kill more Americans.[1]

(Dennis C. Blair)

On April 16, 2009, the Director of National Security Dennis C. Blair made a statement to all those involved within the US Intelligence Community. His statement was based on the media outcry about the interrogation techniques used against personnel detained in United States custody with regards to the War on Terror. These methods had been approved for the sake of National Security by numerous leaders within the US government during the Bush Administration. Dennis Blair admitted to the necessities of using such methods at the time, but stated that they should no longer be used in an attempt to appease the international community. He also suggested that he would continue to support those involved in using such methods in the past and would defend them from legal or civil actions. A major debate occurred within the United States not just because of interrogation techniques, but because of all tactics being utilized to fight the War on Terror. The greater debate however lies in the ethical standards held among the United States leaders and the Intelligence Community.

No matter the fact that the debate relates to tactics used to fight the War on Terror, the most notable missing piece is the understanding of international perception in relation to such tactics. The United States lacks cultural understandings of the Muslim extremists that are being fought. Iraqi and Afghan persons made similar statements towards their perceptions of the United States prior to 9–11. "When we saw soldiers waving traffic, when the statue of Saddam fell, we laughed and became confused as to why you weren't shooting all of us" and "we lost respect for you when we saw you waving traffic."[2] These are two of many similar statements made by indigenous persons abroad during the War on Terror.

Those who are being fought understand harsh brutality. In many ways, they respect such brutality as it has been the method used to control their populations for centuries. This does not mean that they are brutal or violent people, rather a culture that understands brutality due to years of oppression. The belief that the United States is a super power has been ingrained into them, a social conditioning that often makes them believe that in order to be a super power one must be the most ruthless. During the invasion of Iraq, the United States proved such beliefs to be wrong as it catered a peaceful approach towards those who were not engaged in the insurgency battles. This kinder and gentler means of warfare led the locals to lose respect for the monster they thought the United States was.

Director Blair's statement is a double-edged sword. One side shows his ethics as a true leader as he openly admits to flaws within the system. Further, he refuses to allow individuals who were engaged in such acts because of orders from above to be personally targeted. On the flip side, although his statement appears to be a mechanism to prove his abilities to lead, it has great potential to increase world violence. Blair notes that he understands the importance of such interrogation practices, but that he believes that they should no longer be used. Had he had an understanding towards the international cultural dimensions where War on Terror operations exist, Blair would have known that such a statement could be a social conditioning mechanism utilized by opposition groups to promote further actions against those serving abroad.

Blair indeed conducted appropriate actions based on his individual moral beliefs. Because of this, he should be applauded. His actions, however, have great potential to backfire and may cause grave "harm." Often times, US military considers actions to have potential to create a second or third order of effect. This simply means that when an action occurs, more often than not the action itself creates more than one outcome. The action or reactions based on the initial action can be greater "harm" than the situation existing prior to the initial action itself. Social Scientists construe this concept related to second and third orders of effect as "Interlocking Spheres."[3] Often times, identity of malfeasance and malfunction (or harm) with intelligence has potential to promote harm to the subject's vital interests, such as their own personal needs. Blair, because of his position as Director of National Intelligence, can be construed as the center sphere with multiple spheres interlocked around him. His words and actions can easily allow him and his spheres to crumble. The concept behind "Interlocking Spheres" means that when one interest or principle is damaged or destroyed, a chain reaction or domino effect may result damaging multiple spheres of principle within a node, tie, network, or system.

> Therefore, 'harm' is the setting back, thwarting, damaging or the violation of an individual's vital interests. Alternatively put, if an individual's vital interests are violated, then that individual is said to be harmed in that he or she is prevented from achieving their needs, goals or activities. (Bellaby 2009)

These interlocking spheres can easily be related to not just individuals, but also to entities or organizations. If one organization were to fall within the intelligence community, imagine the impact this could have among all other intelligence organizations and the ultimate effect on National Security. The situation with the questionable interrogation techniques could be construed as an element or sphere that has caused an ethical violation, which could later be used against the United States, preventing intelligence and government officials from achieving their ultimate goal of protecting National Security. Today, there are still outcries within America's social and political domains about these interrogation techniques. An ethical edge of debate exists and will continue to exist because of such an incident, with little hope of resolution from those for or against the actions that occurred.

Resolving and coming to an agreement with regards to interrogation techniques is unlikely because definitions of ethics are cultural in nature and not legal. This is because the greatest debate related to interrogation techniques is based on ethics. Like the word terrorism, the word ethics is difficult to define because of the vast array of cultural values that constitutes ethical/moral behavior. A need for a legitimized profession of SOCINT will never be observed unless a governance structure can impose sanctions resulting from unethical practices.[4] Most professionals see minor unethical behavior daily without any recourse. Intelligence disciplines are no different. The problem with this is the question as to "when are minor unethical acts considered major unethical acts?" When do multiple minor unethical acts aggregate to cause the equivalent of one large unethical act? Unfortunately, many professionals in the multiple fields of intelligence believe that an ethical policing body could never exist in the intelligence community.

The art of ethical collection

With an understanding of intelligence and actions needed to collect intelligence to preserve National Security, it is easy to fall into such a trap as to believe that addressing unethical behavior is virtually impossible. One of the greatest allies to the United States in the Middle East, Israel, could easily argue such a belief. Dr. Shlomo Shapiro from the Department of Political Studies within Bar-IIan University states:

> The world of intelligence has been full of expert liars, and indeed, telling the truth is often considered the least desirable option. Agents and case officers, working under false identities over long periods of time, develop different perceptions of the 'truth' or 'truths' in plural. But the truth, or true and full reporting, is the core of effective intelligence work. (Shapiro)

In his work *Speak no Evil: Intelligence Ethics in Israel* (2007), Shapiro mentions the fact that the individual intelligence operative continuously faces ethical dilemmas.[5] He believes most individuals would be incapable of acting appropriately when faced with a dilemma that could lead them to jeopardize national security. Often times the intelligence operative must engage in acts needed to protect individual sources/informants, protect secrets related to national interests, interrogate individuals, and/or act or behave in means for survival. Most persons are incapable of acting or operating in such manners. These actions may protect the operative through laws, however when laws are not written for specific circumstances, the individual's morals must take over. Because of the wide array of actions to which intelligence operatives may be subjected, the country of Israel has set up stringent ethical practices.

Multiple personal characteristics are sought after when looking for or recruiting intelligence operatives. Loyalty, integrity, honor, honesty, respect, etc., are characteristics needed to fulfill high-risk missions. No matter the situation, one must be capable of believing in oneself and those above in the system in which one works. SOCINT, because of its nature, would need individuals with such characteristics even more so than any other intelligence discipline. While many may believe this is an opinion, it indeed is a fact. SOCINT would be construed as the only intelligence discipline where operatives actually live, interact, and understand societal systems within geographically designated areas. While their operations would construe understandings of sociocultural norms, they would continuously be learning the systems of interest. This means that they would be reliant upon their ethical and moral principles for survival when laws related to the situation are lacking or missing.

Through respect for others as individuals and as large systems and networks, friendships grow. In order to promote peace, a distribution of goods and the respect for cultures must remain open and prevalent. A rethinking of strategy must start by analyzing sociocultural practices within the networks and social systems being persuaded for an end result of peace.[6] While many individuals may believe that manipulation of individuals is wrong, such perception and belief is based on the negative connotations of the term manipulation itself. In reality, manipulation is a very simple concept used to move or influence whatever needs such movement. A means of manipulating a society is the simple removal or implementation of a tie or node within a system or network that differentiates the social structure. In order to conduct such an operation, a trained "Social Agent" (which later will be construed as the SOCINT Operative) should be sought after. This person should be aware of the social phenomenon of mass society and of the machinery of mass persuasion and social control.

The ethical tasks of the SOCINT operative

The social agent should be construed as an intelligence operative. The social agent/SOCINT operative must have excellent personal ethics, morals, interpersonal skills, and sound rapport-building techniques. This person will be forced to acquire assets and sources for data that will later be analyzed by a team of sociocultural analysts for production and dissemination known as a SOCINT report. The greatest importance of the social agent or SOCINT operative is to gain trust from the local indigenous persons, build friendship, and promote some form of sociocultural manipulation of the local systems and networks.

> The aim of law and politics is to build peace, not through the militarization of states, but by establishing bonds of friendship and, where possible, legal bonds as well. Precisely because it is a practical reason which orders one to build peace, those who engage in practical work to this end act rationally. (Cortina 2007)

Without a doubt, the SOCINT operative will be responsible for the security of numerous entities besides him/herself. Security will be required and he/she will have a moral obligation to protect individuals along with national interests simultaneously. Individual and National Security are concepts that have not been truly defined, however they are understood concepts that go hand and hand.[7] National security is a concept to secure the interests of the people. Instead of strictly securing one specific node (individual security), an entire system of hundreds of networks are secured. Unlike Human Intelligence operatives who deal predominantly with one person as a source, the sociocultural operatives will be dealing with an entire system. Because of this, they will be subjected to secure not one node, but an entire network of nodes that are tied together. Unfortunately, with irregular warfare and the lack of international laws protecting terrorist—unlike existing laws that protect uniformed service members within nation-states—emphasis on moral obligations in the protection of individual rights has never been so apparent. Because of international observation and the pursuit of new laws in dealing with terrorists, havoc and defense against such needed principle will most likely occur the moment numerous social science-based organizations find out about an intelligence discipline operating via local indigenous populations. Because of this, the ethical standards promoted among such a discipline must be extraordinary.

> As its name implies, the "lesser evil" approach agrees with the moralists that some actions are always wrong, even if they are effective. However, with the consequentialists, it maintains that there are circumstances in which consequences matter so much—say, for example, saving the lives of innocent people from a terrorist attack—that necessity may require that a liberal democracy's principle of self-defense compels it to take a course of action that strays from its own foundational commitments. (Pham 2004)

The SOCINT operator must be skilled at mediations and negotiations. He/she must be accepting of multiple local systems views and understanding of such needs as well. The operative must be willing to articulate in a language common to single and multiple parties. Morality is not necessarily an individual concept, rather a principle based upon the social systems in which we live gained through practical reasoning. Morality is not a universally accepted principle due to the diversity of cultures. With language, practical reasoning becomes better structured. In this case, language does not have to be a universally understood spoken/verbal form of communication, rather a more simplistic communication form understood by all parties involved with the communication process.

> In order to lie to someone, we must first share a language with him. And whereas self-interested reasoning may counsel each of us to defect from the cooperative practice of truth telling, which therefore has the incentive structure of a prisoner's dilemma, language has the incentive structure of a coordination problem, in which self-interested reasoning counsels each of us to converge with others rather then make an exception for himself. Even when self-interest oppose(s) telling the truth to others, it still favors speaking their language.[8] (Velleman)

When speaking of language in this context, one must truly be in the mindset of understood communications. Prisoners have language unknown to those who have never been in jail. Gang members have multiple languages ranging from their clothing, hand gestures, to actual vocalized utterances. Military members speak a language filled with acronyms. These forms of communications assist in the reasoning of the individual and individuals being interacted with. They are crucial for performance and, more importantly, survival.

Communication is not just about the delivery of messages. It is also about grasping the message, analyzing the message, and understanding the message. If the SOCINT operative is to be a mediator and negotiator, he/she must be apt at recognizing, witnessing, and visualizing their surroundings and future surrounding outcomes based upon the manipulation promoting change. The greatest tactic to do such an operation is through mediation, because mediation solves a crisis among two or more parties by having all parties come to some form of agreement to end some form of suffering. Because suffering is different depending on the individual, many persons have great difficulty describing it. Thus an enhanced ability to recognize and interpret suffering must prevail. This cannot occur unless an understanding of the local methods of language (again not necessarily through verbal means) exists. With such understanding, an ability to mediate to resolve such pain can greatly be enhanced.

> It promised a humane alternative to relationship-destroying adversarial proce-dure, a way for parties "to own" their dispute and its resolution, and to craft (with the help of a neutral, impartial, and processually virtuosic third party) an agreement that preserved relationships, transcended split-the-difference com-promises, and sustained itself. And yet, from its inception, mediation was never entirely free from the vapors of ethical skepticism.[9] (Cobb 2004)

Related to ethics, negotiations and mediations will often take place with party members who may have "bad blood on their hands." Whether these individuals are liked or not, neutrality must exist pertaining to the feelings towards such individuals in order to achieve the overall end state desired, such as the promotion of peace and understandings into a designated area. The refusal to negotiate among those with so-called "bad blood on their hands" will hinder the overall mission and make very little sense anyway. Those who can make decisions among parties are powerful. No matter how much blood they have on their hands, they can continue to promote violence in turn adding more bloodshed. At times, human rights violations may even have occurred. Through ethical, practical reasoning, only one question must be asked, "Will human rights violations continue if I don't negotiate with these individuals?" More often than not, the answer would be yes. While human rights violations may have occurred, they indeed will continue to occur unless some form of agreement is made with multiple parties. This can only be done successfully if the mediator is fully aware of the situation presented.

> The conflict management perspective holds that the goal is to end the violence as quickly and with as few casualties as possible, with "justice" if possible, with-out it if necessary. This means negotiations with people and organizations with blood on their hands, not because we approve of them but because they often have the power to continue the war.[10] (Licklider 2008)

It is inevitable that compromise occurs daily in any person's lives, and many times that compromise must occur between two people through a negotiation. The severity and depth of the negotiation will depend on the gravity of the situation. Many times, we can conduct these negotiations very simply, while at other times approval to compromise must exist prior to such negotiations.

Leadership roles in the ethical elements of SOCINT

Leaders must be fully informed of the ground truth atmospherics in order to make appropriate decisions based upon whether negotiations and compromise should occur. To obtain such data, leaders often times conduct ill advancements promoting a top-down approach to the situation.

> All in all, this requires that we more recognize the role of social ties, local values and existing ethical frameworks in order to enhance the full participation and ownership of the contract of those involved in, and affected by, the violence and war. (Hellsten 2006)

The situation does not take place in an office in Washington D.C., nor at a corporation headquarters. It takes place in a specific geographic area of concern. The top-down approach is a disastrous method in achieving a desired end state. The top echelon should only be approving actions based upon the recommendation of the sociocultural operative and not on preconceived notions. The institutional levels need a bridge for understanding the grassroots level of understandings for better informed decisions.

The contracts that Hellsten discusses are social contracts.[11] These are agreements among multiple parties through some form of negotiations and or mediations related to an unresolved issue that must come to an end. Agreements made between national and international law is the focus related to social contracts when such laws are missing or misinterpreted among multiple entities. Unfortunately, it is very difficult to identify realistic social contracts because of misunderstood grass root levels of sociocultural data.

Social contracts occur less often than compromise, however they do occur frequently. An individual can observe social contracts through religious aspects of marriage, monetary donations within politics, "your enemy is my enemy therefore you are my friend" within the military, etc. "The concept of justice and the normative framework justice offers to lasting social harmony needs to be considered in relation to local social ethics, values, and to the public ethics requirement of impartiality" (Hellsten 2006). The principle behind the social contract is to promote unification between multiple parties.

The ultimate means to resolve issues is through identification of key factors within the surroundings that can cause some form of explosion throughout. Sociocultural factors have been studied for years in an attempt to identify key indicators of stable locations that are on the brink of turning unstable. These are considered "tipping points." Tipping points are crucial for the SOCINT operatives who have a moral obligation believing in their work to identify, understand, empathize, and conclude appropriate actions deemed necessary in their designated areas of operations. The operatives must identify these tipping points and mitigate prior to disaster.

Sheptycki, J. (2002) identifies in his work *Postmodern Power and Transnational Policing: Democracy, the Constabulary Ethic and the Response to Global (In)Security,* that for too long, paramilitary or military peace keeping or policing has been standardized to deter, detect, and apprehend or destroy violators.[12] Today, with an uprising of social scientists, observation and interaction to better understand systems and networks in specified geographic areas are needed to predict and interfere with tipping points to hostile factions. To conduct such operation a Constabulary Ethic apparatus needs implementation. Sheptycki argues a very basic and one-dimensional approach to principles that would be found in SOCINT, if such an intelligence discipline were ever be formalized into an official capacity.

> In these conditions, democratic policing requires at very least the combined attentions of social scientists, human rights NGOs and policing leaders to the social harms arising from the reality and perceptions of insecurity that pervades our cities, held together with the normative glue provided by the principles and notions that describe what I call the constabulary ethic. (Sheptycki)

America is currently facing one of its most difficult times due to the War on Terror and the economic crisis. Because of such difficult times, American perception allows individuals to believe the United States is continuously losing its allies. At no other time has it been so crucial to unify organizations and nation-states to deter, detect, and destroy threats. The plethora of threats today places the United States and every other country in the world at grave risk. Without the unification and determination among nation-states, irregular threats such as terrorists, rogue regimes, cyber crimes, and climate change will become threats difficult to defeat. As President Harry Truman once said, "No one nation alone can bring peace. Together, nations can build a strong defense against aggression and combine the energy of free men everywhere in building a better future for all." Unfortunately, elitism and nepotism among leaders is one of the greatest hindrances in achieving the goal of unification.

The ethical defeat of elitism and nepotism is not as simple a problem as it may appear. Too often intimidation, bullying, and hostile workforce environments are difficult to resolve especially when such environments result from the initiation stemming within leadership of organizations. Work force bullying occurs throughout every industry. Because the US government is built the way it is and the government salary pay system is structured uniquely, work force bullying is rampant in the US government and more often than not continues without appropriate action. The means to stop the bullying are greatest when it starts at the top. Unfortunately, when the bullying occurs at the top, a complete organizational meltdown is likely.

> Workplace bullying comes in many varieties, overt and covert, direct and indirect. It is intentionally hurtful, typically repeated, and often malicious in nature. Among the most frequently reported behaviors are yelling, shouting, and screaming; false accusations of mistakes and errors; hostile glares and other intimidating non-verbal behaviors; covert criticism, sabotage, and undermining of one's reputation; social exclusion and the "silent treatment"; use of put-downs, insults, and excessively harsh criticism; and unreasonably heavy work demands. (Yamada 2008)

Leadership has an ethical obligation to take care of their people. Many can construe leadership as the shepherds and their people as their flocks. They must protect their people and ensure their individual's assurances to promote the ease needed to fulfill their daily tasks. It may happen that leadership be forced into situations where laws will not guide them, and they will be required to rely on their self-driven morals and ethics, and certain actions may be necessary for the greater good. American leadership as a whole should serve the people as if they were their children. When it comes to national security, the American public may not be privy to key data that would allow full understanding of situations, but more often than not, the public does not need to know such information.

> Children typically lack the understanding needed to protect their own long-term interests. They can be illogical and poorly informed. They commonly give priority to short-term desires and peer approval. They lack judgment. They are easily victimized. Adult caretakers therefore play a vital role in the protection of children.[13] (Allen 2008)

American Government leadership must act as the responsible party ensuring the safety of their constituents, which in this case are the people of the American society. In doing so, they must utilize key judgment in their critical thinking and practical reasoning, which will be dependent on their self-driven moral and ethical values.

As an example of ethical decision making, let's look at the Insurance Society of Philadelphia. This is an organization that follows a very simple methodology for its ethical decision-making process, which can be found in their *Insurance Ethics: a Business of Trust* Power Point slide presentation.[14] In it, five key steps are outlined to ensure key judgment is made for ethical decision making:

1. determine if it's an ethical question
2. gather all the information
3. identify and evaluate alternatives
4. Reach a decision
5. then monitor the decision

Using a decision-making tool enhances the ability to not only think critically about the situation, but also to visualize outcomes by writing them out in a systematic way. People in leadership positions have to make decisions and must do so with the reliance of individual's assessments towards the situation. Their tools for such decision making are crucial as they can be forced into ethical dilemmas continuously. Because intelligence is a very unique and challenging practice, ethics are crucial. When dealing with human subjects as SOCINT, ethics become even more important than in any other intelligence discipline. When adding multiple human subjects and conducting intelligence operations within entire networks and systems, the value of ethics could be life saving not only for the nodes and ties that makes up the network but also to the SOCINT operative.

Notes

1. Media allegations continued to attack the intelligence community for numerous acts of interrogation methods used against terrorist since the 9–11 attacks. For a full recount of his statements see: Blair, D. (2009) Director of National Intelligence (Dennis C. Blair) Statement to the US Intelligence Community. (PDF Transcript). (April 16, 2009).

2. Interviews occurred with Iraqi persons in 2007 while attending a course on military and cultural needs. Statements such as these were made on numerous occasions by such individuals in attendance throughout this course.

3. Bellaby, R. (2009) *Many Spheres of Harm: What's wrong with Intelligence Collection?* International Intelligence Ethics Association Conference Paper. Presented at Johns Hopkins University at Mt.

Washington on February 20, 2009 during the annual International Intelligence Ethics Association Conference. This paper is an attempt to identify malfeasance and malfunction (or harm) with intelligence collection so a philosophical foundation can be thought to mitigate objectionable current collection methodologies that promote or have potential to promote harm to the subject's vital interests such as their own personal needs.

4. Prescott argues that definitions of ethics are cultural in nature and not legal. A need for a legitimized profession of Competitive Intelligence will never be observed unless a governance structure can impose sanctions resulting from unethical practices. Additional arguments continue and claims that individuals know unethical behavior when they see it, yet prior to this statement Prescott mentions that minor ethical acts occur daily. Such a statement makes one wonder when a minor ethical violation becomes a major one.

5. The individual intelligence operative continuously faces ethical dilemmas. As an individual, he/she must protect sources, national interests, arrest, interrogate, and or act/behave in means for survival which the normal person would be incapable of acting. These actions conducted may protect the operative through laws however when laws are not written for specific circumstances, the individual morals must take over. Because of the wide array of actions which the intelligence operative may be subjected to, the country of Israel has set up stringent ethical practices for such operatives. Shapiro provides an extremely solid case for such ethical guidance.

6. Cortina wrote an excellent paper discussing the needs to promote peace through the distribution of goods and the respect of cultures. A rethinking of strategy must start by analyzing social practices within the networks and social systems being manipulated for an end result of peace (of note, Cortina is against manipulation of individuals, however mentions nothing about the social structures or systems of which the people are a part). One unique principle written about relates to the usage of "social agents."

7. Individual/Personal and National Security are concepts which have not been truly defined however are understood to go hand and hand. National security is a concept to secure the interests of the people. Instead of strictly securing one specific node (individual security) an entire system is secured. Unfortunately, with irregular warfare and the lack of international laws protecting terrorist unlike laws that exist protecting uniformed service members within nation states emphasis on moral obligations in the protection of individual rights has never been so apparent. To better appreciate this principle, it is encouraged to read *Law, Human Rights, Realism and the "War on Terror"* (Pham)

8. The introduction of the book *How We Get Along* (Velleman 2009) identifies the main theory that morality is not necessarily an individual concept rather a principle based upon the social systems which we live through practical reasoning. Morality is not a universally accepted principle due to the diversity of cultures throughout. With language, practical reasoning becomes better structured. Recognition, witnessing, and visualization to later analyze and interpret to mitigate subjectivity for an ethical approach to mediations is crucial. Because suffering is a concept, many individuals have great difficulty describing; an enhanced ability to recognize and interpret the suffering must prevail. With such understanding an ability to mediate to resolve such pain can greatly be enhanced. Read, *Witnessing in Mediation: Toward an Aesthetic Ethics of Practice.* (Cobb)

9. Recognition, witnessing, and visualization to later analyze and interpret to mitigate subjectivity for an ethical approach to mediations is crucial. Because suffering is a concept, many individuals have great difficulty describing; an enhanced ability to recognize and interpret the suffering must prevail. With such understanding an ability to mediate to resolve such pain can greatly be enhanced. Read, *Witnessing in Mediation: Toward an Aesthetic Ethics of Practice*. (Cobb)

10. Negotiations are often times crucial to bring peace to a specified area. Ethically speaking, the greater good may at times include speaking with those who indeed have "bad blood on their hands." These individuals also are the ones who can continue with the violence in the area. While human rights violations may have occurred, they indeed will continue to occur unless some form of agreement is made with multiple parties. This can only be done successfully if the mediator is fully aware of the situation presented.

11. Agreements made between national and international law is the focus related to social contracts. Unfortunately, it is very difficult to identify realistic social contracts because of misunderstood grass root levels of sociocultural data. Too often a top down approach to understanding the realities in mitigating violence and bringing peace to an area occurs. That top down approach occurs from leaders who are ill informed to the situation. The institutional levels need a bridge for understanding the grassroots level of understandings for better informed decisions.

12. For too long, paramilitary or military peace keeping or policing has been standardized to deter, detect, and apprehend violators. Today, with an uprising of social scientists, observation and interaction to better understand systems and networks in specified geographic areas are needed to predict and interfere with tipping points to hostile factions. To conduct such operation a Constabulary Ethic apparatus needs implementation. Sheptycki argues a very basic and one dimensional approach to SOCINT.

13. When is it ok to spy? Anita Allen demonstrates excellent argument as to when it is and is not ethical to spy. Bringing the practice of spying out of the private world and into the state and federal government inevitably protects individual's privacy much greater than the later. The government can be viewed as the parents to all Americans with an obligation to protect its children. In doing so they must be informed as to their surroundings to better equipped action for protection.

14. Over 110 Power Point slides in reference to ethics predominantly related to the business of insurance exist within the *Insurance Ethics: A Business of Trust* lecture presented by Lyons. While these are related to the insurance industry, they are excellent examples of the "Do's: and "Don'ts" in any industry. A great ethical decision-making process exists within this lecture which states, "Determine if it's an ethical question, gather all the information, identify and evaluate alternatives, reach a decision, then monitor the decision."

CRITICAL THINKING AND SOCIOCULTURAL INTELLIGENCE III

The Need for Critical Thinking within Sociocultural Intelligence

7

Chapter Outline

Critical thinking versus analysis

Battlefield information, however, is of limited value until it has been analyzed. Through analysis, this information becomes intelligence. The intelligence analyst integrates the seemingly insignificant bits of information from multiple sources to produce an overall picture of the battlefield. This picture reduces the uncertainties about the battlefield and the situation.

(FM 34–3 1990)

Although some individuals within the Intelligence Community (IC) may believe the aforementioned quote taken directly out of US Army Field Manual 34–3 (chapter 1 page 1, second paragraph) to be accurate, many might argue against it. Malcolm Gladwell, Nassim Taleb, Theodore Dalrymple, and Charles Clayton are some of the people more likely to disagree with such a statement related to intelligence.[1] They are acclaimed authors in fields related to the social sciences and not intelligence operatives, but they have assessed the means, or lack thereof, of critical thinking, which is the key to any analysis.

The United States and other countries based on similar Western scientific philosophy have missed a large chunk of knowledge that was discovered by Charles Sanders Peirce in the late nineteenth and very early twentieth century. Peirce detected that a portion of Aristotle's Philosophy had been deleted from philosophy in the fourteenth century. This fundamental change in philosophy came about when the proponents of our present doctrines (Nominalism and Humanism) ejected the Scholastics from the Colleges of Europe and consequently threw "Form" out of Aristotle's definition of "Substance" (form is the basis of knowledge for the Reasoning Mind and Knowledge Science) while simultaneously throwing out the teaching of "Logic, the Art of Reasoning, and the art of Debate" (Critical Thinking).[2] Since then, the West has made little advancement in "Logic," "Art of Reasoning," and in the "Knowledge Sciences." Without such practices, however, the social sciences and intelligence communities will never be fully prepared to face the constantly evolving global circumstances that we face today and will face tomorrow.

The lack of courses on critical thinking is an unfortunate tragedy in American education. It is a concept that left most of Europe and never really reached the United States. We understand philosophy and theology, but those are not end-all, be-all within critical thinking and instead should be construed as only parts of it. Arguments have been made that the United States teaches instead numerous forms of mathematics such as geometry, algebra, and trigonometry, which are all crucial elements to enhance critical thinking and practical reasoning skills. Most schools today do not even offer debate as a class, but as an extracurricular activity after school.

Even though we know—or assume we know—what is needed to become a decent or even possibly a good critical thinker, very few can accurately define the process. Because critical thinking should be construed as a process, the most suitable definition for such an argument comes from CriticalThinking. net. The excerpt below shows that critical thinking involves a multitude of key attributes.

> Critical thinking is here assumed to be reasonable reflective thinking focused on deciding what to believe or do. This rough overall definition is, we believe, in accord with the way the term is generally used these days. Under this

interpretation, critical thinking is relevant not only to the formation and checking of beliefs, but also to deciding upon and evaluating actions. It involves creative activities such as formulating hypotheses, plans, and counterexamples; planning experiments; and seeing alternatives. Furthermore critical thinking is reflective—and reasonable. The negative, harping, complaining characteristic that is sometimes labeled by the word, "critical," is not involved.[3]

One of the first key attributes used in defining critical thinking is "reflective thinking" or thought. To look back at the past is essential to understand the historic principles of a situation. This in itself could be construed as the "breadth" of critical thinking. Reflective thinking serves as the foundation needed to provide a baseline of thought. It encourages individuals to look back at their past experiences to formulate ideas about the present.

Also used as well in the above definition is the term "formation," which is crucial with regards to SOCINT because, as already discussed, SOCINT specifically deals with networks and systems that are built through multiple nodes and ties, be they individuals or entities. In order to gain greater understandings of these systems and networks, an individual will need to conduct more narrow focused research outside the breadth of critical thinking. This phase of the process could be construed as the "depth."

Next, "checking and evaluation" are identified as elements needed to formulate either a median between the information being processed or an end decision of focus and reason based on a compare-and-contrast approach. Checking and evaluation could be conducted through experimentation or "wargaming,"—an approach that would enhance the knowledge of thought while proving or refuting ideas of actions.

Lastly, "creative activities" are identified to ensure that the presumed end thoughts are validated into a tested hypothesis for accuracy. These final two phases of critical thinking—checking and evaluating along with creative activities—constitute a process known as the "Application" phase. These two elements go hand in hand and should serve one another in unison to reach a conclusion based on the presented data. All these elements form the entire process of critical thought which enhances the formulation of knowledge.

Within SOCINT, nothing is more crucial than the implementation of critical thinking for numerous reasons. First and foremost, it assists "Western Thinking" understanding the numerous cultures and societies where operations exist. In the end, SOCINT should assist decision makers by offering viable options that are in accord with the societies and cultures deemed critical. To be effective, critical thought from application is necessary.

Technology dependency

As one can observe, using critical thinking to understand very complex networks and systems is indeed a very demanding process that cannot be done in milliseconds. The simpler the system, the faster one will be capable of formulating a conclusion. Critical thinking is key for an individual to fulfill task and purpose, and one should not strictly rely on a computer system to obtain needed answers.

Computer systems are often used inappropriately for analysis and become relied upon for the actual critical thinking needed for understanding. This in itself can result in disaster. (Note that the term analysis and the utilization and reliance on computer systems versus the need for understanding are and should remain different processes.) Computer systems and analytical tools are just that, tools. They help the critical thinking process of an individual trying to visualize the situation confronted. But they are not to be relied upon for understanding the principles of the "5 W's."[4]

Because the United States developed from an agricultural society to an industrial society, and into a technological society, we have lost some of the fundamental processes of critical thinking and inappropriately rely upon technological analytical tools for answers. Consequently, threat identification, international tipping points, and domestic needs have been partially identified, but with multiple gaps of understandings that could have been presented with greater acknowledgment. The appreciation for critical thinking and practical reasoning with lesser reliance upon technical analytical tools will be crucial for anyone seeking to understand sociocultural elements.

Filling the gaps of critical thought

Without critical thinking and practical reasoning, such gaps of information and knowledge will exist. The missing data could have prevented any disaster via mitigation or destruction before they became problems. Neither mitigation nor destruction operations will ever be deemed successful without such needed principles of thought.

A few maverick geniuses tapped into Peirce's vast storehouse of knowledge in the 1960s, and their work is embodied in some of our most advanced weapons systems. However, the most advanced weapon system is indeed the human mind. Unfortunately, that burst of knowledge was soon eclipsed by a tsunami of Software Simulations and Software Tool Designs. We have been laboring under the illusion that reasoning and analysis is only software-based and can be only accomplished by Software Programmers. An individual can see the results of such thinking today due to the current presented intelligence failures within National Security.

> Analysis is the determination of the significance of the information, relative to information and intelligence already known, and drawing deductions about the probable meaning of the evaluated information. (FM 34–3, Section 2–4, p. 19)

Analysis is an element of critical thinking, but it is simply a means to visualize the topic of concern. In SOCINT, analysis alone could be construed as an accident waiting to happen. Analysis in itself is the picture that shows what we already know. Multiple pieces of information for understanding the sociocultural elements are missing without critical thinking.

At best, analysis may show some history and present data, but it will always lack the multiple nodes and networks perception to the situation and in turn will only allow a one-dimensional perspective based on the analyst self critique. The analyst, who must be a critical thinker, must also be capable of "digging deeper" into the equation for understanding. Virtually every renown author of critical thinking states that a series of questions must be answered in order to "dig deeper" into the critical thinking process to better understand the situation. To do so, additional observation must occur. To succeed in obtaining such observations, deeper infiltration into the known system or network must exist. In an attempt to infiltrate the system deeper, a series of questions must be asked. Within the SOCINT framework, critical thinking questioning should consist at a minimum of the following:[5]

1. What is the truest objective in understanding such sociocultural matters?
2. What are the numerous nodes and/or networks that make up the system? What views or perspectives do they have, based on the situation past, present, and future, including formal and informal factors that constitute such views?
3. What existing methodologies can help formulate a conclusion about the situation based on the multiple nodes and/or networks that it encompasses?
4. What prejudices exist among those formally and informally involved within the situation?
5. Based on what is known, how many courses of actions can occur and which would limit the amount of collateral damage within the area of concern?
6. If decisions or actions are made or taken based on the known situation, what effect will they have among the nodes, networks, and overall system, including second and third orders of effects?
7. What means are present to mitigate any negative reactions based on decisions made or actions taken?

The critical thought process

Answering such questions is not simple and will take time. Numerous steps must be achieved just to answer such questions. First, collaboration of ideas to fully understand the customer's truest desires must be met. Often times what the customer believes he or she needs is not necessarily so and instead there is a greater and more thorough need.

Through such collaboration, strict understanding of what the customer believes he/she requires must be met. At times, and more importantly, meeting the needs of what the customer truly does not know related to underlying principles must also be achieved within the planning of collection operations. This is crucial because more often than not, too many individuals "do not know what they need to know." Such collaboration of ideas should be incorporated into a collection plan.

The first step in understanding a network is through the development of a collection plan that will be formulated from an operations cell. This plan must be formulated with a sound understanding of the task and purpose stemming from the initial desires of National Security leadership. The plan itself must be thorough and goal oriented. The lack of gaps in questioning should prevent gaps of information at the end of all collection efforts, understanding that the initial process will not be complete and that unforeseen relationships will be discovered.

Something, someone, some entity must be known about the network prior to conducting any research. This information should be readily available through the identification phase of the initial network analysis, fully knowing that networks have many similarities as well as distinct differences and purposes. Prior knowledge related to the network should be obtained through past experiences and literature.

The goal behind the plan is not to reinvent the wheel of information, rather to obtain further detailed information pertaining to the network that is not known through open source information. The collection plan must include questions that identify who, what, why, when, where, and how. Through gap analysis, the operations cell will be the overarching determining functioning system that will either integrate or deplete ties connected to nodes within systems.

This process will occur for influential purposes to achieve desired effects including second and third orders of effects within the battle space. In all, such operations will be conducted to assist all battle space players in achieving their desired end state. In order to be effective in assisting in such a process, the operations cell must be familiar with DOD, DOS, DOJ, Host Country Organizations, and NGO operations/protocol and literature, including maintaining rapport with key influential leaders within such organizations for collaboration applications/operations.

Second, a SOCINT collection team must be capable of identifying the numerous nodes and ties within the network of concern. They must be capable of formulating their own sub plan based on the operations cell's plan to infiltrate the network in an attempt to obtain answers to such questions derived from the numerous perspectives stemming from the informal and formal outliers. This operation in itself could take the majority of time in concluding the end state.

This collection cell will be the ultimate responsible party that makes or breaks the SOCINT operational process and, historically, it is the most neglected. Commanders Cultural Intelligence Requirements (CCIR's) are often neglected due to the demand of lethal targeting responsibilities maintained by traditional Defense Intelligence Operatives. With current doctrinal requirements holding responsibility among Civil Affairs and the vast array of Provincial Reconstruction Team (PRT) projects, it has become evident that neither current traditional Defense intelligence nor Civil Affairs (1) has the training to conduct adequate Cultural Intelligence let alone collection needs and (2) is too overwhelmed with current tasks to achieve success in Cultural Intelligence protocol.

Because of these two crucial points, another asset must be utilized to achieve such Cultural Intelligence requirements. The asset, in this case a SOCINT team, must have freedom of movement and limitless rules of engagement stemming from conventional forces and their operations. This last point is stressed because with such limitations, the current Human Terrain System (HTS) will inevitably never gain the momentum needed for proof of concept without a sister organization like SOCINT.

Third, with the obtained data collected from the SOCINT collection team, analysts must be capable of thinking like the nodes within the system to gain a greater sense of appreciation towards the collected data. They must be capable of presenting detailed questions for collectors to continue with their endeavors and reach enough insight into the situation for completeness. This in itself should be construed as the conducting of "gap analysis."

As the gap analysis process is fulfilled, understandings towards the multiple layers of the overall system must also be achieved. Such network layers could be, but are not limited to, infrastructure, media, politics (local and national), internal and external factors, religious elements/factions, etc. Lastly, the analysts must be capable of "Wargaming" numerous options of activities in an attempt to understand effects (first, second, and third orders of effects).

The analyst cell must then be responsible for disseminating the data analysis in a language understood by the ultimate decision makers who have access to the action arm to be used later to persuade, influence and, if necessary, manipulate the overall system. In the end, a decision to act or not act will be made, and in time, the ultimate outcome shall exist. As drawn out as this process may seem at times, it may be very quick due to the collectors and or analysts adaptive intuition.

Time and thought

Prolonged amounts of time are not always needed for appropriate critical thinking and to promote practical reasoning. Gladwell expresses that an adaptive unconsciousness is more often referred to as "a kind of giant computer that quickly and quietly processes a lot of the data we need in order to keep functioning as human beings" (Gladwell 2005a). This shows that we have two elements of critical thought to allow such mental processing: intuitive and non-intuitive thought.

Non-intuitive thought is that which comes from study. It is gained from books, lectures, movies, etc. Some social structures, such as academia, are dedicated to assist non-intuitive thought. At the same time, intuitive thought is based more or less on instinct, feelings, or a sense not unlike a "sixth sense."

Intuitive thought is just as learned a concept as non-intuitive thought. More often than not, such learning comes from informal training and experience. We learn to ride a bicycle not from a book, but rather from falling, getting back up again, and trying until we get the principal methodology needed to successfully ride the bicycle. Riding a bicycle is not a natural act for the human body and no matter how long or how far our mothers, fathers, grandparents, etc., push the back of the bicycle for us, the truest of means in learning how to ride that bicycle comes from personal experience.

Years can go by without ever riding a bicycle again, but when the time comes to get back on the seat, the adaptive unconsciousness built predominantly through intuitive learning experiences kicks into gear. This in itself allows the individual rider the understandings of the situation to successfully ride again. It is the intuitive cycle of thought that will impose the necessary means of survival for the SOCINT elements.

Delving deeper into the complexity of the power of critical thinking and the differentiation between non-intuitive and intuitive proponents of thought, another crucial factor must be mentioned. This element within cognition is dependent on speed and is called "rapid cognition." Rapid cognition is a hidden gem of brain power. When facing a situation here and now, the brain can easily recognize "slices of patterns" based on previous situations, a process better known as "thin slicing."

Rapid cognition is a smaller entity hidden inside the adaptive unconsciousness. Once the brain identifies these patterns, a rapid analysis is conducted to provide understandings towards the current situation. This rapid cognition based on the thin slicing principle is virtually impossible to achieve unless individual experiences exist.

In the land of the Blind, the one eyed man is King. (Afghan Proverb)

Good will hunting syndrome

The Intelligence Community, possibly unknowingly, as a whole has become a group favoring non-intuitive thinkers much more so than intuitive ones. They have become the "Good Will Hunters of Intelligence." The following scene from the movie *Good Will Hunting* will help understand what is meant by this phrase:

Sean: Thought about what you said to me the other day, about my painting. Stayed up half the night thinking about it. Something occurred to me ... fell into a deep peaceful sleep, and haven't thought about you since. Do you know what occurred to me?

Will: No.

Sean: You're just a kid, you don't have the faintest idea what you're talkin' about.

Will: Why thank you.

Sean: It's all right. You've never been out of Boston.

Will: Nope.

Sean: So if I asked you about art, you'd probably give me the skinny on every art book ever written. Michelangelo, you know a lot about him. Life's work, political aspirations, him and the pope, sexual orientations, the whole works, right? But I'll bet you can't tell me what it smells like in the Sistine Chapel. You've never actually stood there and looked up at that beautiful ceiling; seen that. If I ask you about women, you'd probably give me a syllabus about your personal favorites.

You may have even been laid a few times. But you can't tell me what it feels like to wake up next to a woman and feel truly happy. You're a tough kid. And I'd ask you about war, you'd probably throw Shakespeare at me, right, "once more unto the breach dear friends." But you've never been near one. You've never held your best friend's head in your lap, watch him gasp his last breath looking to you for help. I'd ask you about love, you'd probably quote me a sonnet. But you've never looked at a woman and been totally vulnerable. Known someone that could level you with her eyes, feeling like God put an angel on earth just for you. Who could rescue you from the depths of hell. And you wouldn't know what it's like to be her angel, to have that love for her, be there forever, through anything, through cancer. And you wouldn't know about sleeping sitting up in the hospital room for two months, holding her hand, because the doctors could see in your eyes, that the terms "visiting hours" don't apply to you. You don't know about real loss, 'cause it only occurs when you've loved something more than you love yourself. And I doubt you've ever dared to love anybody that much. And look at you... I don't see an intelligent, confident man...I see a cocky, scared shitless kid. But you're a genius Will. No one denies that. No one could possibly understand the depths of you. But you presume to know everything about me because you saw a painting of mine, and you ripped my fucking life apart. You're an orphan right?

[Will nods]

Sean: You think I know the first thing about how hard your life has been, how you feel, who you are, because I read Oliver Twist? Does that encapsulate you? Personally...I don't give a shit about all that, because you know what, I can't learn anything from you, I can't read in some fuckin' book. Unless you want to talk about you, who you are. Then I'm fascinated. I'm in. But you don't want to do that do you sport? You're terrified of what you might say. Your move, chief.

This scene from *Good Will Hunting* is more than just about a certified psychologist conducting a partial psychoanalysis of a non-intuitive orphan. There is a very deep underlying factor that must be acknowledged with regards to the entire society of Americans. The Good Will Hunters dominate the US Intelligence Community.

As a majority, the US Intelligence Community has a multitude of "Will Huntings" out there. Too few have ever experienced the physical livelihoods of those about whom they conduct intelligence. Too few know what it's truly like to face the enemy as they are being shot at. They are underprivileged and do not go out and work with the operatives, who are often referred to as the "shooters, movers, and communicators" within the military. Because of this, they undermine some of the greatest factors that would enhance their skills. In all, they lack the intuitive conceptualizations of discipline towards intelligence. Social scientist, too, face this dilemma, but less often than the intelligence operatives.

Gladwell, neither a labeled intelligence operative nor a social scientist by trade, is a staff writer for the *New Yorker* and served as a business and science reporter for the *Washington Post*. He is a journalist and a very good one at that. He is good at what he does because of his systematic approach in fulfilling his works.

Gladwell conducts broad-based research, and then identifies gaps of information analysis based on his non-intuitive learning. He later goes out and actually attempts to bring his own intuitive experiences into an application of learning via interviews, observations, and multiple gambits of perspectives identified through obtained human sources within systems of interest. Unofficially, Gladwell, along with an entire network of journalists and freelance writers, could be construed as the epitome of SOCINT operatives.

Most intelligence operatives lack workforce diversity outside their profession. Diversity in the sphere of SOCINT is crucial. Like a journalist, the sociocultural operative must be willing to go out into the unknown and be capable of transitioning from an intelligence operative into a doctor, a law enforcement official, a farmer, or even a reporter. This does not mean that they must be capable of becoming experts in these disciplines, rather become students of such.

Theodore Dalrymple, for example, is a doctor by trade who works in the United Kingdom. He is also a writer who has traveled extensively throughout the world and is therefore capable of making observations based on numerous past personal experiences. Such observations have allowed him to reach viable conclusions about the world around him that threatens the cultural stature of the United Kingdom.

In his works, he shows the extensive knowledge he gained working around law enforcement in prison systems. He has witnessed the rise of office support workers who have virtually surpassed the actual law enforcement practitioners. This alone has not caused decline in the culture, but the effects of such enhanced structures have played a large role.

Because of such workforce structures, Dalrymple claims that incident and arrest report writing has increased dramatically. Increased paperwork leads to more opportunities for mistakes. This in turn often allows criminals to avoid incarceration because of inaccuracies found in the cases later, when going to court. In all, what appeared to make sense when restructuring the entire criminal system has caused greater risk to society. Such failures in society cause greater work functionaries and needs for government intervention, which mistakenly misconceives a need for more employment and staffing.

> A child who does not learn to read properly often behaves badly in school and this becomes the subject of inquiries by educational psychologists and social workers....They always find that the child in question lacks self esteem and therefore should be allowed to attend only those classes that he feels he can cope with. The so called senior management team in the school-teachers who have retired into a largely administrative role—deals with all disciplinary problems by means of appeasement, for lack of any other permissible method available to them. (Dalrymple 2008, p. 129)

This observation from Dalrymple is strictly garnered from years of experience in working among social workers. Here, he presents an observation based on time, experience, associations, perception, etc. This does not mean that he is necessarily right or wrong about what he believes, but that through multiple properties of mnemic phenomena, he has reached a conclusion using critical thought.

As mentioned, his conclusion is neither right nor wrong, but incomplete because it lacks one essential element of critical thought, which is "testing." Dalrymple and many other professional social scientists may not always have to physically test their conclusions. This step may at times be reduced or eliminated when enough critical elements of evidence present themselves to the situation for agreement. In this case, Dalrymple had enough evidence of the situation, enough historical knowledge of what is or was to draw such conclusion accurately with minimal to virtually no argument based upon his presentation of logic.

What Dalrymple has displayed is the epitome of Bertrand Russell's Lecture IV, "Influence of Past History on Present Occurrences in Living Organisms." The overall theme of this philosophy is based upon the reasoning that

> as hitherto observed facts are concerned, can only be brought under casual laws by including past occurrences in the history of the organism as part of the causes of the present response...past occurrences are part of a chain of causes leading to the present event. (Russell 2005, p. 45)

Earlier, we examined the necessity of experience through the scene from the movie *Good Will Hunting*. The following six attributes allow to gain the mnemic phenomena that Dalrymple identifies (Russell 2005, pp. 44–53):

1. Acquired Habits of Habitual Knowledge
2. Images of Acquired Sensations
3. Association of Experiences
4. Non-sensational Elements in Perception

5. Memory as Knowledge more related to as Definite Knowledge
6. Experience based upon modification of behavior

Dalrymple exemplifies the understandings of cause and effect through probable and improbable means. He uses the example of an individual consuming a toxic poison—the cause—and the death following such consumption—the effect. Many scientists believe that the sun rising will inevitably cause the effect of night in time. While this probable cause-and-effect relationship may appear sound, in itself it may result in the improbable.

Cause and effect

The improbable effects of such causes may include, but not be limited to, medical caregivers saving the life of the poisoned victim, an eclipse occurring during the day or night, etc. The aforementioned attributes resulting in mnemic phenomena assist in influence related to past history in concluding or hypothesizing results/effects caused by causes/occurrences.

The causes or occurrences are not as simple as many would like to believe. Every cause is an action that results in a process causing the end effect. While the cause is important, the process is just as crucial to understand and, if anything, is more important. Like a doctor who diagnoses a patient, an evaluation of circumstances and process must be observed prior to any recommended prescription to resolve the illness. Similarly to the physicians approach to cure an ailment, critical thinking within the social spheres of SOCINT must also be possible.

Material objects may appear to be one-dimensional substance, but in reality no material object is proprietary in itself, rather it is a system of multiple components that can be manipulated. Knowing this, a material object can be destroyed with just an understanding of its simplistic form. On the other hand, by understanding the system of multiple elements that form the object, one could systematically take it apart and put it back together differently for the better. An example of this is a wooden chair. The chair itself is more than wood. It is a multitude of objects tied together to make the actual object of the chair itself. Some other nodes within the system of the chair could be glue, nails, a saw, sand paper, stain, etc. They are all "tied" through actions that put them together, thus creating the overall material object, that is, the chair. (Of note, a wooden chair can be put together in numerous ways hence no guaranteed pattern of structure exists.)

Identifying cause and effect and utilizing numerous critical thinking skills about the object will allow a wood worker to take the chair apart, manipulate it, and recreate it into a better/different working system. In this case, the identification of the wooden chair can be taken apart and restructured into a child's rocking horse. There may be a need to introduce different objects/nodes and actions/ties to the structure that were not used for the creation of the original object, in this case, additional wood, different saws, extra material, etc. These are additional nodes implemented into the ties of the system.

SOCINT is a discipline that is used to identify a system and understand what makes the system into a complete element. Through understandings, means to influence or to persuade, and manipulation of the system can occur. The existing social and cultural structures in a designated area and the reformatting of such is a process little to no different from restructuring a chair into a rocking horse. However, it takes a highly skilled critical thinking team of disciplined individuals to achieve such success. Without non-intuitive and intuitive team members, the SOCINT discipline will inevitably fail.

Incorporation of critical thought in SOCINT

More often than one would like to admit, intelligence operatives fail in their mission. They fail because of dependence upon non-intuitive thought, which they were taught. The intelligence operatives specifically in SOCINT will depend equally if not more on intuitive thought. They will not be bogged down looking specifically for patterns (pattern analysis) like most other intelligence operatives. Although identifying patterns are important, Taleb identifies in his book, *Black Swan*, that patterns are not always the key in finding the highly improbable. "History is opaque. You see what comes out, not the script that produces events, the generator of history" (Taleb 2007, p. 8).

Unfortunately, some highly skilled individuals within Clandestine and Covert Operations may disagree with Taleb's statement when it comes to the programming of human nature. Although they would most likely agree that as a whole, human nature lacks appropriate programming to identify the highly improbable, social programming through training can occur. It is known that the most important tool in any fight is the human mind. Thus

SOCINT must specialize in the invariable focus of what every day persons see, smell, taste, feel and must be capable of observing and witnessing what most persons never understand exist in the present, past, and future.

Those operating in the SOCINT discipline must not be strictly capable of identifying past, present, and future observations, but must also be capable of mentally storing this information for later use. Such storage of information is necessary to fulfill the intuitive needs in understanding sociocultural dynamics no matter their geographic operational locations. At the same time, these operatives must be capable of storing such data in their minds in a manner that such experiences and information will not hinder their psychological mentality, which is needed for continued operational success.

Lastly, the mental capabilities of any SOCINT operative cannot be accessed through quantitative testing such as SAT or ASVAB testing used to assess those who wish to enter college or the military. Such testing is too often relied upon for educational measures and not used to identify true intelligence and probable capabilities of an individual's critical thought. Because of this, a multitude of assessments ranging from psychological, physical, practical, and social testings should be used to identify natural abilities and evaluate the critical thinking capabilities of individuals. In all, this will prevent the narrowly focused norms of current social standards to meet specific desires to promote the current caste system that exists in today's intelligence community.

By testing in such a unique means, SOCINT operatives will stand out and prove their abilities to operate anywhere and anytime throughout the world. It will also show their ability to think critically and form judgment based on practical reasoning for actions needed by decision makers to influence, persuade, and at times manipulate a system of concern. This in itself will shield SOCINT operatives from the focus of well-defined sources of uncertainty among the intelligence community, which will promote their thinking in means to emulate such a process where they operate later in time. This is another way to naturally enhance their intuitive thinking for future needs.

All critical thinking proponents are needed for successful SOCINT operations at all times. The critical thinking dimensions are crucial in the end when analyzed products are created and ready for dissemination throughout the Intelligence Community, which will be later used to introduce some form of action in an area of concern. The breadth of the scope behind these products lie in the critical thinking needed. However, with a more focused depth, analysis to make such sociocultural products must also be observed.

Notes

1. Malcolm Gladwell, Nassim Taleb, Theodore Dalrymple, and Charles Clayton are prominent authors who have written books such as *Blink, Black Swan, Not With a Bang But a Whimper, The Re-Discovery of Common Sense*, along with others. These books, while not necessarily considered books on critical thinking, truly expose the world around us in ways that lead the reader to think critically as well as analyze and comprehend that which at times seems to be incomprehensible.

2. To obtain a greater insight of Charles Sanders Peirce, read Nozawa, E.T. (2009) *A Short Synopsis of the Profound Knowledge of W. Edwards Deming and Charles Sanders Peirce's Scientific Semeiotic*. A great amount of insight related to this thought stemmed from conversations between "Achteck" and this author through e-mail threads. His insight and in-depth understanding of Critical Thinking through philosophers such as Peirce is impeccable and I cannot thank him enough for the education he provided me on the subject.

3. This definition was taken out of the http://www.criticalthinking.net/ web site. It should be also credited to The Critical Thinking Company as well.

4. In the case of the "5 W's", the questions of Who, What, Where, When, Why, are included, but also as important is the question of How. All six questions are construed as the 5W's needing answers for generalized understandings of a situation.

5. The listed questions have been conceptualized from FM 34–3 (1990). *Intelligence Analysis*. Selection from Chapter 1 "The Intelligence Mission" titled "The Intelligence Analysis System." Section 1–6. Although these questions are not directly taken from the publication, they have been developed through understanding the publication and combined within a sociocultural perspective.

Current Research in Critical Thinking and Analysis with Sociocultural Intelligence

8

Sociocultural intelligence signs

Sign, sign, everywhere a sign
Blockin' out the scenery, breakin' my mind
Do this, don't do that, can't you read the sign?
> *(The 5 Man Electrical Band,*
> *http://www.fivemanelectricalband.*
> *ca/signslyrics.html)*

The world around us is filled with signs. Every social, political, economic, cultural, military, and religious system is surrounded and filled with signs meant to offer clues to understand such systems. Those unknowing or unwilling to observe the multitude of signs in the world will never be capable of understanding and appreciating those among whom we live. Observing the world around us only promotes observation, but does not induce the critical logic needed for understanding what needs to be done in relation to the observations.

The Department of Justice, Office of Justice Programs released its *Highlights of the 2007 National Youth Gang Survey.*[1] Juvenile gang problems have increased to an all-time high since the year 2000. During the 1996–1998 period, major gang-related issues were identified in the United States. Gang activity then declined up until recently. The methodology identified in the report shows how the quantitative analysis was conducted, but the key missing piece throughout the report is the underlying principles as to why such an increase occurred.

The report lacks key elements of indicators that would promote critical thought and practical reasoning towards means and methods to reduce such criminal behavior among today's youth. Signs exist throughout any geographic area in the United States that would allow criminologists a greater understanding towards probable continued increased juvenile gang-related activities. Such signs could also demonstrate locations where one could observe possible decreases in such activities. This in itself could be considered an understanding of the "why" factor.

Some of the signs related to increased probabilities of gang activity include, for example, increased divorce rates that lead children living with single parents to search for fatherly figures or group acceptance. Other signs may be related to economic crisis in specific geographic locations, as was observed recently in the city of Detroit after the devastation of the American automobile industry, which forced young people to use extreme measures to find means of providing economically for themselves and their families, as they knew their parents may no longer be capable of doing so themselves.

Another sign may be the evaluation of a transnational crisis stemming from the country of Mexico. The growing Mexican drug war can also be construed as an internal revolution that could easily force young people from neighboring American towns, such as Nogales, Arizona, to be socially conditioned to increased numbness to violence, especially when so many of those youth have family members living across the border. The lists of signs are limitless and it becomes a matter of observing and seeking out which are the signs that can allude to such an increased activity.

Current intelligence activities rarely identify such signs through observation. Intelligence operatives have been socially conditioned to present only known facts related to current issues. They rarely think outside the box in an attempt to understand why specific incidents and activities occur. They track incident patterns, associations, and linkages towards matters of concern. They lack the time it takes to leave their offices to wander the streets where they live in an attempt to observe and understand signs, symbols, indicators, etc. that have meaning in unspoken languages.

The ability to observe and understand signs is part of the semiotic analytical process.[2] Today's threatening environments of political distraught, domestic and international terrorism, insurgencies, climate change, disease, etc. are filled with signs. Such signs of increasing threats range from the H1N1 Swine Flu epidemic, increased acts of piracy, domestic violence from "lone wolf" terrorists, greater snow melt on Mount Kilimanjaro, and more. Within the discipline of SOCINT, individuals must have the ability to not only observe, but also to understand the meanings of such signs and symbols.

Triadic Theory, a portion of Semiotics, exemplifies the means in which learning through symbols and signs is proven as a critical element of knowledge and understanding. Unfortunately, Charles Sanders Peirce did not gain credence in his philosophical concepts of learning until many years after his death. While cause and effect assists in our understandings of subjects, not all subjects of desire have an actual cause and effect relationship.[3] Because of such instances of missing cause and effect, Peirce identified the necessity to observe signs and symbols to understand meaning. Through the utilization of analytical software, an individual can observe nodes and ties that identify signs, symbols, and relationships. However the understanding of why these exist, and the ways in which they do, will continue to be missing as long as strict reliance on such analytical software remains a proponent of the Intelligence Community and National Security.

Until the incorporation of SOCINT arises, the United States and its Intelligence Community will continue to analyze the pre-existing "knowns" of threats and such known activities (the here and now), but will never be capable of understanding the future threats and capabilities stemming from them (the then and there). Hindrance in understanding why such subjects of concern operate in the ways they do will never be understood, rather simply assumed. More importantly, understanding viable means to mitigate their operations and induce permissive environments will never occur unless of course a new tool such as SOCINT is implemented to promote such logic and critical thought.

Signs are concepts and or clues that present understanding towards a greater image if they are observed accordingly. To obtain a visualization and understanding of the sign itself, indicators are present. These indicators are considered signifiers that could easily be construed as codes, objects, etc. These are the subcategories that allow an individual to infer the meaning behind the overall picture. The signified is the compilation of all signifiers combined. To gain a greater sense of understanding signifiers and the signified, let's look at the example of an individual's office.

This individual parks his car in what appears to be an industrial parking lot flanked with high-rise buildings. On the exterior wall of one of the buildings hangs a large construct with writing that states, "The Law Offices of X." After simply observing the construct of the words to confirm that he is at the proper location, he must then enter the building and go into an office to meet its occupant. It is easy to simply walk through a building, but how does this individual know he is at the center of gravity of where he must go? Continuing on, he walks into a room, filled with mops, brooms, a dirty old chair, and some cleaning products. Because the individual he seeks to meet is an attorney, such observations would lead him to conclude that the room he entered was not the appropriate location for the meeting. In fact, this is a janitorial room. The products that we observed are the signifiers and the full picture of all the materials within is the signified.

Walking on to find the proper location of the meeting, he sees an office with an open door. Through observation, he notices a beautiful wooden desk, a leather-cushioned rolling chair, a brass lamp, a computer, and so on. The objects identified acting as the signifiers allow him to assume that this is an appropriate room that matches his preconceived notions of an attorney's office. The total picture signified that the total objects identified one major sign, which allowed the brain to analyze what was observed to draw such a conclusion.

The systematic approach to understanding

Unfortunately, preconceived notions can hinder our ability to analyze appropriately, leading to poor judgment being made. In relations to National Security and Intelligence, our preconceived notions have allowed analysts to categorize inappropriately nodes, ties, networks, and systems. *The Miniature Guide to the Art of Asking Essential Questions* (Elder 2005) exemplifies the baseline for a means towards understanding topics of interest. The guide is based on "Critical Thinking Concepts and Socratic Principles."

Intelligence disciplines have template questions needing answering. Unfortunately, intelligence operatives become socially conditioned in asking only template questions, which conditions them to lack an "outside the box" thought and ask further detailed and necessary questions to individuals. Because of this, their intelligence analysis contains essential gaps of information. If such answers were obtained with adequate questioning, intelligence in understanding social systems and networks would improve and lead to better decision making.

> The quality of our lives is determined by the quality of our thinking. The quality of our thinking, in turn, is determined by the quality of our questions, for questions are the engine, the driving force behind thinking. Without questions, we have nothing to think about. Without essential questions, we often fail to focus our thinking on the significant and substantive. (Elder 2005)

The ability to observe signs and symbols and understand their meanings is crucial. When limited means of understanding such signs and symbols exists, essential questions must be asked and answers must be sought. Yet even when such answers are obtained, more often than not complete understandings towards the situation's future remains missing. Because of this, simulation must also occur. Simulation is an exercise that gives individuals an opportunity to experiment with mock scenarios that will enhance understandings related to cause and effect. Many social scientists may construe this process of observing signs and symbols, questioning, and then simulation as a breadth, depth, and application system of learning. This thought is relatively non-arguable because in a very practical means, it is. Through the incorporation of SOCINT, simulation would serve equally to all other aspects of the total SOCINT discipline. Simulation is rarely taught in large academic environments. However it is a proven methodology for learning success.[4] Because of its proven ability to promote greater understandings and enhance the learning process, simulation would be an incorporated methodology within the SOCINT discipline. It would be necessary in wargaming, in communication, and when among local indigenous persons to understand better their systems and networks.

While wargaming is mentioned, the concept of brainstorming must also be introduced into the critical thinking process. Brainstorming is also a systematic approach to critical thinking needs. It should never be conducted individually, but in a group that should be as diverse as possible. Brainstorming with individuals from different technical, cultural, and academic backgrounds fosters the introduction of new ideas and principles. This in itself is crucial as it will provide numerous members within the group an opportunity to understand ideas from those with loose affiliations to the problem.

> This technique can maximize creativity in the thinking process, force analysts to step outside their normal analytic mind-sets, and suspend their typical "good

judgment" about the practicality of ideas or approaches. More generally, brainstorming allows analysts to see a wider range of factors that might bear on the topic than they would otherwise consider. (Central Intelligence Agency 2009)

Brainstorming as a group is often overlooked, yet deemed critical. It is often unused in the professional workforce among those involved in Intelligence and National Security. Although recent implementations of "Fusion Cells" exist domestically and internationally for those working the intelligence spheres, they are often one-sided discussions because the supposed moderator (a crucial element in any brainstorming session) has his/her own prejudices related to the topic discussed or is in a position of superiority compared to the participants to the session.

To eliminate such negative issues and promote positive outcomes of the brainstorming session, rules must be laid out and agreed upon among the group. All comments and opinions, no matter how "outside the box" they may appear, should always be considered and looked into equally. Also, an appropriate amount of time should be designated for the session. Were reasonable conclusions to the situation not be reached within the allocated time, then a new time and date for continuation with all original participants along with possible additions to the group should be agreed upon. Brainstorming is an excellent tool to assist the critical thought process, but it is not the only one as there are many tools available—some of which being the technical means available through today's technology. To assist in greater stimulation of the human mind for critical thought, technical and or virtual necessities should be sought.

Current issues with critical thinking within the Intelligence Community

The Intelligence Community continuously relies on the virtual or technical world to assist in our analysis. More often than not, such tools are used as data management systems. The data stored in these systems are old, however, because they consist of already obtained or collected information. Although this is not always a bad thing, it may lead to grave dangers by promoting preconceived notions about entities in existence, unless proper management of such data exists along with the means to critically think about the situation of the known and unknown. Analysts continuously become reliant on past and present (here and now) data acquisition with little means for future prediction (then and there).[5] There is a continuous search for greater technological capabilities that involve little to none of the basic means of critical thinking and analysis needed for the observation of signs that would lead to adequate understandings of the situation. Still, technical means are needed to support the simulation process in understanding the social and cultural systems as well as networks of concern.

The Combating Terrorism Technical Support Office released a Broad Agency Announcement (BAA) 09-Q-4590 titled "Human, Social, Cultural, and Behavior Modeling (HSCB) Program." This announcement was issued under the provisions of paragraph 6.102(d)(2) of the Federal Acquisition Regulation (FAR). This is a solicitation announcement for work proposal via the Combating Terrorism Technical Support Office related to the HSCB. Although it notes in the synopsis that multiple entities have initiated the collection of Human, Social, and Cultural data, the missing piece of storing, analyzing, and wargaming such data is obsolete. There is a library of data that has already been procured for over three years in Afghanistan and Iraq via organizations similar to the Department of Defense's (DOD) Human Terrain System (HTS), yet such data is seldom used adequately to reach progress in the country due to an inability to understand and operate in non-conventional/irregular warfare contingencies.

Millions of dollars have been spent incorporating such organizations as the HTS, who have been constrained due to the mismanagement of information and the inability to think critically about such data. This in turn enhances the ignorance displayed among the international community and the communities in which such operations exist, such as Afghanistan and Iraq, due to mismanagement and inadequate decisions that leadership promotes for continuing operations. This could easily be mitigated if the right persons were operational who would maintain the proper situational understandings, critical thinking, and means to fulfill such tasking while collection and analysis processes simultaneously took place.

To better understand and appreciate the HSBC Program that released, under the Combating Terrorism Technical Support Office, a technical/virtual system work proposal, a journal was created within the organization. The Spring 2009 issue included an article titled, *Human Social Cultural Behavioral Modeling Program*.[6] The article demonstrates a simulation principle that does not yet officially exist. The intent is misleading in the fact that it portrays a sense of incorporation of a tool that will allow users a greater understanding of the "Human, Social, Cultural, and Behavioral" aspects. It has already been noted that in order to understand a system or network of individuals, physical interaction must take place. This physical interaction not only assists in the identification of language and communications, but also allows observations of signifiers throughout the geographic domains in which the systems exist. The HSCB program is meant to induce simulation engineered software that will ultimately produce timely analyzed products for consequent decision making. The United States has been socially conditioned to rely on technical and virtual means. We have lost complete understandings of the necessities to promote understanding, reasoning, and equality of others throughout the world in which we live.

The promotion of critical thought for enhanced analytical skills will be a socially changing challenge within the United States Intelligence Community. Most recently, it has been noted that the United States Army Intelligence School in Ft Huachuca, Arizona, has begun the process of educating students in the discipline of critical thinking.[7] While in Europe, specifically in France and Russia, critical thinking and semiotics have been taught for years, this has not been the case in the United States, which is just now starting to understand their importance. One of the most difficult aspects of instilling critical thinking in any US academic environment is finding proper educators. It is too often assumed that critical thinking must be taught via the expressions and findings of famous philosophers, such as Peirce and or Saussure. This in itself is not accurate. Critical thinking is a skill, which is obtained not through traditional learning alone, but also through stimulating mental exercises that include scenario development. Although it is wonderful to know each and every famous philosopher who sought critical thinking, it is not necessary. Wide arrays of tools are readily available to persons seeking to hone their skills in critical thinking.

Additional tools for critical thinking and Sociocultural Intelligence

CriticalThinking.org is an organization that has already established a strong foothold in the critical thinking spheres. It offers a wide array of seminars and publications, one of which is titled, 'Analytic Thinking: How to take thinking apart and what to look for when you do the elements of thinking and the standards they must meet' (Elder 2007) and can be found in "The Thinkers

Guide to Analytic Thinking." This guide uses systematic diagrams to illustrate the critical thinking process, which consists of eight steps that should be overly familiar to those working within the spheres of National Security, and even more so to those working in the profession of intelligence. The critical thinking process is similar to that which is known as the Intelligence Cycle, but there are major differences, as follows:

Intelligence Cycle	*Critical Thinking Process*
Planning and direction	Purpose
Collection	Question at issue
Processing	Information
Analysis and production	Interpretation and inference
Dissemination	Concepts
	Assumptions
	Implications and consequences
	Point of view

As one can observe through compare and contrast, the current intelligence cycle is missing crucial steps in formulating an in-depth end product for sound decision making. It would be easy for a professional intelligence operative to argue that the steps found in the critical thinking process are hidden elements found throughout the intelligence cycle. This argument, however, is very weak considering that those involved in the intelligence process would be required, as individuals, to subjugate themselves to go a few steps further to get the details required by the critical thinking process. With such an argument, so long as nothing is set in stone in some form of mandated National Security Publication requiring such steps for all to understand and implement within the intelligence cycle, times will prevail when such data and thought is missing.

> AS A SPECIES, we possess remarkably little genetic variation, yet we tend to overlook this homogeneity and focus instead on differences between groups and individuals. At its darkest, this tendency generates xenophobia and racism, but it also has a more benign manifestation—a fascination with the exotic. (Yong 2009)

Individuals from different parts of the world think differently. In the East, people could be construed as more analytical while in the West they might be more holistic in thought.[8] This does not mean that one is right or wrong in their logic, rather just different. To be capable of combining the two cognitive means would bring total completeness in critical thinking. Such differences do not occur only among Eastern and Western cultures as they can be observed in the United States, between the different professions for example.

The joint environment and its hindrance on critical thought

The Defense Department shows internal differences when it comes to the means in which observations for critical thought are meant. The Army, Navy, Air Force, and Marines all conduct their business very differently. In order to operate differently, they must think differently, too. In today's Joint environment, they must be capable of meeting the necessities of one another for unification and for the creation of a professional operational environment. Even today, mutters can be heard related to the prejudices between the Armed Force's different services. These prejudices not only hinder relationships, but also cause turmoil in credibility of informational sources within intelligence products, which in turn causes major concerns in decision-making processes. It can easily be deduced that such differences within the numerous branch services have created an atmosphere of xenophobia that blocks the much-needed critical thought from the intelligence system.

Prejudices continuously exist among the numerous branches of service. Now, in an attempt to mitigate and eliminate such prejudices, a Joint Doctrine is being written. This Joint Doctrine should not be deemed a tool identifying who does what and when among the numerous branches of the armed forces, but should delve deeper. A quarterly publication known as the *Joint Force Quarterly*, although not to be considered doctrine, but rather guidance for professional enhancement, is also available as open source for anyone to read. An article, *Effects Based Thinking in Joint Doctrine*[9] it outlines the necessities for those working in a joint environment to initiate a systematic approach in its critical thinking and practical reasoning. This approach, as written out, is meant to allow the reader an opportunity to understand that every problem needing resolution cannot be answered strictly through observing the problem as a whole.

Problem solving, especially when related to National Security and Intelligence, almost always concerns many more issues than the original concern/problem. Because this is known, the problem must be broken down and categorized as well as prioritized. If a village becomes a focal point of concern, one must ask why it is so. This in itself is the supposed problem. Systematically, observation must be made to solve the problem. Questions must be answered to identify which systems within the village induce such concerns. At times the system thought to be of concern may not exist in the actual geographic domain. This means that an outside approach in observation must first occur, and then observations must push internally until the center of gravity is reached.

Although it may appear that the answer to the question of why was reached, that does not mean the problem has been solved. It only means that an understanding has been reached. Next, moving through the systematic approach, answers to more questions must also be found to rectify the problem. Such questions include, for example:

- What assets are readily available to resolve the problem?
- How feasible is it to use those assets in the current situation?
- What are the initial supposed outcomes along with secondary outcomes?
- How long can outcomes reasonably be reached?
- What can be done during the phase of time that the outcomes are not reached (short-term resolutions)?

This in itself is considered "effects based thinking." It is a systematic approach at

1. understanding and accepting the fact that a problem exists;
2. observing the surrounding areas all the way to the core of the geographic location of concern;
3. identifying numerous means to solve the problem;
4. timing the resolution reasonably;
5. continuously observing the situation after the resolution has been implemented.

Current joint doctrine promotes a "Systems Perspective of the Operational Environment" (see JP 3–0, chapters II and IV). This perspective—or better understanding—"supports operational design by enhancing elements such as centers of gravity, lines of operations, and decisive points." This allows commanders and their staffs to consider a broader set of options to focus limited resources, create desired effects, avoid undesired effects, and achieve objectives. (Joint Staff J7 Joint Doctrine and Education Division Staff 2009)

Although it is nice to see an effort of Joint Doctrine and siding elements such as open source publications supporting it, it would be foolish to believe that such doctrine will promote harmony among the numerous branches of service. The armed forces as a whole are a major system made of multiple players. If each node was identified within the system along with understanding their relationships through their ties, it would be observed that the system—while not needing total restructuring—does need another tie to induce the harmony needed for continued joint operations. The tie that needs to be inserted in the armed forces system is SOCINT.

Prejudices are found in all elements of society. As previously mentioned, numerous branches of Armed Forces, too, have their rivalries that also induce prejudice thoughts. The conventional Army has its prejudices among its Special Forces. Special Operatives as a whole face continued ridicule based on their operational spheres. The Joint Special Operations University (JSOU), which is open to all elements within the Defense Department and not just meant as an educational system for Special Operatives, continuously exemplifies the professional atmosphere for continued, up to date educational courses and forums. It has a publication department that releases open source data for anyone to read for self-educating opportunities meant to promote "outside the box thinking."

The JSOU released a publication titled, *Educating for Strategic Thinking in the SOF Community* (JSOU Report 07–2).[10] The report identified the probable dilemmas the Special Operations Forces (SOF) Community will face in its future. Former Secretary of Defense (SECDEF) Donald Rumsfeld believed the Special Operations community would take the lead in defeating insurgencies and terrorism as a whole. Because of his confidence, he delegated the SOF community to take the lead in planning and instituting such plans in the War on Terror immediately following the September 11, 2001 attacks.

Special Operatives have been used in operations that were not originally intended as priority within their community. Most notable was their extensive utilization in Direct Action (DA) operations. Special Operatives were originally meant to serve as advisors, trainers, and mentors for indigenous forces abroad. Although they are still training elements, such as the Afghan Commando Forces, they are more often observed as performing the tasking of DA. Thus, people, such as former SECDEF Rumsfeld, have virtually caused the SOF community to wear multiple hats, which they are not used to wearing. One such service they now are required to provide is taking the lead in critical thinking for the War on Terror.

Knowing that today's War on Terror is being planned by the Special Operator community, one must understand that this principle should be considered commendable as Special Operatives as a whole are trained in working closely with indigenous persons. They are socially conditioned to empathize and go out of their way to truly understand the local populace in which they operate. Unfortunately, the SOF Community is now stretched very thin. Many SOF operatives serve only a few years in their official capacity, then leave the Armed Forces to seek employment as Defense Contractors mostly due to the large sums of money they can obtain in that capacity. The SOF community has very few Officers with deep academia, again, mostly because to the difficulties in continuing education due to deployments. Although schooling is readily available for such operatives in Critical Thinking and Strategic Planning, more often than not numerous open seats remain in such academic environments. Even when such persons exist within the SOF Community, they are rarely listened to today among their conventional armed forces counterparts due to the prejudices previously mentioned.

It is noted that because of the prejudices and xenophobic mentalities throughout the Intelligence Community, a vast array of social and professional barriers have been raised. This is nothing new within the IC. So long as these barriers are understood formally or informally, the means to conduct abduction and deduction reasoning to limit the negative impacts on the barriers becomes increasingly promoted. Abduction is the process of deriving consequence by what is inferred, speculated, or implied based on reasoning. Such reasoning is driven through the signs and symbols observed. Deduction means the process of deriving consequence by what is assumed based on pre-existing facts. Through abduction and deduction reasoning, complete change within a system may not be needed, but the introduction of a tie into the system might be.

> The human mind has no natural guide to the truth, nor does it naturally love the truth. What the human mind loves is itself, what serves it, what flatters it, what gives it what it wants, and what strikes down and destroys whatever "threatens" it. (Paul 2004)

Within the Intelligence Community, through understanding the existing barriers, the needed tie into the system is a social element that conducts observations seeking signs and symbols, evaluates such observations, fulfills practical reasoning to identify viable means to solve the problem, and implements such actions as persuasion, influence, or even at times total manipulation techniques to resolve matters.[11] This is one of the most viable and cost-effective measures in understanding ourselves that is needed prior to understanding others. This concept may seem threatening to many professionals working within the Intelligence Community, however the overarching principle is a much-needed entity to resolve the unknown sociocultural matters that exist within the Intelligence Community. Because of this, it is evident that SOCINT will fulfill multiple roles, all of which will need operatives with exemplified means to conduct and promote critical thought for social change internally and externally among today's Intelligence Community.

> A standard recommendation for reform—one made regularly by people discovering these problems for the first time—is to encourage "outside the box" analyses that challenge conventional wisdom and consider scenarios that appear low in probability but high in consequence. To some, this sort of intellectual shake-up might well have led the intelligence system, rather than Tom Clancy, to anticipate the kamikaze hijacking tactic of September 11. (Betts 2002)

Richard Betts may very well be correct in his assessment concerning intelligence reform. A complete overhaul is not necessary within the Intelligence Community. What is needed are individuals with the ability to think outside the box "challenging conventional wisdom."[12] A group of individuals within their own system who would understand the sociocultural dynamics of any system in which they are introduced could be deemed the necessary ingredient. They may appear to be somewhat rough around the edges because of their continued abilities to question the world around them, but they would serve as the epitome of professional unconventional intelligence. SOCINT has the ability to fulfill such necessities to increase the capabilities and successes within the Intelligence Community and assist in thwarting threats domestically and internationally. Such persons should have extraordinary diverse backgrounds within Academia, Military, and the Social Science spheres. Too many "Think Tanks" currently exist within the United States. They lack a means to promote action into the world in which we live. Because it would be considered an intelligence discipline, SOCINT would not only serve as a think tank, but would also have the ears of those in authority to act reasonably based on the cognitive analysis presented among the SOCINT elements.

Notes

1. It is evident that a social problem exists within the United States related to juvenile gangs. An increase of juvenile gang activity appeared in the 2007 records. Although analysis of this data exists and a systematic approach to obtaining a sound methodology was initiated, failure to understand the "Why" factor remains. Without understanding the why factor, some criminologists may conclude that an

increased police force is needed throughout the United States to mitigate the threat of juvenile gang activity. This may appear to be the logical approach, but in fact it is not. If a greater understanding of the social spheres of influence promoting such gang increase were presented, a vast array of multiple solutions to the problem would exist. While SOCINT has been focused predominantly on international conflict, this example exemplifies the needs for SOCINT domestically as well.

2. Sociocultural Intelligence is a discipline built in understanding people who make up a network that often influences a larger system in one way or another. Semiotic analysis becomes crucial to understand the sociocultural dynamics. To identify individuals is easy, but to understand them is much more complex. One means to do so is through the understanding and incorporation of semiotic analysis. This in itself refers to identifying signifiers and the signified that make up the signs. Once signs are observed, an ability to identify relationships becomes more evident. In dealing with language, it is codes and conventions that make the signs in the total narrative of the communication being transferred between the communicator and the receiver.

3. Breadth and depth of logic has been and continues to be an extremely overlooked principle in critical thought. Peirce was meticulous in his research and understandings. As society stands within Western thought, individuals such as Peirce lacked credence until after his death. Peirce was astute in understanding that many elements of knowledge cannot be learned from cause and effect, but rather through symbols (triadic theory). Such knowledge can be learned from symbols and understandings/meanings of such better known as semiotics. With the amount of technological advancement, semiotics and triadic theory can easily be found in analytical software that assists in programs such as link diagrams.

4. Simulation is a known element of learning where students have opportunities to apply their knowledge and skills. Traditional means of education lack extensive simulation exercises. Simulation can be construed as the third most important means of cognition if the breadth and depth constituted the first two necessities for understanding. Because human nature continuously dominates in learning, the social sciences must also promote simulation experiences in the field. With the incorporation of SOCINT, simulation serves as a necessity in wargaming and also as a needed entity in communication and understandings among local indigenous persons for better understandings of their systems and networks.

5. The continued inability for intelligence officers to formulate conclusions based on data collection inhibits decision maker's abilities to act appropriately and in a timely fashion. This document is meant to assist those working within the intelligence spheres in formulating systematic approaches of intelligence analysis through proven structured techniques.

6. HSCB has been introduced as a simulation process to assist users within the DOD in understanding the Human Social Cultural Behaviors in operational environments deemed crucial for purposes of National Security. It is a program that is meant to induce simulation engineered software which will ultimately produce timely analyzed products for consequent decision making.

7. This statement is based on information obtained from multiple discussions among intelligence representatives that took place on May 07, 2009 between the author and individuals working within the US Department of the Army's Training and Doctrine Command (TRADOC) and the Intelligence School House in Ft. Huachuca.

8. Psychologists and many other social scientists have continuously researched how and if cognitive thought differs in the west and east. Knowing the analytical methods of cognition used in the west and the domination of technological advancements, probable grave disaster that precludes understanding societal evolution will result in the future.

9. "Current joint doctrine promotes a 'Systems Perspective of the Operational Environment' (see JP 3–0, chapters II and IV). This perspective—or better understanding—'supports operational design by enhancing elements such as centers of gravity, lines of operations, and decisive points'. This allows commanders and their staffs to consider a broader set of options to focus limited *resources, create desired effects, avoid undesired effects, and achieve objectives*." Although Joint Doctrine may be perceived as the over arching principle of written guidance within the DOD, one can assume that in all practical purposes, it is not even in today's day and age of Joint or Inter-agency operations. Without a Joint Doctrine identifying and stressing an importance of effects based operations, those working in such environments will continue to be on different pages of understanding their environment. While a systems approach is identified, the dichotomy of understanding the multiple dimensions of known or unknown systems is lacking. Systems design and structure cannot be understood within only one or two chapters of any DOD publication considering engineers take years to understand networks and systems. Lacking current doctrine depletes the abilities of those serving positions of understanding areas of concern.

10. It has been noted that the term manipulation is a concept that many steer far away from. Unfortunately, our minds are the greatest of manipulators within ourselves as individuals. We must learn to understand all aspects of human society to block certain preconceived notions or fallacies which manipulate our own critical thought.

11. The Intelligence Community continuously faces severe scrutiny although it has been a successful system thwarting terrorist attacks within the United States and against interest deemed critical towards National Security. However, the Intelligence Community still faces dilemmas concerning its truest of strengths and weaknesses. Many recommendations exist and none comes remotely close to what was recommended by the National Commission on Terrorism: "roll back the additional layer of cumbersome procedures instituted in 1995 for gaining approval to employ agents with 'unsavory' records—procedures that have had a chilling effect on recruitment of the thugs appropriate for penetrating terrorist units." SOCINT does not need "thugs" so to speak, but needs individuals who are street savvy, maintain a sixth sense, and those with an ability to critically think on ethical base lines to better understand the situation for informed consensus needed among decision makers.

MIND, BRAINS, AND ANALYSIS IV

Intelligence Analysis for Sociocultural Intelligence

9

Chapter Outline

When spider webs unite, they can halt even a lion.

(African Proverb)

Linking everything to something

The world in which we live is like a giant spider web. The larger the web, the stronger it is. However, the smaller the web, the less likely it will survive its purpose. The strongest societies have great linkage within them and some are global, like that which exists inside the United States. The American society has links and ties to numerous internal factors along with external factors. The ability to visualize and understand these associations improves situational awareness in regard to social and cultural matters related to sociocultural intelligence (SOCINT).

The American society can be observed as the largest of spider webs. The difficulty in understanding our society stems in visualizing our truest global impact, that which makes us strong. Imagine looking at a map of every country in the world. Now, draw a line starting inside the United States and continue that line until you reach the center of another country. Repeat the process until every country is connected to the United States. What you have just done is provided yourself with a visual analysis of the external network within the United States. Why would one do such an exercise? Because it proves that the United States is linked somehow, in some way, and for some reason to another part of the world no matter the circumstance.

The linkage may be known or, many times, may be assumed. Hence at times, the analyzed visualization line may be fully filled (for those known associations) while at other times the line may be dashed (for those assumed associations). If associations are strong, the line could be thicker than the one representing a weak association. The point is that a line links two entities. The diagrams below depict two nodes and one tie. The nodes are the rectangles and the tie is the line. The two nodes in the first case are directly linked because the tie is a solid line (Figure 9.1). If the line is dashed, then the relation is an indirect or suspected link between the nodes (Figure 9.2).

Claims are made every day about products rumored to be "American Made." While it sounds nice, not all of them are. Wark, in his book, *Gamer Theory*, explains that even American-made computers often utilize columbite-tantalite, which serves as an excellent electric conductor dug out of places afar such as the Democratic Republic of Congo. Whether we know it or not, we are all linked globally. This should matter to anyone involved with International Affairs or Public Policy, and even more so with Intelligence or National Security.

The Democratic Republic of Congo (DROC) has been a country faced with extreme internal violence. Is it truly to be blamed on internal struggles that result in violence? Maybe, but then again, maybe not. Wars have been fought over the substance columbite-tantalite.[1] Similar wars have been fought over diamonds in places such as Sierra Leone. Today in Afghanistan, we observe a crisis among villagers and farmers due to opium eradication efforts within. It is evident that the place with the resource may face austere conditions, but is it because of this resource or is the problem larger than that? Without a doubt, an individual can conclude that world demand has played the greatest vital role in the atrocities that occur in the places mentioned.

Figure 9.1 Two nodes with direct linkages

Figure 9.2 Two nodes with indirect linkages

Picturing the link

Understanding such atrocities and the underlying issues related to them are often overlooked among analysts because they don't see nor visualize the bigger picture. They lack visualization externally and, more often than not, they visualize on the internal strife. This is a very easy mistake to make. It's even easier in attempting to manage a smaller problem than a larger one such as the global demand that causes such issues.

The greatest unfortunate element today with analysts is that more often than not, they analyze very little, if they actually analyze anything at all. The majority of analysts today are simply serving as data entry personnel. They obtain data from sources, then simply input that data into a software data bank system. What they actually do, related to true analysis, is very little.

Today's intelligence analysts rely on software programs used as a false perception for the discipline of analysis. They rely so heavily on these programs that they often allow the latter to provide a false sense of understanding towards the situation for analysis. The individual often fails to input crucial data needed to complete the visualization process within the analysis process. Through reliance on the tool itself and dependency of the collected source data, they marginalize their own self-initiated analysis of the situation.

The greatest of navigators first understand the sun, stars, and terrain, which allow them to move in the right direction on their journey. They then learn the utilization of a lensatic compass and map. When they become proficient enough, they learn how to utilize a Global Positioning System (GPS). In a nutshell, they learn to crawl before they learn to walk and then to run. Unfortunately, and indeed arguably, intelligence representatives today within National Security elements learn a very opposite methodology in their analytical skills.

While navigating in any environment, it is crucial to know where you are located at all times. More often than not, individuals only concern themselves with navigation needs after they are already lost. Today, in Afghanistan, it appears as though the United States and its coalition are lost. They must find themselves politically, militarily, economically, socially, religiously, etc. One methodology in finding oneself or coming to conclusion about a situation among social scientist is through triangulation. Triangulation, through a land navigation principle, is the concept of finding three different compass bearings then referencing them to one's map to identify their exact location. It is often used in conjunction with the terms resection (referencing two known points that an individual can physically observe, then finding them on a map without the assistance of a compass) and intersection (the means in utilizing two known compass bearings then referencing those bearings to the map).

Triangulation among social scientist is not about simply utilizing three known points or pieces of data to conclude a determination of the situation. It is a concept/methodology that is limitless when utilizing referenced materials. Validity in understanding their research is the key and triangulation is their key methodology.

> Triangulation has been used as a metaphor by social scientists for the use of data from different sources, the use of several different researchers, the use of different perspectives to interpret a single set of data, and the use of multiple methods to study a single problem. (Beebe 2001, p. 19)

With over eight years into the war in Afghanistan, it is somewhat evident that the United States is lost. We lack a means of honing in on our desired path (our navigation) to meet our truest objectives to achieve victory. A strategic SOCINT initiative is more important than ever before. If for any other reason of its importance, it is the means in identifying where we are as a coalition and identifying the proper path to move forward. Normally, this task would be accomplished by strategic operational planners along with their strategic intelligence sidekicks.[2] Such obligations and necessaries by such parties have lacked understanding and objectives, which continuously risks the lives of soldiers, sailors, airmen, and marines along with their civilian counterparts.

Today's intelligence analysts are taught to identify individual targets of interest. They then learn how to input those targets into a software program that will link them to other targets, thus creating a network of targets. In the end, they compute the inputted data to formulize a picture of understanding and refer to this picture as their analyzed product. This process is software/information technology (IT) dependency and should not be construed as true human analysis. The truest of human analysis means that not only can a person visualize the situation, but more importantly can understand the situation.

Gladwell discusses the importance of understanding "Mavens, Connectors, and Salesmen" in his book, *The Tipping Point: How Little Things Can Make Big Difference*. This typology will be discussed later in the chapter. What is important to understand for now is that such types and characteristics are rarely understood in the world of analysts. More often than not, an analyst will identify an individual who is linked with many persons and hone in on that one individual as a key principle of concern. With SOCINT, that one individual may be identified as a key principle, however a greater unknown underlying principle about the situation may be discovered and identified as the truest of concern. This identification may be deemed necessary for operations to exist affecting the identified sociocultural main principle through measures taken using an unorthodox approach in a non-lethal effects based operation.

Open an employment search on the Internet for any government intelligence vacancy, and the odds are an individual will find that IT has taken over such professional industries immediately upon reviewing the job qualification requirements. Today, intelligence representatives are required to utilize such technology. It serves as a false sense in understanding situations around us. Such technology only serves as a tool to support a picture of the situation, but it does not fulfill the analytical needs in understanding to better provide accuracies for decision makers that will allow them the best possible solutions towards their problems.

There are many theories concerning what analysis is and is not. One such theory in identifying what analysis "is not" would be that analysis is not the technical dependency in utilization of software programs that provide a visualization of inputted data. Such programs should be strictly construed as tools for visualization. In the most simplistic of means, analysis "is" the process that allows pieces of information to come together to obtain a total picture of the situation and a means in fully understanding that picture. Not only will the picture be observable, but, more importantly, it will be understood as to why the picture exists the way in which it does.

> There are many different ways to win and many different styles of play. But regardless of the path you take, there are very few universally accepted axioms that apply to the game no matter how it is played. (Gordon 2005, p. 5)

Netting the sociocultural elements

Phil Gordon is, arguably, one of the world's greatest Texas Hold'em Poker players. He has theorized and studied the game with great passion and stands as one of the world's most renowned players in the game. His principles are very unique in that they can be translated into any "game" decided to be played, to include that of intelligence analysis—in this case SOCINT analysis.

When fulfilling analytical needs within SOCINT, everything lays on the geographical space. Every matter in dealing with any social and or cultural domain falls on some form of topography. Unless we live in space, all humans live on some form of topological domain. Because of this, initiating sociocultural analysis must begin with our immediate surroundings. Gordon has a very simplistic means in his poker analysis.[3] First, he assesses himself. Second, he assesses the individuals against whom he is playing. Third, he assesses the cards the dealer has dealt him. Based on all three factors leading to his play, he will make a decision to act. What Gordon is truly doing is a mental ontology analysis by visualizing his social network "net." His methodology is through a concentric ring approach that is crucial in understanding any social network. This is construed as capturing the "Social Net."

The Israeli armed forces utilize a concept of defense for their facilities known as rings of defense. The United States utilizes an identical concept, known as defense in depth. Both concepts of defense for assets utilize a three-ring approach. The first ring is the closest ring to the asset. This ring uses not only physical armed guards to protect the asset, but also Access Control measures, Close Circuit Television (CCTV) monitors, alarm devices, etc. The Second ring is often times a perimeter fence line that also utilizes a similar approach to protect the asset at hand with tools such as armed security patrols, CCTV, alarm devices, gate entry systems, etc. Lastly, the furthest ring is not a physical ring at all, rather an imaginary perimeter based on infrastructure, social and political assets, and terrain. This third ring uses some armed patrols, such as local law enforcement for deterrence operations, intelligence operatives, and local town watch systems. Utilizing such rings of defense makes penetrating the asset protected much more difficult considering the opposition force must penetrate through two of the three rings of defense before it actually reaches the asset itself.

The Rings of Defense or Defense in Depth concept is a proven approach to make penetration of an asset much more difficult than without the rings. Now, imagine the utilization of SOCINT operatives in a similar approach to the defense in-depth concept. It is clear that the conflict in Afghanistan is heavily influenced by activities that occur in geographic locations surrounding the actual area of operation, such as Pakistan. Iraq also has serious players that affect the operations, such as Iran. If the War on Terror moved conventionally into the Horn of Africa, one would notice that issues in Kenya are influenced by Somalia. All of these influential countries have their own terrorist issues, whether it is as support bases for terrorist activity through financing, intelligence, weapons procurement, etc. such as Iran, while others simply face their own terrorist activities with bombings, assassinations, intimidation, etc., such as Somalia and Pakistan.

If the utilization of the Rings of Defense approach were implemented for Human Terrain in such geographic locations as Pakistan, Somalia, Iran, etc., the third and most outer ring, which in a defensive approach would be the first ring to deter, detect, and neutralize (through either kinetic or non-kinetic maneuvers), would succeed in defeating the opposition. It is obvious that today's Department of the Army's Human Terrain System (HTS) concept has serious possibilities as a tool to assist in winning the War on Terror. One must ask, however, "Is the HTS concept being used to its fullest abilities to gain the greatest results if they are only operating inside the immediate area of concern?" By simply using the defense in-depth concept of operation and observing a quick compare and contrast analogy, one could only conclude the answer as no.

If the War on Terror is intended to come to an end one day, we must first understand the actors of influence for the opposition. Once we understand them, we must find a way to penetrate them. If this can be done in a non-kinetic approach, then we must come forward and meet their needs to neutralize them. If we cannot succeed in this approach, a kinetic avenue must be accomplished through all out war. This is something none of us would like to witness. There is a reason why the Department of the Army's HTS

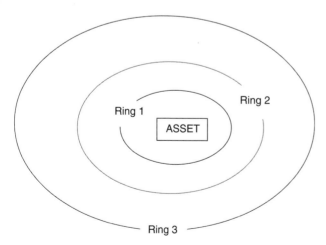

Figure 9.3. An example of an ontology in visualizing a Social Net or Rings of Defense/Defense in Depth

was implemented recently in the War on Terror; the world cannot afford to see another world war. Unfortunately, the HTS is an ad-hoc band aid with numerous limitations that hinder success. We must understand the people's needs. This must be accomplished successfully through inserting a professionally trained SOCINT discipline within the intelligence community in the areas that pose the most influence of the opposition not in just the areas of US military operations.

While conducting analysis for SOCINT, the systematic approach that Gordon describes should be no different. The analysis must understand themselves first (in the example shown in Figure 9.3 it would be the asset) and all associated factors in which they are allied (ring 1), plus all the exterior factors outside the immediate concerns (ring 2) to fulfill their analysis. They then must be capable of identifying the surrounding areas representing their geographical areas of concern (ring 3). Once they complete this tasking, which could arguably be construed as the most challenging, if done through eliminating all biases, they then must determine with the tools available the best means in continued source collection methodologies to hone their analysis by linking all elements within the Social Net.[4]

Identifying the social net is conducted to fulfill a portion of the SOCINT analysis. It should be construed as one of the first steps in the sociocultural analysis. This is done so that some form of geographic location is identified for a suitable action that can be determined upon the needs of superiors and decision makers. That said, one must not forget the link diagram needed to assist not only a picture of the social networks in existence, but the understanding the social network itself.

We must understand that the world we live in is not a utopia rather it is an "atopia." The difference between the two is tremendous. The term "Utopia" is based on a fictional geographic space of perfection. Some could argue, depending on their religious beliefs, that God has created the Earth and because it was created by God, the earth is perfect and hence it is an "Utopia" itself. While this belief can be construed as argumentative and debatable, the intent of even mentioning "Utopia" here is to understand the difference from "Atopia."

In today's technologically driven world, it is evident that we live in a world without borders. It is a known fact that because of man, borders have been established between states. These borders are rudimentary in nature. They are primitive. With technology, any person can go into a foreign land through the utilization of a computer (in the virtual world), aircraft, boat, etc. Wars are still fought with borders though. This is a mistake. Revolutionists see no borders, nor do terrorists. They utilize all available assets whether they are internal or external in nature. The Irish Republican Army depended on its United States supporters to provide funds and weapon systems. They were capable of targeting outside influencers to assist in their cause. South American revolutionists relied on Cuba and the old USSR for active and passive support. Today, the Taliban and other opposition groups fighting in Afghanistan rely on Pakistan along with other outside influencers/elements for their support. Such groups understand the atopia in which they live to achieve their objectives.

Fighting the Taliban, Al Qaeda, Hezb Islami Gullbidine, and other opposition groups in Afghanistan has caused major issues among the United States and its coalition partners. The greatest issue is caused because of our means in which we fight warfare today and the failure to change our outlook on how we need to fight such wars. We must first understand that borders created by man are a false sense of an utopia that our enemy does not observe. By understanding this, we must now operate in a manner that demonstrates our willingness to accept that we live in an atopia world, that is, a world without boundaries.

While fulfilling such analytical needs, the SOCINT analyst must be capable of properly mapping their analyzed works. Each step taken in their analyzed process, be it "Social Netting," "Link Diagrams," etc. must be layered with topographical maps. These maps should contain contour lines that demonstrate elevation. Lakes, streams, and rivers should be understood in the area of concern. High vegetated areas, roadways, etc., all need identification and understanding. Such topographical identification allows a greater means in understanding the community and economics towards the area of concern. Maps have borders; however, the world we live in today is relatively borderless.

To be successful in analyzing the SOCINT data, and understanding that the world is mapped today with borders (a utopian map), the SOCINT team must look at the world from above. To do this, they must obtain a map of the world that they will serve. It could be a map of a city, state, country, or the entire world if needed. They must then not observe the borders that are predesignated by the map's creator, but rather begin to observe the map through an understanding that it is an atopia.

Hypothetically, if a situation or concern about the area of Trenton, New Jersey were to be discovered and the request to implement a SOCINT team were to be utilized, the first task conducted would be to identify the area of

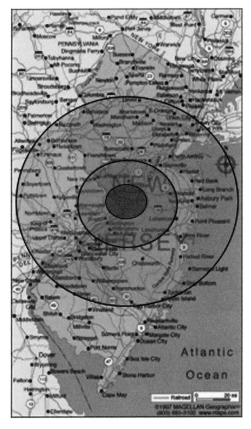

Map 9.1 Map of New Jersey representing a systematic area ring analysis

concern and all surrounding areas. They would then prioritize all three areas of concern based on the collected data they obtained. Next, they would begin to dig deeper into the situation in an attempt to identify networks causing such issues.

Understanding that several networks exist within systems, researchers must conduct the most time-consuming aspects of understanding such networks and systems. This time-consuming process is the actual research needed to fulfill essential elements of information requirements that are necessary in order to identify, assess, analyze, and determine the level of value within the network and its influence on other components and networks. Figure 9.4 below represents a system that has multiple networks tied together. Each network is deemed critical for the systems survivability. In this example, each node in the specified system is boxed and colored in shades of gray. The circles represent the sub systems/networks which directly links all four into one large system.

Through observation of the above system, an individual can depict the center of gravity which links all networks together through the nodes and ties. The darkest areas due to the blending of shading are the center of gravity which all elements would be linked to directly or indirectly and have a cause–effect relationship with. When attempting to analyze any systems' center of gravity, the researchers and analysts will find it most difficult to gain knowledge of the system itself without initiating their research on the outer rings of the system (the system example identified below depicts the outer layer). As time continues, the researchers and analysts should attempt to gain enough confidence of the portion of the system already researched to move into the next layer.

In the case of Figure 9.5, the next layer is the middle layer. Research and study should be ongoing until an understanding of the center of gravity exists and coincides with the fulfillments of the essential elements of information

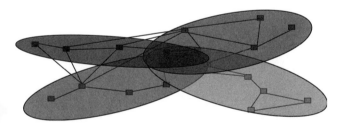

Figure 9.4 Multiple networks within a system

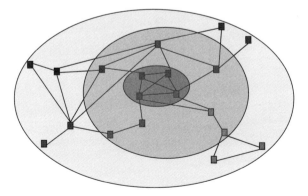

Figure 9.5 Concentric rings of multiple networks found within large systems

found in the original collection plan.[5] The center of gravity in the below example is the darkest color.

Putting all of the analysis together is a process. First, the topographical map must be presented. Then, the spheres of influence must be added on top of the map based on the known concerned areas. Once this is accomplished, link analysis must be completed starting with the greatest area of concern and working outward. After the link analysis is accomplished, a prioritization through understanding the entire network and or systems should occur. This prioritization will allow decision makers an opportunity to determine the best means in enacting some form of task to fulfill their desired goals. In the end, the total visualization piece may appear somewhat disorganized and sloppy but with a trained analyst, they will be capable of understanding their visualized tool and be capable of briefing such to their superiors.

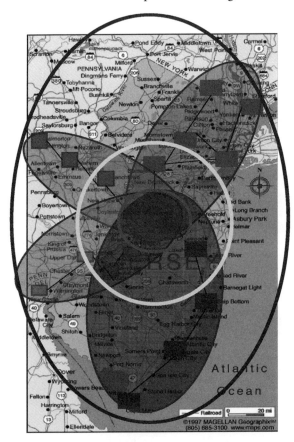

Map 9.2 Completed area analysis with prioritization of a Social Network

The big three

As previously mentioned, there are three main elements of concern which will be identified as "Mavens, Connectors, and Salesmen." Understanding these three entities is crucial especially when attempting to analyze collected sociocultural data and identifying what many refer to as the spheres of influence or social circles. It is important to note that these three entities are not always going to be individuals. They can be persons, places, or things. As Gladwell notes, "My social circle is, in reality, not a circle. It is a pyramid" (Gladwell 2005, p. 38).

The "Maven" serves as the "brains" behind the situation. In a social or cultural setting, the "Maven" will virtually always be a person dead or alive. The Maven may have great historical roots especially when dealing with Political, Military, Economic, Social, Infrastructure, and/or Religious elements.

"Connectors" may appear as "Mavens" at first, but they often are not true "Mavens." The "Connectors" obtain the information presented by the "Maven." Once they obtain the collected information, they pass it on to others. Often times, the "Connectors" have a strong social or professional network of individuals that will be utilized to spread the "Maven's" information to a larger system. Not all connectors are persons. This book or the publishing company of this book, for example, could/would serve as a "Connector" while the author would serve as the "Maven."

Lastly, to fully understand the importance of the three entities needed in understanding SOCINT analysis, an individual must understand the so-called "Salesmen." The "Salesmen" are those who can easily be construed as followers in social spheres. While they can be observed as followers, they often times have a large following themselves. These are the individuals who obtain the information from the "Connectors," who originally obtained their information from the "Mavens." Once the information is obtained, the Salesmen pass the information onto a larger network or networks. Numerous "Salesmen" can exist. Again, while it would be assumed that most "Salesmen" would be individuals, they are at times not people at all. Using this book as an example again, the "Salesmen" could be the bookstores where the actual book is sold or an Internet site from which the book could be obtained.

As an individual can observe, the influence that a single Maven can have is tremendous (Figure 9.6). It is obvious that the above diagram simply represents a book. The masses can become much larger depending on the Salesmen and those influenced. Most marketing today is enhanced simply

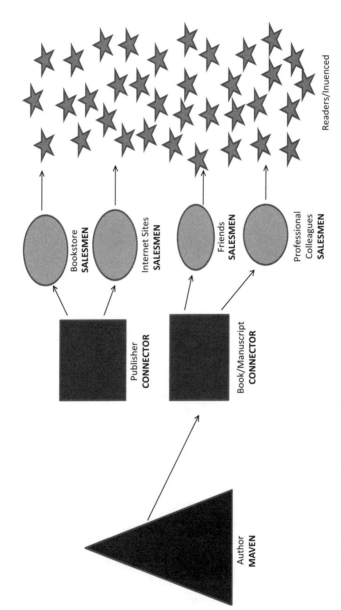

Figure 9.6 Influence one single Maven can have on a society

through word of mouth. Now, imagine the above diagram not representing a book, rather an insurgency.

Gladwell stated that his social circle is truly a pyramid like the above example. What happens when the Maven is so strong that it has connectors all around? Imagine the above diagram having the identified "Connectors" on the right of it, but also having them on the left, above, and below. Now, expand your mental visualization and picture each one of those connectors having equal amounts of salesmen and each salesmen having the same amount of stars (influenced) in the pre-existing illustration all around them as well. Multiple networks have been established simply off the one Maven identified. That Maven no longer has a network as the above illustration demonstrates, rather it has a system established. This system now can have rings all around it. A small ring circling the Maven, an outer ring circling all the Connectors, another outer ring circling all the Salesmen, and one additional circle surrounding all those influenced. These circles encompass the social spheres of influence within the system created by the Maven.

Most intelligence operatives do not target the Mavens or the Connectors rather they (intentionally or unintentionally) target the influenced and or at times the Salesmen. Very few intelligence operatives go after the largest of targets, such as Osama Bin Laden or his close associates, and when they do, decision makers are often reluctant to act upon the intelligence received due to collateral damage or public blow back. When operatives target the lower end individuals, their workload is increased and success is limited because the information created by the Maven and originally disseminated by the Connectors is already out in the public domain.

Because of today's process of intelligence analysis, one could assume that reason (lacking SOCINT initiatives) exists as to why the current war in Afghanistan has not resulted in victory to date. Assets are wasted when they can be spared. Intelligence focuses on targeting those influenced or lower end targets rather than the Mavens and Connectors. Our intelligence operatives are simply targeting the wrong entities and it's greatly caused by a lack of understanding SOCINT which will be proven in the upcoming chapter.

Notes

1. Columbite Tantalite is a mineral substance often utilized as an energy conductor for technical devices such as cellular phones, computers, etc. Wars have been fought over this substance due to its

value and needs within items as those mentioned. To understand how Columbite Tantalite affects persons daily, read: Wark, M. (2007) *Gamer Theory*. Harvard University Press. Boston, Massachusetts.

2. In the case of those working side by side among Strategic Intelligence representatives are numerous "other" representatives, such as Strategic Planners, Operations, Logistics, etc. Although intelligence is necessary for any Strategic Organization, all other elements are of equal value. Take one of the entities away from the entire staff; the total force will be jeopardized as it is virtually impossible for actions to occur without one another.

3. Those with an interest in understanding the game of Texas Hold'em Poker should read any book by Phil Gordon. He is considered one of the world's greatest players. His abilities are through systematic play that entails detailed analysis of the situation which he faces.

4. Systematic Approaches to analysis may be varied depending on the situation in which analysis operates. In the case described, there will be times when this process must be completed in reverse order starting with the farthest outside areas and working ourselves inward to the smallest sphere of influence.

5. Networks and the systems connected may have several layers and if viewed in three dimensions could be represented as spheres thus the term spheres of influence. The more the layers, the longer and more difficult it may be to gain adequate insight to understand the center of gravity. An incredible source for understanding networks, systems, and spheres of influence is Wasserman, S. (1994). *Social Network Analysis: Methods and Applications (Structural Analysis in the Social Sciences)*. Cambridge University Press. New York, New York.

Current Research for Analysis with Sociocultural Intelligence 10

The sociocultural intelligence analyst

In this paradigm, individual analysts are assigned to specific production lines based on the capabilities of the former and the needs of the latter. However, for this model to work, staffers need to know what assets the analysts in the work force possess. Similarly, when intelligence agencies use precious few hiring allocations to bring in new intelligence analysts, they must maximize those opportunities, and only hire qualified personnel.

(Moore and Krizan 2003, p. 95)

One would believe that the US Intelligence Community (IC) only hires the best of the best to ensure national security remains intact. Unfortunately, like virtually any other business in existence, the US IC, too, faces dilemmas that often times allow individuals who are unqualified, or not as qualified as one would assume or like, to enter into the intelligence system.

Understanding that virtually every large corporation faces issues in their hiring processes, such information about the IC should come as no surprise. It takes an extremely unique individual to serve in any intelligence capacity to meet the needs of their customers and possibly even more so if they are to serve within a sociocultural capacity.

Individuals working within the IC will be faced with the stresses of secrecy, pressure from bureaucratic politicians, and pressure from knowing their finalized products will be used to save the lives of fellow countrymen and women. They will also be required to work extensive hours, and possibly deploy into austere conditions, along with having to face many other situations that cause increased stress. After understanding the environment in which intelligence professionals work, one could conclude that an individual must possess certain characteristics to be successful.

Intelligence operatives must have a very unique sense of humor. They must be willing to challenge their peers as they will often be faced with group discussions and numerous pressures. They must be motivated to fulfill tasks that may not be of interest or whose importance they do not fully understand. Controlled curiosity must be present as well. However, intelligence operatives must understand how far they can push their curiosity without crossing the line into the imaginary.

They must be willing to agree to disagree, yet still move forward with the mission at hand. If they are serving in a sociocultural capacity, they must also be willing to live with locals, adapt to their customs, courtesies, and values. Besides possessing these personal traits, they must also have and maintain professional qualities as well.

Professionally, intelligence representatives must be capable of utilizing numerous computer software programs and learning other unfamiliar systems rapidly. They must be excellent communicators, both verbally and in writing, as well as be excellent listeners. They must be capable of seeing signs or items that the ordinary civilian would most likely not be capable of observing and interpreting, as well as be capable of utilizing their "sixth sense." The knowledge of whom and how they serve must also be present.

Understanding the IC as a whole must be sound, along with understanding the numerous interagency and national level policies. Like any good supply sergeant in the military, they must also be resourceful. Their resourcefulness must stem from interpersonal skills and rapport techniques that allow them to obtain and maintain as many contacts as possible.

Too often, an individual can witness or observe an appearance of "users" that exists within the IC. Too many people working within the system will contact others with requests for information or insight about a situation, but will never return the favor. Numerous excuses as to why this happens are expressed. However, they are just that: excuses. Maintaining relations takes a bit of time, but it is time well spent as it helps ensure success.

Lastly, individuals performing in such capacities should be gamers at heart. This is not implied that we need "Madden Mayhem" fanatics, rather individuals who also enjoy traditional and non-technical games such as Chess, Sudoku, Stratego, etc. Such games allow an individual to perform mental analysis as situations continuously and rapidly change. They also allow mental conditioning in rapid deductive and inductive reasoning. These games are important, as one will find that observations and the ability to interpret such signs are the baseline for any good intelligence analysis.

Grabbing the indicators

What we observe from day-to-day of what goes on in foreign states—even in those areas in which our collection and basic intelligence is the best—is actually something less than the tip of the iceberg. Disasters—natural and man-made— insurrections, major internal struggles even including the ouster of key officials, mobilization of thousands of men and a host of other military preparations have been successfully concealed from us and almost certainly will be again.

(Grabo 2002, p. 34)

Surprise attacks on the United States like those witnessed at Pearl Harbor on December 7, 1941 or on September 11, 2001 occurred with little warning. Or did they? Many critics of the IC have made claims that we "fell asleep behind the wheel." The truth is that no one within the IC was sleeping, rather grave mistakes were made that cost many American lives.

One of the greatest mistakes is the likeliness that an Unconventional or an Asymmetric Indicator Lists was never developed. These indicator lists are complied hypothetical situations or actions that adversaries towards the United States could perform to hinder the security of this nation or its interests. They are complied with three major sources of knowledge: History of the adversaries' past actions, doctrine utilized by opposition groups, and lessons learned or after action reports stemming from recent conflicts in which the opposition was engaged.[1] These lists are of great importance as they allow analysts a written cheat sheet to monitor continuously known or perceived activities that could trigger concern among the IC to take caution of future activities.

Strategically these list may be overly broad, however as the analyst focuses more on a tactical perspective, they can be honed in towards a more in-depth focus. As greater insight and knowledge is obtained by the analyst, such list should be tweaked and updated with newer information expressing such possible indicators. Indicator lists should never hold 100% certainty towards providing insight for the analysts, but should strictly serve as guides. As Grabo states, "The mere ticking off of items on an indicator list has never produced warning, and it never will. It is a tool but not a panacea" (Grabo 2002, p 29).

As actions occur, they must be annotated chronologically by time and date of action and not the time and date of the reporting. This is crucial when attempting to identify patterns that will later assist in the indicator and warning principle of assisting in predictive analysis. Unfortunately, some may perceive the indicator analytical technique as somewhat straightforward. In many regards it is. However, too often we believe we know everything there is to know about a situation and often lack the fortitude to dig deeper into understanding the situation.

If an individual is incapable or unwilling to do the right thing, even when no one is watching, by delving deeper into the situation, the indicator methodology could be a great waste of time as missing pieces to the puzzles will never be found. Those lacking desires to delve into the situation for understanding often realize that obtaining such insight is painstaking and needs meticulous analytical skills—something many in the IC are not willing to sweat over because it's easier to simply serve as IT data processors than do hard work as true analysts.

An individual must keep in mind that although some indicators may be observed or witnessed, many more indicators that actually exist will never be recognized. There may be several reasons why analysts do not make observations of such indicator signs. The greatest reason is simply because analysts are not prone to identify with the actual culture and socio-complexities for the geographical areas of concern that they are analyzing. This in turn provides even more reasons to implement an official SOCINT discipline within the US IC.

As Ms Grabo points out, the Intelligence Community must avoid treating the warning function as only a by-product of other intelligence production. To "work" a warning problem is to anticipate events in their fullest political, military, economic, diplomatic and cultural context. If the attacks on the World Trade Center and the Pentagon came as a surprise because "nothing like that had ever happened before in the U.S.," then the events truly echo those of December 1941.[2] (Jan Goldman 2002, Editor's Preface, p. vi.)

The differences of analysis

A debate exists within the profession of intelligence, specifically intelligence analysis, based on the determination of intelligence analysis as either "art or science."[3] The greatest concept of declaration of intelligence analysis as an art is based on its subjectivity and intuitiveness. On the flip side, the intelligence analysis debate of being a science lays on its principles of structured, systematic, and methodological nature.

Needless to say, this debate will continue because it is known that analysis has structured systematic methodologies, but also has and will continue to have a great amount of intuition and subjectivity within the end product. Because of this, encouragement to end the debate leads to realize that intelligence analysis is neither truly an art nor a science, but a combination of both, making it a discipline.

Intelligence analysis is a discipline because it requires even the most novice intelligence operative to understand that the incorporation of art and science is needed to achieve the greatest analytical product for the end user. Analysts must be confident to know and understand when and how they must incorporate both debatable concepts into their own work. Because of this principle, intelligence and intelligence analysis are referred to here as disciplines to eliminate the debate of art versus science.

The need for an extensive understanding of every analytical methodology is unnecessary. What is necessary is an understanding that a great push throughout the United States government exists to promote enhancements within the IC, specifically analytics. Reasons exist for this push and they stem predominantly from numerous intelligence failures that have jeopardized National Security.

It is evident that the United States IC as a whole fails to rely on truly structured methodologies in the analytical trade. Today, more and more accounts of poor intelligence are presented because of analysts relying on their intuition of the situation rather than creating and obtaining an account or log of this information and the means and methods in making the necessary analysis of the information. As Marrin (2007, p. 7) states, in his document titled, *Intelligence Analysis: Structured Methods or Intuition*, this would serve as an "Audit Trail."

If any individual has ever read the infamous 9–11 Commission and WMD Commission reports, they too would gain a sense that a lack of structured analytical techniques exists within the IC due to both reports identifying a need for additional money for such use to eliminate intuitive thought. Unfortunately, the authors of these reports fail to mention that hundreds of analytical methodologies already exist. The issue is not to reinvent the wheel, rather to enforce a standard that analysts must utilize and annotate the analytical methodologies used for their finalized products.

The necessity in the creation or utilization of a structured analytical methodology, outside of having some form of audit trail, has multiple reasons. It allows new analysts readable and understandable insight to the situation that they may need an understanding of. It provides decision makers with opportunities to reflect and check information after presentations in a readable form. Such a log will allow others to check for mistakes, inaccuracies, and or biases. Lastly, it will hopefully hold individuals accountable when adverse actions occur. Marrin has stated that while working at the Central Intelligence Agency:

> No one I knew—except for maybe the economic analysts—used any form of structured analytic process that was transparent to others. No quantitative methods; no special software; no analysis of competing hypotheses; not even link charts. (Marrin 2007, p. 9)

Marrin is truly an expert on intelligence analysis. With that said, he too understands that, at times, intuition will occur and will most likely be needed. The principle is an attempt to eliminate the vast amounts of intuition among analysts and ensure that utilization of more systematic analytical methodologies occurs within the IC. Marrin does not necessarily condone the creation of more analytical techniques to be developed, rather encourages the utilization of those that already exist.

The issue today is not necessarily individual analysts not wanting to implement scientifically produced analytical techniques, such as the Bayesian Method, rather the greatest issue lays with time and demand.[4] Time is of the essence for decision makers. They want their intelligence here and now.

Using pre-existing methodologies

The 9–11 Commission and WMD Commission reports express a need for additional funding into the IC for analytical purposes. The money needed could be considered for greater technical means and methodologies for expedited analysis. Unfortunately, today's intelligence analysts do not need more tools readily available for the discipline, but greater time to fulfill their intelligence analysis requirements for accuracy and understanding.

Intelligence analysis is the discipline of obtaining numerous pieces of information, organizing, interpreting, and producing an understandable product to assist decision makers in identifying a credible means in solving a problem through the incorporation of as many variables as possible. The goal behind any intelligence analysis is to identify the most predictable outcome of a situation. This is often referred to as intelligence analysis estimation.

There are multiple programs of intelligence analysis, such as opportunity, linchpin, and analogy.[5] Opportunity analysis is a means in attempting to identify gaps such as vulnerabilities within opposition or interests entities, groups, key leaders, etc. By identifying these vulnerabilities, the analyst presents such opportunities to decision makers so they then can determine a means and method to exploit such opportunities to provide a greater advantage.

Linchpin analysis is a means to fulfill a systematic "checks and balance" of intelligence being derived internally. This is a very unique methodology to ensure that inaccuracies have been mitigated among the data being analyzed. It ensures that all hypotheticals have been observed and assessed to reach the end stated analyzed product. Not only is the linchpin analysis a check of the finished product, it also serves as a proof read so decision makers have limited means to misinterpret the finalized product.

Analogy is the comparing and contrasting of at least two entities or situations. While identifying similarities is important, it is also important for the analyst performing the analogy to identify the dissimilarities. By fulfilling a compare and contrast on the entities, the analyst will be capable of identifying reason towards the existence of the entity. This identification of reason towards existence will assist in identifying the entities capabilities and hopefully a means in dealing with that specific entity or element. As Rodgers states, "Clearly, humans cannot assess all that is being presented. They need to reduce or simplify the information presented" (Rodgers 2006, p. 623).

One of the greatest difficulties in analysis, whether it be from a sociocultural perspective or done by a medical practitioner, is the means in understanding what is relevant and what is not. Not only identifying the relevant information, but also sorting it into a manageable system of importance is necessary as well. While this may appear to be a simplistic task, because of our demeanors as human beings, we often tend to have difficulties differentiating the relevant versus the non-relevant.

We are filled with self-induced biases and beliefs about items of self-interest that lead us to push more towards certain aspects of information to be observed versus that which may "bore us." This could be based on our previous experience or self-expectations. Human information processing is affected by three elements. Rodgers describes them in relation to intelligence analysis as

1. the tendency to see patterns where none exist,
2. the tendency to seek confirmatory evidence, and
3. the use of preconceived biases.[6]

A unified system within the IC still lacks adequate procedures for National Security needs. While this systemic element has improved dramatically since the horrific attacks that occurred on 9–11, the repository itself is still extremely weak and partially broken. Not one single entity serves as the repository for all intelligence analyzed products. The DOD, DOJ, DOS, CIA, etc. all hold on tightly to their intelligence products, ensuring a need to know exists prior to release internally within their own organizations as well as externally.

With the dramatic rise of intelligence blogs and wikis in existence today, enhancements have been achieved. However, as previously stated, the system is still partially broken. One main reason that a break exists is not necessarily due to the lack of intelligence products, but to misguided principles within the IC itself.

It's only history, not analysis

The United States has incredible means to collect virtually any data desired throughout the world. This provides a false sense of greatness within our own IC simply because we fail to truly understand our greatest of shortfalls. Today's IC has become a regurgitator of information strictly based on the reliance of historiography.

Historiography is the study of past qualitative evidence formulated as words and sentences in natural language.[7] It is the historical means and method of intelligence analysis within the US IC. Historiography is based on somewhat informal past elements. Because of its reliance on past information, difficulty in prediction exists, which also means such information becomes overly futile in nature. Rational expectation on the other hand stems from "estimative forecasting based on available evidence and formal analytic methods" (Smith 2006, p. 6). This is the crux where critical thinking and scientific analytical methodologies must meet. By implementing the scientific analysis with critical thinking, a means in predictive analysis becomes less futile than the traditional means of historiography analytics.

We as individuals often overevaluate information as well. This occurs very easily as we discover patterns and make false assumptions about the information through simplistic analysis without ever truly identifying why such events occur. While utilizing quantifiable measures to perform our analysis, such quantifiable methodologies can at times hinder analysis unless the identification and understanding as why such quantifiable situations exists.

Probability, in regards to analysis, is more often than not reached when lack of difficulty in prediction occurs. We dismiss factors and hypothetical scenarios when it becomes too difficult to understand. As one can imagine, this could be overly costly when dealing with national security.

As a society, we have our own cultural belief systems. It is overly easy for a society to make predictions based on how we understand a situation stemming from our own cultural norms. When dealing with cultures we are not accustomed to dealing with, it is paramount to throw away our own belief systems and cultural norms, and mentally think like the culture that is being analyzed for greater analytical predictable outcomes.

Rodgers utilizes the case of when analysts and decision makers conduct mirror imaging.[8] Mirror imaging is a catch phrase for a very simplistic concept of "wargaming." This is when a scenario is presented to a group of individuals and they attempt to determine what will occur if they fulfill the acts of X, Y, and or Z. They are attempting to make a determination of the reaction based off their action. This is overly difficult to do accurately if the team playing the Mirror Imaging game has limited understanding of the sociocultural elements of the geographic domain which they are operating.

Medical malpractice exists more often than not because of unintentional misdiagnosis of the patient through inappropriate analysis of the information obtained. Although it is noted that such misdiagnosis is often very unintentional, lives could be mistakenly lost due to such inappropriate analysis. Likewise, when dealing with National Security, such misdiagnosis can not only cost the life of one individual, but can lead to the total destruction of an entire nation.

Cooper identifies in the Introduction of his document titled, *Curing Analytic Pathologies: Pathways to Improved Intelligence Analysis,* four major pathologies within intelligence analysis: (1) identification of individual analytic impediments and determination of their sources, (2) promotion for analysts to detect the systemic pathologies that result from closely coupled networks and to find the linkages among the individual impediments, (3) each of these networks, and thus each systemic pathology, usually spans multiple levels within the hierarchy of the IC, and (4) the framework highlights the need to treat both the systemic pathologies and the individual impediments by focusing effective remedial measures on the right target and at the appropriate level.[9]

One of the greatest concerns Cooper outlines is the minimal intelligence analysis updates between the Cold War era and today as we face unconventional and asymmetric threats. The threats today are very different from yesterday when we fought conventional armies and their political likes. Today, we fight very unique, determined, and aggressive oppositions with little state support. With such little state support, these threats rely on the people. Within the people lay a society and within that society exists a culture that we, as Westerners, simply are not familiar with.

Educate analysts for success

Because of such differences between yesterday's means and methodologies and today's practice of intelligence analysis, a change must exist. That change does not necessarily constitute a change in analytical methodologies, but a change in the mental capacities of the intelligence analysts. Individuals must be held accountable and take responsibility for their flawed intelligence estimates. This is reason for the implementation of a formalized SOCINT discipline within itself. It is also reason to promote social change within the IC for educational purposes as well.

> Like a guild, each intelligence discipline recruits its own members, trains them in its particular craft, and inculcates in them its rituals and arcana. These guilds cooperate, but they remain distinct entities. Such a culture builds pragmatically on practices that were successful in the past, but it lacks the strong formal epistemology

of a true discipline and remains reliant on the transmission, often implicit, of expertise and domain knowledge from experts to novices. Unfortunately, the US Intelligence Community has too few experts-either analytic "masters" or journey-men-left in the ranks of working analysts to properly instruct and mentor the new apprentices in either practice or values. (Cooper 2005, p. 6)

Intelligence analytical techniques are abundant. Schoolhouses that teach such techniques for agencies within the IC are still the ideal locations for such delivery to new analysts. Understanding that it is the schoolhouse that teaches technique and the numerous methodologies of intelligence analysis is not enough. To hone in on skills and individuality within intelligence analysis, more educational systems throughout university settings are being built to assist in the greater need to better our intelligence capabilities.

These systems of higher learning are building a very new principle of intelligence education for one of the world's oldest professions. Although secrecy must remain for some educational principles within intelligence, such as collection and analytical techniques, having university settings to teach national security or intelligence programs allows professional intelligence operatives, or those with desire to one day become professionals in the field, a greater scope of understanding numerous diverse key factors. Some of those key factors stem from global issues, international affairs, political science, military history, and critical literature.

Many of these topics would be overlooked among individuals serving in such capacities of intelligence. Implementing university academics to the intelligence fields serves three purposes:

1. It allows those already serving within the field a mental expansion that they may not already have in an attempt to think even more "outside the box."
2. With young collegiate personnel obtaining degrees in National Security and or Intelligence, a new recruiting ground will be established based not just on foreign language or global cultural matters, but on academic grade performance that demonstrates that the graduate fully knows and understands the work at hand and is capable of successfully performing such tasks in the professional world.
3. Lastly, such academic environments allow those already serving in the field an opportunity to rotate their assignments from the intelligence tasks and bring those experiences into a collegiate setting. This will assist in sound research that will expand through dissemination of literature also relevant for the intelligence professional, along with diversity by working with others who are not in the field and strictly work in the academia setting. This last point will build greater professionalism within the intelligence arena simply by observing and working in a setting to which they are not traditionally accustomed.

Educational institutions are not the end-all be-all cure to rectify issues that exist within the IC. The private sector is filled with extraordinary organizations that have exemplified their success through the utilization of intelligence analysis for business. Such companies have a lot to be learned from.

The world of intelligence analytics does not strictly occur within National Security. Numerous private corporations also have their own intelligence elements such as Wal-Mart, Amazon, Nike, Capital One, hotels such as the Marriott, etc. Some may not call such entities "Intelligence" but in the end their work performance is just that: Intelligence.

Many of the greatest of corporations that are still making excellent headway during current economic hardships should be observed to see what they are doing to make them continuously successful. Their results and the means to achieve them should be observed by the US IC in an attempt to improve intelligence analysis production. The key in understanding how private industry success in their intelligence capabilities is that they do not strictly serve as data managers like many intelligence officers unofficially serving in such capacities within the US IC.

Corporations do not hire analysts to strictly plug data into a computer data bank system, rather the private sector representatives review the data, perform a *quantitative* assessment, cross reference with other elements, then make recommendations in gaining the greatest impact through a finalized analyzed product. By performing in this capacity, they reduce assumption and provide *quantitative* deductive reasoning to truly understand and know the insight needed for their superiors to make sound decisions. The statistics used for their deductive reasoning that these private organizations produce is not the end-all be-all approach to their success.

They also perform complex modeling for predictive analysis. This modeling optimizes results of the statistical equations that lead to the earning of greater profits because instead of having one idea to act or perform, the leadership has several alternative avenues for maneuver. Indeed, National Security elements perform modeling exercises, but they often reduce the amount of modeling when thrown into a war zone simply because they get overwhelmed by the current tactical events occurring around them. Even when they do perform the modeling experimentations during their war time contingency operations, rarely will they be utilized with the incorporation of statistical deductive reasoning stemming from analyzed intelligence products.

Some may construe this approach as a similarity in utilization of the analytical methodology called the Bayesian Model. Although this may not necessarily be the case, similarities indeed exist between the two approaches. This methodology is appropriate as it serves as an additional tool for the analysts to obtain a greater sense of understanding the situation.

The Bayesian Methodology is a relatively simplistic analytical process. This methodology, like many, utilizes real events to assist the analyst in identifying future probabilities based on hypothetical scenarios. To utilize the Bayesian methodology, first, full understanding of defined hypothesis of future scenarios is needed. Next, analysts must insert, based on their own understandings towards the situation, their own data to prove each hypothesis is true. Once analysts complete this task, they move on to the third step, which consists of inserting known collected data into the equation to obtain a quantified probability of the outcome for the hypothesis.

This is fulfilled in an attempt to obtain equated ratio probabilities to determine why events would or could take place. In all, this process is a true quantifiable process of elimination or deductive reasoning to determine events or future events for predictive analysis. This methodology, while still entailing some bias towards the end analysis, is an excellent methodology through the means of adding quantifiably understood data into the numerous hypothetical equations to make a nonsubjective prediction. As more events occur, the addition of such information should be added continuously to gain insight and greater accuracies for SOCINT concerns.

Corporations are inclined to continuously perform internal assessments on not just their production and sales, but also on their analytical elements to determine accuracies of assumptions and success rates. When performance drops, an unbiased assessment must occur to identify flaws. Once those flaws are identified, critical necessity exists in rectifying the issues causing such flaws. More often than not, the flaw is not the analytical methodology, but the subjectivity stemming from individuals themselves.

Initiative, understanding, and a little thought

While operating in Eastern Afghanistan, the discovery of subjectivity has been identified. The subjectivity presented false assumptions about geographical areas of concern. Not only were these areas of concern misinterpreted, areas of little to no concern were left alone allowing "under the rug" activities to take place by opposition groups often referred to as Anti Afghan Forces (AAF).

Areas of Operations are mapped out all over utilizing topographical and or geospatial imagery. Some maps had outlines of the different districts within provinces, while others not only had districts outlined, but adjoining provinces as well. Decision makers would read daily intelligence reports of specific activities that occurred at specific locations and immediately assume, along with most of their staff, that such an area should be considered a bad area.

The analysis to determine that an area be identified utilizes a color system similar to that of a traffic light. Red meant that the area was bad, while yellow meant it was neutral, and green that it was relatively non-hostile or safe. Strictly based on hostile actions, districts on such maps would be filled with the appropriate color.

A serious dilemma represented itself because a large amount of diverse government entities served in the same geographical space. Often times, unnecessary in-depth conversations between the State Department and the Department of Defense (DOD) representatives would take place for hours on end, simply to determine the geographical position of villages, districts, and or provinces. This was time wasted when the only thing needed was for an individual or group of individuals to think outside the box and create a tool that would determine, through quantitative and qualitative reasoning, the true posture of the area of concern.

Unfortunately, very few people found interest in creating a tool such as a District Matrix. One must wonder if individuals just like to argue and pitch their own sense of being to others for some form of pleasure. Needless to say, an initiative was taken by a select group of highly motivated individuals to formulate some type of matrix.

The matrix had to be simple and resemble something already known to those who would partake and/or assist in adding values to it. Virtually every infantryman understands a matrix known as the CARVER matrix, which is a relatively simple tool to understand and utilize.

CARVER is an acronym for Criticality, Accessibility, Recuperability (which is argued by many to truly mean Recoverability), Vulnerability, Effects on Population, and Recognizability. The CARVER matrix was developed by US Special Operations Forces as a tool to assist in targeting adversary's resources. The CARVER selection assists in target selection and eliminates subjectivity.

Each factor must be considered and designated with a numerical value from one through ten. One would be the least desirable while ten would be the most desirable. This value represents the quantifiable determination of each designated factor. Each value is then placed inside the decision matrix itself. Once all values are inputted, a total "score" is provided for the individual target of interest. If done properly, each target of interest is assigned a numerical value that will determine the order of desire for attack among the Special Operations elements.

This is an extremely easy matrix to reduce subjectivity. Because of its ease and understandability, those with an interest in the Districts of Afghanistan decided to produce something very similar to the CARVER matrix. This idea was based on the expedited needs in teaching users how to fulfill the task, along with the desires and likes of simplicity.

Understandably, the end product created for the District Matrix was far from perfect. It was however much better than the subjective bickering methodology already used within working group meetings. Those in high management positions were grateful to those who took the time to create such a matrix and understood its value, but determined that they would not "force" anyone to utilize it as "they already had enough on their plates." Many lower and mid-level personnel were reluctant to incorporate such a tool. Needless to say, these demeanors may be reason enough as to why the war in Afghanistan continues: Failure to adapt and promote internal change.

The District Matrix was referred to as HIRAGE. At the time, the name suited as morale was relatively low among the personnel operating in this specific geographical space within Afghanistan. Many of them indeed were high with rage. The District Matrix was not named after the individuals serving in Afghanistan, nor their morale level. It was named this because like CARVER, it too is an acronym.

This quickly developed matrix incorporated items of concern among US government entities. Health issues are prevalent throughout the country. Because of Taliban control for such a long period, often times women could not enter a hospital during labor and relied on midwives. This still occurs but with time, improvement is being made. Irritable Bowel Syndrome is extremely common, but as simplistic as it is to treat inside the United States, if left untreated under harsh conditions, advanced ailments could occur. These are two very simple issues the US government and its allies face daily in Afghanistan. There is an extreme shortage of medical clinics and hospitals as a whole throughout the country. For this reason, health care became a necessity to evaluate and served as the "H" for the HIRAGE matrix.

Afghanistan is an extraordinary place with extraordinary terrain. Located throughout Afghanistan are some of the world's toughest mountain ranges, such as the Tora Bora and the Hindu Kush. Deserts to the south and roaring rivers in the north make travel long, hot, and tiresome. Such movements are not only difficult on the Coalition operating out of Afghanistan, but also difficult for even those from the country itself to include opposition groups. The "I" in HIRAGE stood for "Isolation Factors." This included how isolated a location was from the rest of the sociocultural system and or how accessible it was as well.

It is known what villages have some formal or informal relationships among opposition groups as well as those that have similar relations with Coalition Forces. Many of these relations took time to understand, but with adequate interpersonal rapport skills, they could be relatively easy to discover when speaking with local indigenous persons. Such relations are extremely important when fighting unconventional or asymmetric warfare. Because of this, the "R" in HIRAGE was dedicated to relationships.

Anti Afghan Forces (the opposition groups fighting against the Afghan Government along with Coalition Forces) conduct numerous tactics in an attempt to obtain their desired end stated goal of ridding the United States and current Afghan regime within Afghanistan. Not all activities were physical, but the threat of physical activities were known often through "Night Letters." Night Letters are handwritten notes that would be inserted into villages threatening some form of physical violence if local villagers were caught working with the United States or the Afghan government. The "A" within the HIRAGE matrix stood for Anti Afghan Forces.

Governance is a serious issue and the United States has still failed to grasp it when dealing with the Afghan government. This is not just simply an issue among the Government of the Islamic Republic of Afghan (the official terminology for the Afghan government) national level, but also on the local level in dealing with tribal elders, district governors, provincial governors, etc. Corruption is greatly accepted within Afghan culture to a certain degree, but not all corruption is acceptable. Many of the locals fail to support their local and national government and because of this, the "G" in HIRAGE represented government.

"Stability Operations" is a phase during war time contingencies that can be construed as the most difficult to accomplish. Jobs must be produced to support the local economic infrastructure. Afghanistan has an abundance of natural resources ranging from minerals, copper, timber, and agriculture. Unfortunately, limited knowledge in managing such resources hinders the economic capabilities of Afghanistan as a whole. To add harsher conditions to the current state of Afghanistan, refugees have been witnessed in recent times coming from Pakistan into Afghanistan. They are migrating from places in Pakistan like the North West Frontier and FATA regions back into Afghanistan where they originally lived during the Russian War and throughout the civil war in Afghanistan thereafter. Many of the Afghan locals are beautiful individuals who are more than willing to share all they have with such refugees, however by supporting numerous individuals simultaneously, they also deplete their own resources off which they live. Because of this, the "E" in the HIRAGE matrix stood for economics and combined such with the current refugee situation as well.

As one can observe, HIRAGE was a matrix that could be utilized universally for villages, districts, and or provinces. Like CARVER, the HIRAGE matrix incorporated a numerical system to support quantitative analysis. Rather than utilizing one through ten principles, it was determined to utilize one through three principles simply to mitigate any confusion and debate between numbers. Understanding that the government at the time would differentiate districts and provinces through a red, yellow, and green matter, the one through three methods made sense at the time. The number one would indicate a principle within the HIRAGE Matrix as green, while the number two would indicate yellow, and the number three would indicate red. This method appeared to be relatively cut and dry.

Prior to fulfilling the HIRAGE Matrix requirements, it was necessary to understand that for it to be successful, multiple individuals were needed for each village, district, or province. The utilization of multiple individuals would rectify a one-dimensional perspective on the area. To complete the matrix, at least three individuals would be utilized. After all three individuals returned with their findings, a mediator (who often served as the sociocultural analyst) would then conduct a debriefing with the three personnel simultaneously ensuring limited gaps of information resulted. The analyst would then find the median between all survey numerical scales of the matrix to obtain a finalized conclusion.

Immediately following the finalized matrix for each location assessed, the analyst would then be required to input that data into a centralized data bank system for safe keeping. As time passed, and a need to reassess such locations arose, the analyst would then be capable of cross checking old data with the new. This was a crucial step as it would allow decision makers a nonsubjective understanding as to where the location in concern is faltering, be it health issues, isolation factors, relations, AAF activities, governance, and/or economics.

Prior to the safe keeping of such data, one last step was crucial; the color coding of the maps according to the outcome of the Matrix assessment. Because virtually every government organization in country had their own maps with similar color codes, times would come when more aggravating meetings would present subjective reasoning to determine which areas were deemed hostile, neutral, and or safe. Needless to say, the team that fulfilled the matrix almost always came out on top of the argument simply because they had a paper trail of *quantitative* and qualitative analysis to support their recommendation.

Below is an example of the HIRAGE Matrix template to allow readers a greater sense of the simplicity needed to fulfill such a tasking. Remember, nothing is perfect, however what little analysts can do to support their conclusions can lead to great accomplishments. More often than not, it takes a little initiative, "thinking outside the box," and understanding of the internal concerns stemming from those of whom the analyst supports and or represents. This Matrix is one means that proved a liking to a very unique advisory team in Afghanistan.

DISTRICT ASSESSMENT—HIRAGE MATRIX

Use the below matrix to determine the HIRAGE scores for assigned locations:

POTENTIAL TARGETS	H	I	R	A	G	E	Total

Health: Health should be assessed in terms of health care accessibility and access to clinics. Use the scale below to determine the numerical value assigned to a particular area.

Criteria	Value Scale
Access to health care and clinic exists within village	1
Access to health care is immediate however no clinic exists	2
No immediate health care or clinic within the three closest villages	3

Isolation Factors: is measured in terms of access for CF along with AAF elements. Use the scale below to determine the numeric value assigned to a particular area.

Criteria	Value Scale
Easily accessible for CF via ground and air with no AAF presence	1
Easily accessible for CF via ground and air with known AAF presence	2
No access for CF exists nor is the area accessible via ground or air transportation throughout the year to include winter months	3

Relationships: measures the relationship between CF and or the AAF within the local population. Use the scale below to determine the numeric value assigned to a particular area.

Criteria	Value Scale
Working relationship with CF and Anti AAF	1
Neutral relationship with CF, neutral relationship with AAF	2
Anti CF and pro AAF	3

AAF Activities: measures if the adversary has conducted kinetic operations, established safe havens, utilization of Night Letters. Use the scale below to determine the numeric value assigned to a particular area.

Criteria	Value Scale
No kinetic activities (CF or AAF) within the past six months, no known safe havens, no known Night Letters	1
No kinetic activities (CF or AAF) within the past three months, rumored safe havens but not confirmed, Night Letters within the past six months	2
Kinetic activities (CF or AAF) continuously, known safe havens, Night Letters within the past three months	3

Governance: measures the local perspectives on the District government. Use the scale below to determine the numeric value assigned to a particular area.

Criteria	Value Scale
No corruption identified or corruption is accepted, supports GIRoA and CF	1
Corruption exists, is not accepted, and support to GIRoA and or CF only occurs for individual gains	2
Corruption exists, is not accepted, fails to support GIRoA and CF	3

Economics: measures the availability of jobs and merchant goods as well as measures the refugee situation. Use the scale below to determine the numeric value assigned to a particular area.

Criteria	Value Scale
Jobs are available with a growing or stable economy and no known refugee status exists	1
Jobs are available yet nonselective, the economy is stable, and a controlled refugee situation exists	2
Jobs are limited or fail to exist, the economy is depleting, and a refugee situation exists which either is controlled with possibilities of worsening or is in need of assistance	3

Notes

1. While indicator lists are compiled utilizing historical data, present actions and changes in political, military, economic, social, infrastructure, as well as religious climate must be observed in the present state for a compare and contrast understanding that will identify the indicators themselves. Grabo displays in-depth details for compiling and utilization of indicator lists in the document Anticipating Surprise: Analysis for Strategic Warning. Chapter 2: Introduction to the Analytical Method. *Center for Strategic Intelligence Research.* Joint Military Intelligence College. Washington, D.C. pp. 25–50.

2. Jan Goldman is a Faculty Member and Course Manager for Strategic Warning & Threat Management at the Joint Military Intelligence College located in Washington, D.C. This quote was taken out of the Editors Preface from the book *Anticipating Surprise: Analysis for Strategic Warning* by Cynthia M. Grabo a publication from the Center for Strategic Intelligence Research the Joint Military Intelligence College (2002).

3. A great debate to determine "Art or Science" for identification of Intelligence continues today. Some believe it is an art while many believe it's a science. This debate may appear rudimentary to many. To limit it in this book, for sake of argument, Intelligence will be considered a combination of "Art and Science" therefore referred to throughout as a discipline.

4. The Bayesian Methodology is a statistical analytic tool to assist in determining probability through quantitative scaling. A hypothesis is formed then inputted into a system identifying such as a historical probability then calculated with current relevant data. In order to achieve the Bayesian results with some accuracy, a mathematical equation is utilized. To understand the Bayesian Methodology in greater detail, it is recommended to read Andrew Gelman's book *Bayesian Data Analysis: Texts in Statistical Science, Second Edition.* 2003. Chapman and Hall. New York, New York.

5. For an in-depth understanding of "opportunity, linchpin, and analogy" read Krizan's *Intelligence Essentials for Everyone* by the Joint Military Intelligence College. Occasional Paper Number 6. Part 5. pp. 29–38.

6. Human processing is the individual's ability to obtain information and compute such information into an understandable form. Unfortunately, as individuals, we have our own biases and acute need to continuously obtain greater insight about the situation in order to change our own opinions that rely on our own preconceived notions. Our biases and preconceived notions often stem from continuous social conditioning found throughout our surroundings. *Improving Analysis: Dealing with Information Processing Errors* by Rodgers outlines in great details how such hindrances affect our abilities to fulfill adequate human processing.

7. Historiography is described as the focus on past information pertaining a specific topic. In relation to intelligence, historiography has appeared to become the trend. Although history is important because it assists in the development of indicator lists, it cannot be relied upon. Smith exemplifies intelligence and historiography in his works, *Predictive Network-Centric Intelligence: Toward a Total-Systems Transformation of Analysis and Assessment*.

8. "Wargaming" is like chess. It is fulfilled by presenting actions and having others determine what impact or reaction will result from the original action instilled. Unless full understanding not of just the opposition but of the local sociocultural dynamics is understood, wargaming will not be close to perfection. Rodgers, in his document, *Improving Analysis: Dealing with Information Processing Errors*, through the *International Journal of Intelligence and Counterintelligence* (Taylor and Francis Group. Vol. 19 Number 4. pp. 622–641) identifies errors in wargaming and lack of sociocultural understanding must be one of the many falters which he identifies.

9. Unfortunately, underlying issues among analysis does not fall on the individual analysts themselves. Like the current crisis in Afghanistan, politicians have interfered with military successes. The difficulty among analysts is not understanding through written doctrine strategic objectives. Argument about Afghanistan even having a strategic contingency plan exists. However media outlets and others have provided a false sense that intelligence failures exist or lack of command and control over coalition forces exists. Needless to say, arguments can be made with such thought, but in the end, no systematic approach has occurred. Pertaining to systematic intelligence, read Cooper, J. (2005). *Curing Analytic Pathologies: Pathways to Improved Intelligence Analysis*. Center for the Study of Intelligence. Central Intelligence Agency. Washington, D.C.

11 Conclusion

Change in culture

The current stature of the United States is very different from when it was first recognized as an independent nation. This change has occurred for so many reasons, that another book would be needed to identify them all. The United States, as a nation, has dramatically changed culturally and socially. To assess this, we can use the same Political, Military, Economic, Social, Infrastructure, and even Religious standpoints that the US government uses when attempting to asses countries abroad.

At one time, the United States was community oriented in a manner much different from today. Any location that is agriculturally dependant survives on its formal and informal community-based ties. Terrain dictates what farming communities can produce, be it livestock, fruits, vegetables, etc. Farmers producing one type of agricultural product rely on their neighboring colleagues for the missing items they cannot produce for survivability. Relations must be strong, and a system of checks and balances must be understood.

The fact that not everyone in this type of society is an actual farmer, but instead some serve as a support mechanism, like doctors, button makers, leather production specialists, metal workers, etc., also needs consideration.

Each member of such societies have a role, which is crucial for the society to survive. Note that survival also means expansion and enhancement.

With expansion comes industrial enhancements. These enhancements occur through individuals who understand what will benefit others in their capabilities. Understanding such needs cannot be accomplished unless rapport is built between parties, to grasp their goals, needs, work environment, etc. This allows one to assume that even societies based on industry also have relatively unique and strong community relationships.

The United States, while still maintaining a relatively small agricultural society in comparison to its past, has transformed into an industrial sociocultural nation as a whole. Means of mass production were created for numerous products and mass production needs caused by World War II saw much industrial growth throughout the defense industrial complex.

Our sociocultural parameters did not stop changing with the Industrial Age though. The diverse population in the United States has led to more changes in our cultural demeanor. Today, we live in what is called a technological culture. Plants that once employed people in industrial lines to put parts together to build something have been taken over by computer systems and robotics that accomplish such work, leading to the replacement of a great deal of human need for occupational success. Farmers have taken a toll with their products as well. Newer technology has replaced human demand to pick crops, bail hay, milk cows, etc. All of these changes within our society as a nation have hindered our abilities to promote and maintain human relations as they once were. The 2008 Presidential Election brought even greater insight towards where some would like to see this Nation head through the mantra President Obama's campaign used, "Change."

The political movements within

Unlike what many within the United States believe, we have never been a "Democratic State." Rather, the United States is a "Republic." In 2008, the people of the United States performed a democratic election that brought a new President to this nation. By doing so, it allowed the "change" mantra used during the campaign to unfold. Most notable are the changes being promoted within the healthcare system, banking, insurance, and the automobile industries as well. Many individuals believe that capitalism within the United States is swiftly turning the tide to socialism.

Some are against change, while others are very "pro" change as sought by the current administration. Politically, the people within the United States are split. One could easily argue that for now a nonviolent revolution is occurring within the United States. The term revolution is not always as harsh as an individual may believe. Throughout this book, the term has been used with its true meaning, a turn or rapid change in power or organizational structure.

Unfortunately, many individuals, liberal or conservative, made unique statements during the campaign. Some were threatening in nature, based on possible outcomes. Others were unique in the blatant unknowing of the deepest of stances between political parties. Many of these statements were simply ignorant. Needless to say, such statements should be of concern to those working National Security, especially within the Intelligence Community.

Of even more concern to those working within the Intelligence Community are the indicators of social disaster stemming from political decisions taking place within numerous state governments. Michael Boldin had written about the State of Alaska signing Resolution 27 (HJR27) in his report titled *Palin Signs Alaska Sovereignty Resolution*. This resolution is based on the 10th Amendment of the US Constitution. This amendment takes the stance that any state has the right to claim complete sovereignty over all powers not granted by the Federal Government of the United States. This was done to protect the people of Alaska from possible additional perceived chokeholds that the current federal government may attempt to impose on the people representing the state of Alaska. Needless to say, the people are scared of the changes possibly being brought about by the federal government. This is not opinion, rather fact since the Alaskan State Government passed this resolution with a one hundred percent vote—without any one representative against such an action.

Enhancing a greater understanding and appreciation towards the political strife taking place internally inside the United States, 37 additional states have also passed some form of resolution resembling that of Alaska. It is apparent that many are against the changes being promoted within today's political federal realms. From a sociocultural perspective, these activities should be alarming and observed as signs and/or indicators that possible future opposition actions will occur internally inside the United States. If an individual was to ever believe that another civil war or a revolution within the United States can never occur as it has in many countries in the world and similar to the movements in South America between the 1970s to today, he/she should think again.

Our social destruction

Socially, individuals within the United States may believe that they are secure and have little to worry about. Unfortunately, such individuals pay little attention to the signs and indicators that are presented virtually daily. Too many lack trust within their elected government, be they right or wrong, this is an issue. For example, although not construed as hostile vigilantes, a mass movement of citizens has taken a stance on illegal immigration and is known as the Minutemen Civil Defense Corp. Many of these individuals have voluntarily decided to attempt to secure our nation's borders by pulling "watch." Their actions are meant to deter, detect, and detain illegal movements crossing the border. Some of those involved within this movement stem from our elements of first responders. They are current or retired Law Enforcement, Fire, Emergency Medical Technicians, and military members, along with even at times individuals holding political positions.

Needless to say, these individuals attempting to secure our borders are concerned about the future of the United States. They live and see the realities of their communities being consumed by waves of illegal aliens. They understand the national issue of our prison systems being flooded by illegal persons. They are tired of local and state tax increases to support illegal persons obtaining education, welfare, medical assistance, etc. They are tired of weak illegal alien laws that hold little bearing on consequences after being tried for crimes dealing with such concerns. In the end, they are simply tired of bureaucratic nonsense being pushed down from the federal government and placed into their own neighborhoods. Many Americans cannot understand their concerns or outrage simply because they are not exposed to the same situation. This movement is large and rapidly growing because more and more Americans are becoming aware of the social issues that have arisen due to illegal alien activities within their own societal settings. Today, this issue is no longer confined to the border regions of the United States, but is an issue throughout every state.

Our social issues do not solely concern the illegal alien crisis. More and more issues are causing grave concerns among citizens. Many role models such as musicians and athletes have failed to hold up to any form of ethical role and serve as true role models for our youth. Many of these individuals have lost respect and audience among those who virtually pay their salaries. The media has taken a major blow because of their single stance in reporting national and international news which has also reduced the amount of audience.

Our religious institutions have also lost a major amount of their congregations due to indecent and immoral acts against their own followers. Church closures have been observed throughout much of the eastern United States. In the Roman Catholic Church, priests have been pointed at for their sexual activities against youth, the failure to annul marriages, and so forth. Although many may believe these activities are nothing to become worried about, they could never be so wrong.

The United States was built by individuals with great regard to self-discipline, moral values, and understanding of risk. Without such moral standings, we, the people of the United States, would most likely never be provided with the opportunities that are presented to us on a daily basis. Political and social changes are taking place all around us, some for the better, but most for the worse. Notably, such changes are prevalent within today's youth.

Many children within the United States today lack understanding of the physical games that many of us once played with friends and family. They are being consumed by the electronic gadgetry that gives many of them the opportunity to remain alone or isolated from civilization. They often can be observed as being isolated from human interaction outside of a school setting. Even today though, changes are made academically for our youth. Many schools allow online training for elementary and high-school students. Such means and methods of education detract from greater human interaction among peers. This prevents tomorrow's leaders from understanding how to de-escalate situations through negotiation and/or mediation face to face.

Our children often seek alternative means for face-to-face interaction. They also seek a means for acceptance. They lack acceptance in their households because many lack a traditional household setting. Male role models that once showed a young boy how to fish, throw a baseball, and or shave are missing. Family vacations are not as common as they once were. Youth activities have depleted. Volunteers to support and work with our youth have been replaced with the ease of providing monetary donations to a cause of interest. Divorce rates are high. Single parenting has become a trend. Yet a greater area of concern is the mass influx of children taking interest towards street gangs.

Their interests lay in a desire to seek out a father figure, sense of true family, and wealth. Gangs have always been around within the United States, but they have never been so large and violent as they are currently. Most children rarely enter a gang because they want to be criminals. They do so for the reasons mentioned. They become socially conditioned in believing the gangster mentality of cheating, stealing, and killing is acceptable. Through a strategic SOCINT standpoint, it is relatively simplistic to observe indicators throughout our society as to where issues have grown or will most likely grow into areas of concern. Simply understanding why situations occur, like youth entering gangs and lack of infrastructure to support healthy environments for our youth, will promote ideas to mitigate such activities better than increasing police forces to simply arrest such individuals.

Asking a privately run juvenile detention center, "What type of outreach program do you have in place for areas which many of the youth originate?" The answer was very simple, yet appalling. Simply put, no outreach program was in place to reduce the activities that bring such individuals into a juvenile detention system. Those questioned stated that was a job and or tasking from the local police departments. Needless to say, this is a very misguided stance within such an institution.

An outreach program must occur within the United States social settings to attempt to make an impact on our youth. This does not mean greater needs for law enforcement DARE programs are needed. This does not necessarily even mean that speeches must be made in schools to scare children away from the dangers presented by drugs, gang activities, or any other individualized criminal act they may be tempted to consider. It means that a principle needs to be introduced within an intelligence capacity that will not only be capable of identifying signs or trends, but also be capable of identifying a means to resolve or mitigate possible increased activities among our youth.

Ideally, those involved with the task of fulfilling such an intelligence role would be SOCINT operatives. Remember, the discipline of SOCINT is not strictly intended to resolve international matters dealing with National Security. It is a discipline designed for National Security as a whole. This means internally as well as externally.

Simplistically, the SOCINT team would identify growing trends or indicators. They would then geospatially map those areas of concern. Once the areas of concern are identified, they would then study the situations that may cause such possible hostile environments to better understand the sociocultural parameters. This information would then be analyzed and would provide mitigation techniques to resolve the issue. Some mitigation techniques could be as simple as speaking with local news media outlets, school administrators, local gyms owners, amusement parks managers, and law enforcement officers. Speaking to such individuals about the matters would enhance situational awareness. It will also allow those being presented with the information time to determine what capabilities they have to promote some form of social change. Such decisions will be addressed so that external monitoring from the SOCINT team can occur. This monitoring of the situation will give professional intelligence organizations the opportunity to understand what is working and what is not working in the resolution of the issue, while helping additional avenues to increase their success. As noted earlier, this technique worked in the past with the Troops to Teachers program and can work again utilizing more out-of-the-box strategies to safeguard the internal grounds of the United States.

To conclude this very basic case study of the strategic SOCINT matters in the United States, we are facing change. Much of this change threatens the internal apparatus of this nation's security. More and more military members are coming home in need for support to get them back on their feet and reenter society successfully. Some are becoming disgruntled with the services to which they are entitled through by organizations like the Department of Veteran Affairs. Sworn government representatives are starting to refuse to adhere to organizational policies in which they may be mandated to enter a war zone, such as those written by Marisa Taylor in her article titled, *Agents say DEA is forcing them illegally to work in Afghanistan*. Increase in violence, including homicide and suicide, has been reported to be greatly induced by economic hardships. Some individuals refuse to conform to government policies. State leaderships are taking similar actions to protect the people who elected them into office.

There is change within the United States and with it comes numerous indicators that the country is currently at a breaking point, which could eventually lead to a violent revolution. Such a revolution could possibly induce another world war since the United States is the leader in promoting and maintaining peace globally through its counterterrorism, natural disaster, and human rights initiatives. Many never considered such thoughts until they observed the realities of such indicators within the United States. Having trained individuals who observe and understand such indicators is now needed more than ever. It is time to formalize and make official the Sociocultural Intelligence Discipline.

Bibliography

AFDD 1. (2003). Air Force Basic Doctrine. Selection from Chapter 2 "Policy, Strategy, Doctrine, and War." Department of the United States Air Force. Washington, D.C.

Allen, A. (2008). The *Virtuous Spy: Privacy as an Ethical Limit*. University of Pennsylvania Law School. Public Law and Legal Theory Research Paper Series. Research Paper No.07–34.

American Anthropological Association Executive Board Statement on the Human Terrain System Project (2007). http://www.aaanet.org/issues/policy-advocacy/Statement-on-HTS.cfm (accessed Nov 09, 2007).

Beebe, J. (2001). Rapid Assessment Process: An Introduction. AltaMira Press. Walnut Creek, California.

Bellaby, R. (2009). *Many Spheres of Harm: What's Wrong with Intelligence Collection?* International Intelligence Ethics Association Conference Paper. Johns Hopkins University. Washington, D.C.

Berger, A. (2004). *Semiotic Analysis*. http://www.sagepub.com/upm-data/5171_Berger_Final_Pages_Chapter_1.pdf (accessed May 12, 2009).

Betts, R. (2002). *Fixing Intelligence*. Foreign Affairs (January/February). Columbia International Affairs Online. http://ciaonet.org/olj/fa/fa_janfeb02/fa_janfeb02e.html (accessed May 12, 2009).

Boldin, M. (2009). *Palin Signs Alaska Resolution*. Stand Up America Blog. http://standupamericaus. com/palin-signs-alaska-sovereignty-resolution:12875 (accessed July 24, 2009).

Blair, D. (2009). Director of National Intelligence (Dennis C. Blair) Statement to the US Intelligence Community. (PDF Transcript). (April 16, 2009).

Blank, D. (2007). *Troops to Teachers: A Model Pathway to a Second Tour of Duty*. Civic Centures Policy Series. www.civicventures.org/publications/policy . . . /pdfs/troops_teach.pdf (accessed October 21, 2008).

Central Intelligence Agency Web Site https://www.cia.gov/about-cia/index.html (accessed April 01, 2009).

Central Intelligence Agency (2009). *A Tradecraft Primer: Structured Analytic Techniques for Improving Intelligence Analysis*. https://www.cia.gov/library/publications/publications-rss-up-dates/tradecraft-primer-may-4-2009.html (accessed May 22, 2009).

Clark, R. (2006). *Intelligence Analysis: A Target-centric Approach*. CQ Press. Washington, D.C.

Clayton, C. (2007). *The Re-Discovery of Common Sense: A Guide to: The Lost Art of Critical Thinking*. iUniverse Inc. Los Angeles, CA.

Cobb, S. (2004). *Witnessing in Mediation: Toward an Aesthetic Ethics of Practice*. Institute for Conflict Analysis and Resolution. George Mason University. Working Paper no. 22.

Connable, B. (2009). *All Our Eggs in a Broken Basket: How the Human Terrain System is Undermining Sustainable Military Cultural Competence.* Military Review. March-April pp.57–64 http://blog. wired.com/defense/files/MilitaryReviewConnableApr09.pdf (accessed March 09, 2009).

Cooper, J. (2005). *Curing Analytic Pathologies: Pathways to Improved Intelligence Analysis.* Center for the Study of Intelligence. Central Intelligence Agency. Washington, D.C.

Cortina, A. (2007). *Development Ethics: A Road to Peace.* Working Paper #339. http://www.ciaonet.org/wps/klg/0002333/f_0002333_1388.pdf (accessed April 15, 2009).

Critical Thinking Project. http://www.criticalthinking.net/ (accessed May 05, 2009).

Dalrymple, T. (2008). *Not With a Bang But a Whimper: The Politics and Culture of Decline.* Ivan R. Dee: a member of the Rowman & Littlefield Publishing Group. Chicago, IL.

Damon, M. (1997). *Good Will Hunting.* The Internet Data Base. http://www.imdb.com/title/tt0119217/quotes (accessed May 12, 2009).

Davenport, T. (2006). Competing on Analytics. *Harvard Business Review.* January 2006. http://hbr.harvardbusiness.org/2006/01/competing-on-analytics/ar/1 (accessed July 27, 2009).

Davis, A. and Fu, D. (2004). *Culture Matters: Better Decision Making Through Increased Awareness.* Interservice/Industry Training, Simulation, and Education Conference (I/ITSEC). Paper # 1852 pp. 1–9.

Devito, C. (2005). *The Encyclopedia of Organized Crime.* Checkmark Books. Los Angeles, CA.

DOD Directive 2000.12 (2003). *DOD Antiterrorism Program.* Department of Defense. Washington, D.C.

Dorronsoro, G. (2005). *Revolution Unending. Afghanistan: 1979 to the Present.* Columbia University Press. New York, New York.

Early, M. (2005). *Troops to Teachers.* PowerPoint Presentation. DANTES. http://www.dantes.doded.mil/dantes_Web/library/docs/TTTBrief.Pdf (accessed October 21, 2008).

Egley, A. (2009). *Highlights of the 2007 National Youth Gang Survey.* U.S. Department of Justice. Office of Justice Programs. Office of Juvenile Justice and Delinquency Programs. http://www.ncjrs.gov/pdffiles1/ojjdp/225185.pdf (accessed May 18, 2009).

Elder, L. (2007). *Analytic Thinking: How to take thinking apart and what to look for when you do the elements of thinking and the standards they must meet.* The Thinkers Guide to Analytic Thinking. The Foundation for Critical Thinking. Item #595m.

—(2005). *The Miniature Guide to the Art of Asking Essential Questions.* Based on Critical Thinking Concepts and Socratic Principles. The Foundation for Critical Thinking.

Eldridge, E. and Neboshynsky, A. (2008). Quantifying Human Terrain. *Naval Post Graduate School Thesis Document.* Naval Post Graduate School. Monterey, CA.

FM 2–0 (2008). *Intelligence.* Department of the Army. Washington, D.C.

FM 34–3. (1990). *Intelligence Analysis.* Headquarters, Department of the Army. Washington, D.C.

Ford, H. (1996). Revisiting Vietnam: Thoughts Engendered by Robert McNamara in Retrospect. *Studies in Intelligence* Vol. 39, No. 5. https://www.cia.gov/library/center-for-the-study-of-intelligence/csi-publications/csi-studies/studies/96unclass/ford.htm (accessed Feb 23, 2009).

Gale, S. (2008). *Terrorists Assumptions and Reality.* (Word Doc). Foreign Policy Research Institute. Philadelphia, PA.

Garra, N. (2001). *Focusing Intelligence: Part 1*. The S2 Company. http://www.s2company.com/files/readings/219.php (accessed Feb 25, 2009).

Gelman, A. (2003). *Bayesian Data Analysis: Texts in Statistical Science*. Second Edition. Chapman and Hall. New York, New York.

Gladwell, M. (2005a). *Blink: The Power of Thinking Without Thinking*. Back Bay Books. Little, Brown and Company. New York, New York.

—(2005b). *The Tipping Point: How Little Things can Make a Big Difference*. Back Bay Books. Little, Brown and Company. New York, New York.

Goodman, M. and Omand, D. (2008). Teaching Intelligence Analysts in the U.K. *What Analysts Need to Understand: The King's Intelligence Studies Program*. Studies in Intelligence Vol. 52, No. 4 (Extracts, December 2008).

Gordon, P. (2005). *Phil Gordon's Little Green Book: Lessons and Teachings in No Limit Texas Hold'em*. Simon Spotlight Entertainment. New York, New York.

Grabo, C. (2002). ANTICIPATING SURPRISE: Analysis for Strategic Warning. Chapter 2: Introduction to the Analytical Method. *Center for Strategic Intelligence Research*. Joint Military Intelligence College. Washington, D.C. pp. 25–50.

Grau, L. (1996). Bear Went Over the Mountain: Soviet Combat Tactics in Afghanistan. National Defense University Press. Washington, D.C.

Griffith, S. (1963). *Sun Tzu: The Art of War*. Oxford University Press. New York, New York.

Guevara, E. (1961). *Guerrilla Warfare*. PDF Download http://smallwarsjournal.com/documents/guevara.pdf (accessed July 28, 2009).

Hellsten, S. (2006). *Ethics, Rhetoric, and Politics of Post Conflict Reconstruction: How can the Concept of Social Contract Help Us in Understanding How to Make Peace Work*. United Nations University-World Institute for Development Economics Research. Research Paper No. 2006/148.

Howard, R. (2008). *Ethics for the Real World: Creating a Personal Code to Guide Decisions in Work and Life*. Harvard Business Press. Boston, Massachusetts.

Irish Republican Army Ireland. (1956). *Irish Republican Army "Green Book."* General Headquarters. Ireland.

Jensen, B. (2008). *Network Bandits: Understanding Recruitment Networks in Contemporary Counterinsurgency Operations*. American Intelligence Journal. Vol. 25 No. 2.

Joint Staff J7 Joint Doctrine and Education Division Staff (2009). *Effects Based Thinking in Joint Doctrine*. Joint Force Quarterly. Issue 53. Second Quarter. pp. 60.

Kant, I. (2005). *Fundamental Principles of the Metaphysics of Morals*. Dover Publications, New York, New York.

Kent, S. (1966). *Strategic Intelligence for American World Policy*. Princeton University Press. Princeton, NJ.

Klein, G. (2009). *The HSCB Assessment Process*. Human Social Cultural Behavioral Modeling Program. Department Undersecretary of Defense. For Science and Technology. Issue 1 Spring 2009. pp. 7–8.

Krizan, L. (1999). *Intelligence Essentials for Everyone*. Joint Military Intelligence College. Occasional Paper Number 6. Part 5. pp. 29–38.

Kuntzel, M. (2007). *Jihad and Jew Hatred: Islamism, Nazism, and the roots of 9-11*. Telos Press Publishing. New York, New York.

Leonard, T. (1999). *Castro and the Cuban Revolution.* Greenwood Press. Westport, CT.

Lia, B. (2006). *The Society of the Muslim Brothers in Egypt: The Rise Of an Islamic Mass Movement 1928–1942.* Ithaca Press. Ithaca, NY.

Licklider, R. (2008). *The Ethics of Advice: Conflict Management vs. Human Rights in Ending Civil Wars.* Saltzman Institute of War and Peace Studies at Columbia University. Saltzman Working Paper No. 4.

Lowenthal, M. (2009). *Intelligence: From Secrets to Policy.* Fourth Edition. Washington D.C. CQ Press.

Lyon, S. (2009). *Insurance Ethics: A Business of Trust.* Insurance Society of Philadelphia Power Point Presentation.

Marighella, C. (1969). *Mini-Manual of the Urban Guerrilla.* PDF Download www.geocities.com/phosphor2013/UrbanGuerrilla.pdf (accessed June 12, 2009).

Marrin, S. (2007). Intelligence Analysis: Structured Methods or Intuition. *American Intelligence Journal.* National Military Intelligence Association. Summer 2007. pp. 7–16.

McFate, M. (2005). Anthropology and Counterinsurgency: The Strange Story of their Curious Relationship. *Joint Center for Operational Analysis.* Quarterly Bulletin. Vol 7. No. 4. pp. 44–59.

—(2006). Cultural Intelligence: "Far More Difficult than Counting Tanks and Planes. *American Intelligence Journal, Vol 23, pp. 16–22.*

Military Advisory Corp Vietnam—Studies and Observation Group Homepage http://www.macvsog.cc/ (accessed Feb 18, 2009).

Minutemen Civil Defense Corp. http://www.minutemanhq.com/ (accessed July 30, 2009).

Mitchell, R. (1993). *The Society of the Muslim Brothers.* Oxford University Press. New York, New York.

Moore, D. and Krizan, L. (2003). Core Competencies for Intelligence Analysis at the National Security Agency. *Bringing Intelligence About: Practioners Reflect on Best Practices.* Center for Strategic Intelligence Research. Joint Military Intelligence College. Washington D.C. pp. 95–131.

Morrison, J. (2009). *Working through Synthetic Worlds: Time Machine & Mind Snaps.* SPAWAR. Systems Center Pacific. http://www.ndu.edu/irmc/fcvw/fcvw10/images/2009/Apr23slides/morrison.pdf (accessed May 25, 2009).

Morse, C. (2003). *The Nazi Connection to Islamic Terrorism: Adolf Hitler and Haj Amin al-Husseini.* iUniverse, Inc. Bloomington, IN.

Ness, C. (2008). *Female Terrorism and Militancy: Agency, Utility, and Organization.* Routledge. New York, New York.

Nozawa, E.T. (2008). *A Conceptual Systems View of Peircean Logic, Art of Reasoning, and Critical Thinking.* IEEE 2008 International Symposium on Collaborative Technologies and Systems. Achteck LTD.

—(2009). *A Short Synopsis of the Profound Knowledge of W. Edwards Deming and Charles Sanders Peirce's Scientific Semeiotic.* Achteck. LTD. 15th Annual International Deming Research.

—(2009). *The Profound Knowledge of W. Edwards Deming and Charles Sanders Peirce's Scientific Semeiotic: A Short Synopsis.* 15th Annual International Deming Research Seminar. Achteck LTD.

Paul, R. (2004). *The Thinkers Guide to Fallacies: The Art of Mental Trickery and Manipulation.* The Foundation for Critical Thinking. http://www.criticalthinking.org/. (accessed May 18, 2009).

Peters, R. (2005). The Case for Human Intelligence: Our Addiction to Technology is our Greatest Weakness. *Armed Forces Journal*. July 2005 Issue. pp. 24–26.

Pham, P. (2004). *Law, Human Rights, Realism and the "War on Terror."* Human Rights and Human Welfare. Vol. 4. pp. 91–106.

Plante, T. (2004). *Do the Right Thing: Living Ethically in an Unethical World*. New Harbinger Publications. Oakland, California.

Prescott, J. (2006). CI and Ethics: Either You Have it or You Don't. *Competitive Intelligence Magazine*. Society of Competitive Intelligence Professionals. Vol. 9. No. 2. pp. 6–10.

Rodgers, R. Scott (2006). Improving Analysis: Dealing with Information Processing Errors. *International Journal of Intelligence and Counterintelligence*. Taylor and Francis Group. Vol.19 No. 4. pp. 622–641.

Ronfeldt, D. (2006). *In Search of How Societies Work: Tribes, The First and Forever Form*. WR-433-RPC. RAND Pardee Center. Washington, D.C. pp. 7–28.

Rose, A. (2006). *Washington's Spies: The Story of America's first Spy Ring*. Bantam Publishing. New York, New York.

Russell, B. (2005). *The Analysis of Mind*. Dover Publications. Mineola, New York.

Scales, R. (October 2007). *Statement for the Record*. Senate Armed Services Committee. Washington, D.C.

Schama, S. (1990). *Citizens: A Chronicle of the French Revolution*. Vintage Books. Hopkinton, MA.

Shapiro, S. (2007). *Speak no Evil: Intelligence Ethics in Israel*. International Studies Association Working Paper. Chicago, IL.

Sheiffer, M. (2008). *Simulation Use in the Undergraduate Classroom*. Department of Social Sciences, United States Military Academy. West Point, NY.

Sheptycki, J. (2002). *Postmodern Power and Transnational Policing: Democracy, the Constabulary Ethic and the Response to Global (In)Security*. The Geneva Center for the Democratic Control of Armed Forces. Working Paper Series No. 19.

Smith, T. (2006). *Predictive Network-Centric Intelligence: Toward a Total-Systems Transformation of Analysis and Assessment*. Winner, 2006 Galileo Essay Contest Sponsored by the Director of National Intelligence.

Taleb, N. (2007). *The Black Swan: The Impact of the Highly Improbable*. Random House. New York, New York.

Taylor, M. (2009). *Agents say DEA is forcing them illegally to work in Afghanistan*. http://www.mcclatchydc.com/homepage/story/70386.html (accessed Aug 25, 2009).

Traditional Christian Knights of the Ku Klux Klan Code of Conduct. http://www.tckkkk.org/code.htm (accessed March 2, 2009).

Tyrell, M. (2007). *Why Dr. Johnny Won't Go To War: Anthropology and the Global War on Terror*. Small Wars Journal Excerpt. Vol. 7.

Velleman, D. (2009). *How We Get Along*. Cambridge University Press. New York, NY. (Introduction pp. 1–7).

Viar, C. (1990). *The Trust*. Central Intelligence Agency: Center for Intelligence Studies.

Wark, M. (2007). *Gamer Theory.* Harvard University Press. Boston, MA.

Warner, M. (2001). *Central Intelligence: Origin and Evolution.* https://www.cia.gov/...intelligence/.../ Origin_and_Evolution.pdf (accessed March 12, 2008).

Wasserman, S. (1994). *Social Network Analysis: Methods and Applications (Structural Analysis in the Social Sciences).* Cambridge University Press. New York, New York.

Wheaton, K. (2009). *Advanced Analytic Techniques.* ADVAT Blog. http://advat.blogspot.com/2009/04/ summary-of-findings-gap-analysis-3-out.html (accessed May 12, 2009).

White, J. (2002). *Terrorism: An Introduction.* Wadsworth Thomas Learning. Belmont, CA.

Wiedenhaefer, R. (2007). Ethno-psychological Characteristics and Terror-Producing Countries: Linking Uncertainty Avoidance to Terrorist Acts in the 1970s. *Studies in Conflict & Terrorism*, Vol. 30. No. 9. pp. 801–823.

Yamada, D. (2008). *Work Place Bullying and Ethical Leadership.* Suffolk University Law School. Legal Studies Research Paper Series. Research Paper 08–37.

Yarger, H. (2007). *Educating for Strategic Thinking in the SOF Community: Considerations and a Proposal.* Joint Special Operations University. JSOU Report 07–2.

Yong, Ed. (2009). *East Meets West: How the Brain Unites us All.* New Scientist Magazine. Issue 2698. http://www.newscientist.com/article/mg20126981.700-east-meets-west-how-the-brain-unites-us-all.html?full=true (accessed May 18, 2009).

Index